My Dad's Funnier Than Your Dad

My Dad's Funnier Than Your Dad

Growing Up with Tim Conway in the
Funniest House in America

Kelly Conway
with Caroline St. Clair

LYONS
PRESS

Guilford, Connecticut

An imprint of Globe Pequot, the trade division of
The Rowman & Littlefield Publishing Group, Inc.
4501 Forbes Blvd., Ste. 200
Lanham, MD 20706
www.rowman.com

Distributed by NATIONAL BOOK NETWORK

British Library Cataloguing in Publication Information available

Library of Congress Cataloging-in-Publication Data
Names: Conway, Kelly, 1962- author.
Title: My dad's funnier than your dad : growing up with Tim Conway in the
    funniest house in America / Kelly Conway ; with Caroline St. Clair.
Description: Guilford, Connecticut : Lyons Press, [2022] | Identifiers: LCCN 2021034054 (print) |
LCCN 2021034055 (ebook) | ISBN
    9781493057696 (hardcover) | ISBN 9781493066322 (epub)
Subjects: LCSH: Conway, Tim--Family. | Comedians--United States--Biography.
    | Actors--United States--Biography. | Fathers and daughters--United
    States--Biography. | Conway, Kelly, 1962---Family. | Conway, Kelly,
    1962---Childhood and youth.
Classification: LCC PN2287.C584 C66 2022 (print) | LCC PN2287.C584
    (ebook) | DDC 792.702/8092 [B]--dc23
LC record available at https://lccn.loc.gov/2021034054
LC ebook record available at https://lccn.loc.gov/2021034055

♾™ The paper used in this publication meets the minimum requirements of American
National Standard for Information Sciences—Permanence of Paper for Printed Library
Materials, ANSI/NISO Z39.48-1992.

Thank you . . .

Tim Conway, Jr.
Patrick Conway
Jamie Conway
Corey Conway
Seann Conway
Jen and Sophia Conway
The Caregivers
Caroline St. Clair
Jennifer De Chiara
Roger Neal
Rick Sittig, for the perfect title
My Malibu Family
The Village of Erieau and the EYC
Pars, Paige-ee, & Marc-ee
Sammi and Ben Boswell
Jill Pallad
Danielle Ruhnau
Lori Waggner
Beth Einhorn
Karen Beatty
Kelli Abraham
Cathy Dunn
Katelyn Benton
Curt Grosjean
My Snow Summit Family
Radical Media
Secret Weapon Marketing
. . . and God
for letting things happen
exactly how they should

Chapter 1

I HAD JUST POURED A CUP OF COFFEE WHEN A TEXT LIT UP ON MY PHONE. It was from my friend Jill in New York. "Hey," Jill wrote. "Are you okay?"

I sat down at the counter. "Yeah, I'm good," I typed back. "Just getting dressed. What's up?"

"I'm on-set in the middle of a wardrobe fitting," Jill wrote. "But my assistant just told me. I'm so sorry about your dad. I'll call you as soon as I can."

I stared at the message. *So sorry about your dad?* After a moment, I clicked on a national news site. On the front page, there was a picture of my dad, with a headline under it. "Comedy legend Tim Conway, dead at 85."

The words hit me like a blow to the stomach. I couldn't breathe. I had just seen my dad the day before and was getting ready to visit him again that morning. But now he was gone.

The phone vibrated on the counter. Suddenly, calls and messages began pouring in as friends from all over the world learned the news.

My stepmother, Charlene, didn't bother to inform me of my father's death when it happened. I hadn't had the comfort of a few hours, or even a few minutes, to process the news privately before the rest of the world knew about it. My dad's life had ended in a nursing home only a few miles from my friend Beth's condo in Sherman Oaks, where I was staying in order to be closer to him. The condo was so close I could have walked there. But it took a friend two thousand miles away to tell me that he had passed away.

It seemed like my tears would never stop. Had someone been with my dad when he died? Was anyone—Charlene, or Mena, his gentle, kind caregiver—holding his hand as he drew his last breath? When my dad's spirit parted from his body, was he alone? I would never know.

The phone rang and rang but I shoved it away. Outside, a cold wind swayed the palm trees against a gray sky. In the past few weeks, I had taken to wearing an old sweater of my dad's, a slightly frayed cashmere crewneck, and had pulled it on that very morning. Sobbing, I wiped my tears with the cuff. It still smelled like him.

Over the past year I'd watched helplessly as the father I loved succumbed to a terminal illness. Many people who have lost a loved one to a progressive disease compare it to an abduction. For me, there had been another kind of theft outside of my dad's illness. My stepmother, Charlene, had denied me any say in my father's care for the last year of his life. I had been prevented from visiting him, accused of theft, physically attacked, and repeatedly lied to. Ultimately, I would take my fight for my dad to court, and in the process, lose part of a family that I had loved. What had been a close and loving thirty-year relationship with Charlene, and my stepsister, Jackie, was shattered beyond repair. All because I wanted to help my dad suffer less. How had it come to this? It is a question that still haunts me.

I had spent those final, precious visits with my dad, holding his hand and talking to him. We would watch his favorite shows on television, and I would tell him about my day—the errands I was going to run, or a job I was thinking of taking. I patted his face with a cool, damp washcloth when the room felt too warm or pulled up the blanket when it was cool. I just wanted to be close to him.

In those last weeks, leaving my dad after a visit was like getting my heart broken over and over. Whenever I said the words, "Okay, Dad, I have to go now, but I will see you tomorrow," he would instantly dissolve into heaving sobs. No amount of reassurance could console him. "Dad!" I'd exclaim, wrapping my arms around him and trying to hide my tears in his chest. "I promise I will be back tomorrow." It took every ounce of strength to leave him, and I often stayed past my "allotted" visitation time because I couldn't bear to walk out of the room. The fear of angering Charlene and being thrown out by security guards didn't faze me; all I wanted was for Dad to know that it was okay because I would be there with him again the next morning.

The first time Dad cried as I was leaving, I'd just assumed it was part of the illness.

"I'm sure he does this when anyone from the family leaves," I'd said to Mena, his caregiver.

"No," Mena replied, shaking her head. "He only cries when you leave."

When I had left him yesterday, with my assurances that I'd be back again the next day, did Dad know it was the last time we'd see each other? Did he know that he was leaving this world?

I stood up, rubbing the tears from my face. It was time to pull myself together and take charge where I still could. I had my five brothers to think about. I needed to reach out to them before they heard the news in the same cold and dispassionate way that I had. I also needed to reassure my friends that I was okay so they wouldn't worry.

I felt an impulse to go over to the nursing home—part of me needed to see that my dad was really gone—but there was no point in going over there now. I knew I didn't want to see my stepmother or stepsister, but I did want to play some role in helping to memorialize my father, something to share a little of the kind, loving, and funny man who had raised me.

Then I remembered the Willie Nelson song.

"Angel Flying Too Close to the Ground" had hit the country airwaves in 1981. Willie sang it with tremulous emotion against a background of weepy steel guitar. One day Dad and I were riding in the car when the song came on the radio. Dad had turned it up as we drove down Ventura Boulevard in the Valley. When the song finished, he looked over at me. "That's the song that I want to be played at my funeral."

Dad was just forty-eight years old at the time. The idea of him having a funeral seemed as likely as his flying to the moon.

"Dad!" I said. "I can't believe you're talking about your funeral."

"That's the song I want to be played at my funeral," he repeated solemnly.

I was a teenager and thought the song was just silly. And the idea of Dad wanting it played at his funeral was mortifying. I stared at the side of his face, waiting for him to crack a smile to show he was joking. "Oh, sure," I scoffed. "Because you are *such* an angel, right?"

Dad didn't blink. "I'm serious," he said. "You have to play it at my funeral."

I rolled my eyes and looked out the window. "Okay, Dad. I promise we will play 'Angel Flying' or whatever it is at your funeral."

I thought that was the end of it, just one of Dad's many jokes that came with the territory of being his kid. But later, I realized that he was serious.

"Here's my song," he'd say whenever it came on the radio, which was a lot that year. "Remember, when I go, this is the song I want to be played at my funeral."

I picked up my phone, not knowing who to call first. Plans for Dad's memorial were probably already in motion, and I had to let Charlene and Jackie know immediately about the song. I'd promised Dad so many years ago, and I would make it happen. It was so perfect.

But I paused, knowing that my calls would go unanswered. I was the oldest of my father's six kids, and his only daughter, but I would have no say in the decisions about his funeral.

I spent the day making phone calls to friends and family. I spoke with my brother Tim, who also lived in Los Angeles, while my brothers Patrick, Jamie, Corey, and Seann prepared to come into town. Even as we made arrangements to gather, we were completely in the dark. Only when Charlene decided to inform us would we know when the funeral would occur and if we were even invited.

Beth sat with me as I cried in between phone calls. She brought me plates of food and tried to get me to eat. I was so thankful that Beth was there with me because being alone on that day would have been unbearable.

By the time dusk fell, I was exhausted from tears and talking. I went into my room and crawled under the covers, still wearing Dad's sweater. Without the distraction of phone calls, I had no choice but to face the deep, dark hole that Dad's passing had opened within me.

A kaleidoscope of memories flashed in my head. There was Dad in the pool at our house in Encino, tan and strong, with me riding on his shoulders as we chased my younger brothers through the water. Dad, spending his only day off creating a "movie theater" for us and the neighborhood kids at our house, complete with real ticket stubs and popcorn in bags. My sweet Daddy, who always knew where I was and what I was doing. My best pal in the world.

I sat up and felt around for my phone. After a quick search, I found the song "Angel Flying Too Close to the Ground" and pushed play. Putting in my earbuds, I lay back against the pillow as Willie's mournful voice filled my ears. As he sang about broken wings and the healing power of love, I was transported back to the passenger seat of our old car with Dad humming along to the song as it played over the radio. It was one of those classic Los Angeles days, filled with sunshine and blue sky, when I was no longer a child but not quite yet an adult, and I truly believed my Dad would live forever.

When the last bars of the song faded away, I pulled out the earbuds. The wind had died down, and a peaceful silence filled the room. "I didn't forget, Dad." I whispered to the darkness.

———

In the end, the song was not played at my father's funeral.

Chapter 2

ALL MY LIFE, PEOPLE HAVE ASKED ME THIS QUESTION: WHAT WAS IT like to be Tim Conway's daughter?

What was life like with such a famously hilarious father? Were we kids always cracking up? Yes. Was our home a den of playful pranks? Yes. Did my mother sometimes want to throw the whole lot of us—me, my five brothers, *and* Dad—out the window when things got a little too crazy? Oh, yes.

Some of Dad's fans need assurance that he truly was as delightful in real life as he'd appeared to be on television. "Please," they say, "*please* tell me your father was as great as I thought he was!" So often, we idolize a famous person only to find out later that they were the opposite of what we'd imagined. And sometimes in terrible ways. A glamorous movie star who beat her children with coat hangers. An on-screen idealized father figure later revealed to have committed horrendous abuse. There is no shortage of examples like these in the entertainment world.

Rest assured: Dad was exactly the same person you remember from television. He was a wonderful father to my five younger brothers and me for all of our lives: supportive, loving, and yes, a hell of a lot of fun.

Who exactly was Tim Conway? If you're a certain age, you may already know him from the many characters he played over his decades-long career. He might have cracked you up as Mr. Tudball on *The Carol Burnett Show*, or the lovable but not-so-bright Ensign Parker in *McHale's Navy*. Maybe, as a kid on a Saturday outing to the movies, you saw him in *The Apple Dumpling Gang* with Don Knotts. Or perhaps you were one of the millions of fans who couldn't get enough of Dad's salty, short-statured golf pro, *Dorf*.

Whatever character he played, Tim Conway possessed a sharp comic wit warmed by a sincerity that made him something rare in the world of celebrity: a relatable and likable human being. That is something his many friends and fans already know. I still hear from many of them today, delighting in sharing their stories of how much Dad meant to them. And because my career has brought me into Hollywood circles, I have met actors and comedians—many of whom are very famous—whose faces light up when they learn who my dad is. "He's been such an inspiration to me!" they exclaim, naming their favorite sketch or character.

The Tim Conway known to the world was also a father who adored his six children and always made time in his busy schedule to be with them. The dad who played ringmaster to a backyard circus of unruly little heathens. A man who dreamed up a riot of pranks, fun, and laughter for his kids' benefit. Dad believed that anything you could imagine should be put to the test, regardless of how absurd it seemed. The trappings of celebrity never distracted him from the responsibilities of being a father. Even after a long day at the studio, he always had time for a wrestling match of six against one.

While Dad was busy being the biggest wolf pup in the Conway pack, Mom was the watchful and steady presence who always made sure to count heads in the pool and step in when someone was at risk of drowning. She was also a complex, highly intelligent woman often quick to explode under the burden of managing six children. We all knew it was best not to push Mom too far, although it happened frequently. Her style of parenting was as different from Dad's as night and day.

I think having these two very different people as parents is what made the chemistry of our family so special. We kids delighted in Dad's spontaneity, coupled with the pragmatic, disciplined touchstone of Mom. As a family, we had our challenges, but it was a magical childhood set against a backdrop of the Valley and the brightly lit studios of CBS.

Dad was born in 1933, the only child of Dan Conway, an Irish-born stable manager with a quiet, thoughtful manner, and Sophia Murgoi, a delightful Romanian immigrant we grandkids called Magi. They met in Cleveland and married, later moving to a cottage on a wealthy family estate where Papa managed the horse stables. After their only child was born, Magi and Papa moved to the quaint town of Chagrin Falls, Ohio, settling into the small, neat house where my dad would grow up.

You may think my dad would have known from birth that he was destined for stardom, but his boyhood dream was to be a jockey. While helping Papa care for the horses at local racing stables, Dad was in close contact with the compact, tough, chain-smoking jockeys walking around in their brightly colored silks, and he idolized them.

But racing atop a thoroughbred wasn't in the cards for Dad. He was too heavy, and, as he admitted himself, he just didn't have the talent for it. Still, he would love horse racing his whole life; I have many fond memories of placing bets with Dad at Santa Anita Park racetrack in Los Angeles.

My mom, Mary Anne Dalton, grew up in Dearborn, Michigan, a suburb of Detroit. She was the eldest of seven children in a large Irish-Catholic family. Her parents, who ran the local funeral home, both drank heavily and fought loudly. When they went on a bender, Mom would be left in charge of her younger siblings, making sure they got enough to eat and were dressed and off to school on time. Sometimes, when the adults were too hungover, Mom would assist clients in selecting a casket or arranging memorial services for their departed loved one. Where Dad had been the cherished only child who had every ounce of his parents' attention, Mom and her siblings had to yell at the dinner table to be heard over the noise.

After graduating from high school, Mom immediately left home to attend Bowling Green State University, where she met my father. The two were just friends at first, and went their separate ways after graduating from college—Dad to the army, and Mom as a performer in the army's Special Services branch. She had always loved to dance and had spent what little free time she'd had taking lessons, which she paid for herself. I imagine that Mom thrived under the discipline of being a dancer, and I'm sure it provided an escape from her chaotic home life. She had a lithe, graceful body and was a beautiful dancer her whole life.

As a member of a dancing and singing group that entertained US soldiers stationed overseas, Mom spent a year living in Germany. During her time there, she learned to ski on the steep Alpine mountains, sparking a passion that would last her entire life. All of us kids started on skis when we were barely old enough to walk, and to this day, I owe my love for the sport to Mom. After she finished her army service and returned to the United States, Mom and Dad reconnected. A renewed friendship blossomed into romance, and after a brief courtship, they were married on May 27, 1961.

After completing his stint in the army, Dad went back to Cleveland. He worked his way up from writing promos at a radio station to producing an afternoon movie program at WJW-TV with his best friend, Ernie Anderson. *Ernie's Place* aired during the featured movie's intermission, with Ernie interviewing local and visiting dignitaries while Dad ran the camera.

But Dad didn't stay behind the camera for long. Often there was no guest scheduled for a particular day, so Dad would dress up as a famous Italian chef or a Spanish bullfighter, and he and Ernie would improv a funny interview. Soon the Cleveland audience was tuning in to *Ernie's Place* just to see what kind of silly sketch Dad and Ernie would create. People were far more interested in watching the hilarious antics of the two hosts than the featured movie, and *Ernie's Place* developed a sort of cult following.

One of these "interviews" on *Ernie's Place* caught the attention of actress and comedian Rose Marie, a star on *The Dick Van Dyke Show*. While visiting the WJW-TV set during a promotional tour, Rose Marie happened to see the show as it played on a studio monitor. No one can recall which character Dad was playing on that episode, but Rose Marie thought it was hilarious. She met Dad and Ernie and asked if she could take a couple of studio reels of the show back to Hollywood to show her friend Steve Allen, star of NBC's nationally syndicated *The Steve Allen Plymouth Show*. After Steve watched the *Ernie's Place* reels, he offered Dad some guest spots on his show.

Dad flew out to Los Angeles to appear as a frequent guest on *The Steve Allen Plymouth Show*. Realizing that he might have a chance at a real career in television, Dad decided to move from Cleveland to Los Angeles. Mom was heavily pregnant with me at the time, but she believed in Dad, and she didn't hesitate when he suggested they move to California. To Dad's delight, Ernie decided to pack up and try his luck in Hollywood, too.

Mom and Dad packed everything they owned into their VW Bug and hugged Magi and Papa good-bye. Then they pointed west and bounced over 2,300 miles across the country, arriving in Los Angeles just in time for me to be born there. You could say the first gift my parents gave me was the honor of being a true California girl. After moving to Los Angeles, Mom and Dad became friends with Rose Marie and asked her to be my godmother.

Dad plunged into working twelve-hour days on-set while Mom and I settled into a small apartment in Van Nuys. Mom was living in a vast city without family or friends, taking care of a new baby with her husband gone most of the day. A situation like this might have been too daunting for many women, but Mary Anne Dalton Conway was cut from a different cloth. She was strong and determined, and she kept her sights set on the promise of a bright future in her new home.

Although it was on the outskirts of the more-intimidating city center of Hollywood, Van Nuys was a far cry from the placid Cleveland suburbs. Having a baby brought out a new side to Dad—he became an ardent protector of his small family. He worried about leaving Mom and me alone all day while he was working. He reminded her to lock the doors when he left and never open them to anyone she didn't know. Dad probably would have loved for the two of us to stay inside all day, but Mary Anne wasn't going to stand for that, and he knew it.

Occasionally Dad would have to go out of town for work. He didn't want Mom and me to stay alone in the apartment, so he would get us a room at the Sportsmen's Lodge in Studio City. Although it was not a glamorous place, the hotel's lounge had been a popular watering hole for Hollywood stars for decades, with Clark Gable, Bette Davis, and John Wayne among the many celebrities who once gathered at the hunting lodge–themed bar for drinks and gossip.

Even when Dad was home, he worried someone might break into our apartment at night when we were asleep. Always the inventor, he had an idea. Figuring that an intruder would most likely try to enter through the set of sliding doors in the living room, he decided to fabricate a homemade alarm system. He took a brick and held it in place with a small block of wood on top of one side of the doorframe. Then, he ran a length of rope over the doorframe and down the other side. He tied one end of the rope to the door handle and the other end to the wood block. On the floor under the brick, Dad placed a metal bucket. If someone opened the door during the night, the rope would pull the wood block away and release the brick, sending it crashing down into the bucket. *Bang*. The noise would wake my parents so they could scare off the intruder. Dad was careful to set the alarm every night before bed.

One night my parents were jolted from their sleep by a loud bang from the living room. They lay still, holding their breath, listening for the sound of footsteps, but there was only silence.

"Tim," Mom finally whispered. "Go see what's happening."

But Dad was paralyzed with fear. He might have been clever enough to create the alarm, but damn if he would respond.

Finally, Mom threw off the covers and tiptoed out to investigate. She returned shortly and climbed back into bed.

The small block of wood keeping the brick on the narrow wood frame had fallen away on its own, sending the brick crashing down. False alarm.

For a few minutes, my parents lay there in silence.

Then: "Did you remember to set the alarm back?" Dad asked.

"God almighty," Mom groaned. "Just go to sleep."

That story pretty much sums up the parenting styles of my mother and father. The differences became more extreme once my five brothers were born. Where Dad looked at every new day as an opportunity for fun, Mom made sure our rangy gang stayed in some semblance of order along the way. It must not have been easy to manage all of us, and she often had to resort to screaming and cursing in order to be heard, sometimes the only way to get our attention.

Even as a young girl I was just as wild as my brothers, and could be even tougher. I never stood down to any of them, even if it took a tumble in the grass with fists flying to accomplish it. While disagreements among us siblings flared up quickly, there was always a new distraction that made us forget the argument. Before you knew it we'd all be banding back together again as though nothing had ever happened, ready to move on to our next adventure.

As the 1960s dawned, Dad's star was on the rise. Unfortunately, just as he'd started to make a name for himself from his regular appearances on *The New Steve Allen Show*, the show was canceled, and Dad became one of many unemployed entertainers living in Hollywood. It would prove to be only a brief setback, as even better things were just around the bend.

In 1962, Dad was offered a co-starring role on a new television series called *McHale's Navy*, about a naval crew stationed on an island in the South Pacific during World War II. Dad was not a big name at the time, but the show's producer, Ed Montagne, had seen him on Steve Allen's show and thought he would be perfect for the role of sweet, bumbling Ensign Charles Parker. Ernest Borgnine, a bona fide movie star and Oscar winner, would play Lieutenant Commander Quinton McHale.

Ed Montagne's gamble on Dad paid off. His Ensign Parker was a well-intentioned but hilariously flawed foil to the prickly and easily frustrated Lieutenant McHale. When Dad first met Ernest Borgnine on the set, he could hardly speak. The pressure he felt stepping into this important role alongside such a formidable man must have been enormous. But the chemistry between the two sizzled on-screen, and the show was very popular. Working on *McHale's Navy* was also the beginning of Dad's friendship with Ernest. After Dad's shyness melted away, he quickly earned not only the respect but also the friendship of the gruff but warm-hearted actor.

Ernest Borgnine was a regular visitor to our home when I was growing up and remained a dear friend to my father for the rest of his life.

Dad's profile rose significantly after the success of *McHale's Navy*. And something else was growing along with his fame. Between my birth in 1962 and my youngest brother Seann's arrival in 1970, Mom and Dad welcomed Tim Jr., Patrick, Jamie, and Corey into the family. With the addition of each new child we moved to a succession of slightly larger houses around the San Fernando Valley.

After Seann was born, however, Dad was finally able to afford the house that would become our true family home.

Chapter 3

THE CONWAY FAMILY HOME WAS LOCATED IN ENCINO, NESTLED IN what people in Los Angeles refer to as "the Valley." It had been built in the 1940s by an art director who had worked on the film *Gone with the Wind*. He used Tara, the famed Southern plantation home where much of the movie is set, as an inspiration for its design. The house had tall columns and balconies with lacy wrought-iron railings. But the best thing about the house was the space, both inside and out, for our large and highly energetic family. Situated across a sprawling, tree-filled lawn were a swimming pool, a tennis court, and shuffleboard decks. What probably sealed the deal was the expansive brick courtyard set between the pool and the main house. It had a built-in barbecue and bar area with lots of room for people to lounge by the pool, and it was the perfect setting for the many cookouts, birthday parties, and social events to come.

I was nine years old in 1971 when we moved to the "Tara" house on Magnolia Boulevard. After years of living in small homes, Mom finally had a big place that she could transform into the house of her dreams. Her love for decorating blossomed, bringing with it the scent of fresh paint, giant rolls of upholstery fabric draped over chairs, and big books of wallpaper samples lying around.

My parents built a large master bedroom suite that Mom decorated in her signature tailored style, with drapes, bedspread, and accessories perfectly matched. When their bedroom was finished, Mom and Dad had a much-needed private space for themselves, one that my brothers and I still managed to invade whenever we wanted. As the eldest child and only girl, I got the old master bedroom upstairs. The room had tall windows with a built-in upholstered seat that overlooked the front lawn, and a fireplace. While I would have loved to paint the entire room purple, my favorite color at the time, Mom wisely vetoed that idea and helped me decorate it in a young but tasteful style.

With five younger brothers, you would have thought that having my very own room—with a door I could close anytime I wanted—would have been a dream come true. However, having shared a bedroom with one or more of my brothers for so many years, being alone felt strange. With my door shut, I'd get restless and start to wonder what my brothers were doing in their rooms down the hall.

Although each kid had his own room, the boys tended to congregate and even sleep all together in one room that had two sets of bunk beds. There was always a steady stream of shouts, laughter, and mysterious thumps coming from their side of the house. Who was that yelling? Was that Jamie crying, or Corey? I'd have to go see for myself, convinced that I was missing out on something really fun. Why would I want to be alone when I could be busy playing "mummy," which meant rolling our brother Patrick in a sheet until he became so enraged that his face turned bright red? Or consulting with Timmy as we dressed our reluctant Maine Coon cat, Kika, in some of Seann's old baby clothes?

Because the six of us kids were very close in age, we operated more like a unified body than individual children. Although there were enough bathrooms to allow for some privacy, we always ended up brushing our teeth together in one, elbows knocking and heads bumping as we leaned over to spit in the sink. The creative mayhem my brothers and I generated could last all day and into the night, with only brief pauses for meals or sleep. Inevitably, someone would dissolve into a meltdown and "go tell." Then our enraged mother would fly up the stairs after the rest of us, ready to spank whomever she caught. There was a constant battle for one-upmanship, like who could make the biggest leap off the top bunk, or endure an arm-twisting the longest. Ours was not a playground for the faint of heart.

One feature of the house that held no end of delight for us kids was the aptly named dumbwaiter—a small elevator used to move items between floors. The dumbwaiter was just the right size to fit one or two small children, and then, with a pull of the lever, send them up and down. Technically, the dumbwaiter was a dangerous thing and, therefore, off-limits, but we still played with it anyway. The fun ended one day when we put three-year-old Corey inside the dumbwaiter, lowered it down, and then stopped it between floors. Realizing he was trapped, Corey emitted an ear-splitting screech so loud that our mother came running all the way from the other side of the house.

"What the fuck?" Mom screamed. "Get your brother back up here *now*. I told you all no playing in the dumbwaiter, you dumb-asses. You could have killed him!"

Corey emerged from the dumbwaiter a shrieking, red-faced banshee. He chased the rest of us around with his small fists pummeling the air. Corey couldn't catch us, but Mom did, and we all got a spanking and were sent to our rooms. After that, Dad nailed a piece of wood over the doors of the dumbwaiter, shutting it off for good.

When she was really angry, Mom was a terrifying thing, although it was mostly just screaming. She never hurt us beyond a smack on the back of the head or a spanking. Mom had grown up in a loud, turbulent home where screaming was the default for any kind of discipline. It must have been very frustrating to manage me and my brothers; we were wild as a wolf pack. Among us kids, no grudges were held despite how hard we beat up on one another. Once the tears had dried and Band-Aids were applied, the six of us would be back together and deciding what we were going to do next.

Dad had an entirely different philosophy for dealing with misbehaving children. He doled out punishment in a much more diplomatic and humorous way. Dad's love of hockey inspired one of his favorites: the penalty box. He built a small bench and installed a light inside one of the family-room closets where offenders were sent to "wait out the game" and think over their misdeeds. Patrick might kick Timmy, and Dad would yell, "Okay, Pat, you get two minutes in the penalty box for kicking. *Now!*" So Patrick would sit on the bench in the closet while the rest of us fell over with laughter and teased him through the closed door. Each of us kids spent a lot of time in the penalty box, but it wasn't scary. It was Dad's fun way of imposing a time-out when one was needed.

Our house offered limitless opportunities for amusement, but outside was where we spent most of the day playing. The yard encompassed a sprawling acre of land enclosed by a wall. Colossal oak and pine trees cast shade from the blazing California sun, and thick stands of shrubs provided ideal cover for hide-and-seek. Over the years Dad built us a series of treehouses, each one a different style, featuring rope swings and lookout platforms. From the treehouse we could see far over into the adjoining backyards and the streets beyond. It was a favorite place for us to spy on neighbors and drop water balloons on an unsuspecting brother passing below.

On one side of the property was the tennis court where my brothers and I spent countless hours slamming tennis balls or playing hockey, usually more intent on hitting each other than putting it in the net. When we got tired of tennis, we could go play over at the shuffleboard decks.

But our favorite place to be was in the swimming pool. At the far end of the pool was a large covered cabana with a sitting area complete with a bricked fireplace, grill, and a long bar. It was our main entertainment area, and we hosted countless barbecues and swim parties there over the years. As the parents of six kids Dad and Mom were very family-oriented, and most of their friends were, too. Everyone from Carol Burnett, Harvey Korman, and Dad's old buddy Ernie Anderson brought their kids to our house regularly. The adults would gossip over beer and wine while the children splashed and cavorted in the pool.

Weekends at our house were a blur of kids racing in circles around the pool, jumping in, climbing out, and doing it all over again. My mother and her friends would sit in the sun with big sunglasses on, talking as they sipped their icy cocktails. Dad and his friends would be gathered around the grill, poking at hot dogs or flipping burgers while they chatted, occasionally erupting into roars of laughter at something funny someone had said.

But Dad loved interacting with us kids as much as he did his friends. He would make up games and contests for us—there could be as many as fifteen children in the pool at one time—complete with prizes for the winners. All of us kids competed ruthlessly for the glory of being declared the winner, and even more for the trophies. That's because Dad's homemade trophies were legendary. He would take an old vase, glue it to a small box, and cover the whole thing with aluminum foil. With much pomp, it would be presented to the fastest swimmer or the biggest splash-maker. Every kid wanted that trophy for their very own. I remember one swim contest when I was determined to win the latest prize, an especially elaborate Dad-crafted award with a little foil-covered fish shape on top. I could already envision the trophy sitting on my dresser.

I got into position alongside my brothers and a few friends on the edge of the pool. With all the adults watching, Dad shouted "Go!" and we sprang into the water. I swam faster than I ever had, gasping for breath with every stroke and kicking so hard my legs ached. I could almost taste victory. But my brother Tim reached the far edge a full two strokes before me. He climbed out of the pool, wet and beaming with pride. Dad handed him the trophy—*my* trophy—and everyone slapped him on the back and cheered.

I crawled out of the pool mute with fury. I swam faster than I ever had before, and that trophy should have been *mine*. Tears sprang to my eyes at the unfairness of it all. While everyone resumed playing, I wrapped myself in a towel and sat alone, sulking.

After a while, Dad came over and sat next to me.

"What's going on, Kell?" he asked.

I was so bitter I could hardly look at him.

"It's not *fair*," I said. "I am your oldest, and your only girl, and I should have gotten the trophy. I swam so fast, and I was trying a *lot* harder than Tim was." I buried my face in my hands.

Dad put his arm around my shoulder. "But Kelly," he said gently, "Tim swam faster than you. He won the trophy."

"But it's not fair, Dad," I repeated. "I am your *only* girl!"

"I know you swam your fastest, Kell. You did really great, and next time you just might be the winner. But sometimes even when you try your hardest, you don't win, and that's disappointing." He tipped my head up so that we were eye to eye. "Hey, you did good, and you should be proud of that. But Tim was the fastest swimmer today. Train hard and you will win one day. Are we good?"

I nodded. Dad was right, and the way he explained it made me feel better.

A few weeks later, I did swim the fastest, and this time it was me who got the trophy. But Dad's lesson had hit its mark, and I never forgot it.

Sometimes in life you want something so much that it's almost as though you could will it into being from sheer desire alone. You put so much effort into it that you just *know* things will pay off—they *have* to, because you nearly killed yourself trying. But that doesn't always mean you get it. It's a tough lesson for anyone no matter what the stakes. All you can do is jump back into that pool and keep on swimming.

Sometimes there were parties for adults only at our house. We kids would be allowed to come out to say hello and raid the snack table, but inevitably Mom would give us a look that indicated it was time for us to go upstairs to bed.

One night I lay on my bed, unable to sleep after being sent upstairs during one of my parents' parties. I got up and crossed the hall to the room with the bunks, where all of my brothers were fast asleep. The windows looked over the courtyard and pool, and I pressed against one of them, looking down. Below, through the limbs of the giant oak tree that grew from the center of the courtyard, I could see the adults sitting around the fire pit. The flames illuminated their faces, and I could hear the soft murmur of voices and laughter. Although it was dark, I could see Dad standing over the fire, motioning with his hands as he talked. As I watched him, an alarming realization crept over me. Someday, my dad was going to die.

I had an abstract idea of what death was, and knew that all people would eventually die. When we went to church, the priest spoke about the wondrous journey that a saved soul would take to the golden gates of Heaven, where an eternity spent among loved ones awaited. I had heard of people dying—a friend of my parents, or one of my school friends would lose a grandparent. But picturing any of my family dead—in particular, my mom and dad—was a devastating concept.

I looked at Dad as he stood laughing in the firelight down below, and my love for him welled up into a wave of sobs. Someday he would be gone, and I would still be here. The idea of being alive without him was inconceivable.

I fled the darkened room and ran back to my own.

A little later, there was a knock on the door.

"Kell?" It was Dad. He opened the door and stepped in. Light from the hallway spilled over me in the bed, and he could see I'd been crying.

"Hey, Pal!" he cried, sitting down next to me. "What's wrong? Are you hurt? What happened?"

I sat up. "Everyone is going to die, right Dad?"

"Uh, yes," he said. "Everyone dies eventually."

"So what's going to happen when you die? And Mom?"

"Kelly, I'm forty. I'm not going to die anytime soon. Neither is your mother. Nothing is going to happen, and we're not going anywhere." He tipped my chin up. "Okay?"

I rubbed my nose with the edge of the sheet and nodded.

"Now, get back to sleep," Dad said. He kissed me and stood up, shaking his head as he walked out of the room.

When you're a kid, someone who's forty seems so old. But of course, as I know now, as a healthy forty-year-old, my dad was actually very young.

Later in his life, Dad would sometimes start a sentence with, "Now, when I go . . ." I'd clamp my hands over my ears and refuse to listen. Even in the days before his death, when we all knew it was inevitable, I still couldn't imagine my life without him.

Just like that night so long ago when I'd sat sobbing at the window, imagining my father's death, the thought was unbearable.

Chapter 4

In 1975, after seven years of appearing on the series as a frequent guest, Dad became a full-time cast member on *The Carol Burnett Show*. When the show debuted in 1967, Carol and her supporting cast quickly won viewers' hearts with their clever, slapstick-style comedy. This was a group of performers who did not hesitate to make fun of themselves or each other. Instead, they reveled in it. Carol could morph seamlessly from a hilarious portrayal of Scarlett O'Hara to a hunchbacked charwoman dressed in rags to a prim Queen Elizabeth II. The show parodied a popular soap opera with the recurring sketch, "As the Stomach Turns," and "Went with the Wind"—a spoof on *Gone with the Wind* with Carol as a melodramatic Southern belle stumbling around in a gown of green velvet drapes—is still as hilarious today as it was in 1976.

Carol was already a star in the television comedy world when she'd first approached the CBS executives about having her own variety show. They insisted that only a man could successfully lead a prime-time comedy show and offered her a sitcom instead. Carol didn't want to do a sitcom, and she continued to fight for her show. She and her husband, Joe Hamilton, realized there was a clause in her contract, called "push the button" in programming-speak, that obliged CBS to do the show if she wanted. Whatever reservations the studio heads may have had about a woman fronting a variety show soon disappeared. *The Carol Burnett Show* became a hit for CBS, making household names of the cast and producing 279 episodes until it ended in 1978.

Dad's style of ad-lib, and sometimes downright bizarre, humor fit like a puzzle piece alongside that of Carol, Harvey, and the other cast members. The resulting sketches would often go off-script, peaking into a screwball riot that left the actors fighting to keep a straight face and audiences clamoring for more.

It was on *The Carol Burnett Show* where Dad met his comedic soul mate, Harvey Korman. The two had an intuitive ability to play off each other, and they would create some of the most legendary comedy sketches ever seen on television. The camaraderie between them was just as strong off the set. Harvey, a Jewish kid from Chicago, was like the brother that Dad, a small-town boy from Ohio, never had. Harvey, his wife Donna, and their kids, Maria and Christopher, were regular guests at our pool and barbecue parties. Later in his life, Dad would describe his time working on the show as the happiest days of his entire career.

The Carol Burnett Show aired twenty-three shows a year for CBS. Dad and the rest of the cast would go into the studio on Monday for a table read of the upcoming show. Tuesday was for rehearsal, line learning, and reworking anything that didn't seem right. Wednesday would be a full run-through of the show, and Thursday was the dress rehearsal, where the actors would spend the day blocking to figure out how to move through their sketches and musical numbers. Finally, Friday night was when the show was taped in front of a live studio audience. In all, the cast and crew only had four short days to learn new material, rehearse, and get it all right before the taping on Friday. It was a tough schedule with little room for error, but Dad and the other cast members were dedicated pros, and *The Carol Burnett Show* was always ready when the cameras rolled on Friday night.

Friday-night taping of the show was an exciting event with a celebratory feel, so many of the spouses and friends of the cast and crew would attend. It became a kind of social outing for them all, and after the show was "in the can," the whole group would go out for dinner and drinks. Friday was Mom's one night out away from us kids, when she was free to talk and laugh with her friends.

After the show wrapped, the whole group would go to their favorite bar, The City Slicker. It was right across the street from CBS, and most of the clientele were people who worked at the surrounding studios. Despite its proximity to CBS Television City, where some of showbiz's biggest names worked, The City Slicker's atmosphere was unpretentious and relaxed. Everyone from the show's star to the cameraman could cozy up to the bar shoulder to shoulder and gossip over a beer or a gin and tonic. After a round or two of drinks, the group would head out for a late dinner before going home.

Friday-night visits to the set were just for the adults—my parents claimed that an "insurance issue" prevented children from being on-set during a taping. I realize now that this was probably just an excuse to keep us from whining about being left at home.

Kids were allowed to attend on Thursday nights when the show went through its dress rehearsal, so a couple of Thursdays a month Mom would pick up my brothers and me early from school to take us to CBS Television City. We had to drive over the hill to get from the Valley to the studio, and on the way we would stop at an amusement park called Kiddieland. Kiddieland's main attraction was horse and pony rides, so we would spend an hour taking rides on the horses around a circular, fenced-in corral. There was one corral with ponies for the little kids and another with regular-size horses for the older kids. The horses were sunken-backed and droopy with age, but I guess plodding in a circle wasn't too bad a gig for a retired horse. Plus, we would feed them carrots and apples, laughing as their big lips brushed against the palms of our hands.

After our rides, we'd sit at wooden picnic tables to eat hot dogs and popcorn before packing back into the car to resume our journey to the CBS studios. I'm sure the purpose of this stop at Kiddieland was to drain some of our combustive energy before arriving at the busy studio.

The spot where Kiddieland used to be is now the home of the lavish Beverly Center shopping mall. Whenever I drive by the Beverly Center, with its exterior escalators and bright neon lights, I think back to those old horses and eating hot dogs in the dusty sunlight.

When we got to CBS, Carol's kids, Carrie, Erin, and Jodie, were usually there, along with the children of other cast and crew. We'd jump from the car and immediately go tearing through the place like a pack of wild monkeys. *The Carol Burnett Show* only occupied the actual stage space on Thursdays and Fridays, when the show was rehearsed and taped. Monday through Wednesday, Stage 33 was used by the game show *The Price Is Right,* and the entire set would be wheeled into the studio for the taping and pushed back out when it was over. The giant, multicolored wheel that lit up when the contestants gave it a spin would be sitting in the hallways, along with the glittery backdrops and props the show used.

The CBS studio complex was a wonderland for children on the loose. There were so many places to visit and explore that it was hard to decide where to go first. We were always hungry, so the studio commissary was usually top on the list, with its cafeteria line of steaming casseroles, French fries, and, best of all, rows of slices of pie and Jell-O with whipped cream on top. Once we'd eaten our fill in the commissary, we'd race back through the halls, past set backdrops, lights, and camera equipment. Hide-and-seek was a favorite game, with so many dark places to conceal ourselves. There were long black drapes used to section off the studio areas, and these were ideal hiding places for jumping out to scare each other. Or we could climb on top of the huge storage crates and lie there unseen on our stomachs, looking out over the sets and spying on everything going on below.

I remember when Dad was preparing to tape a sketch that required him to fly around the set. The crew buckled him into a harness attached to a cable hanging from the rafters. I was standing next to Dad watching the costume designers make small cuts in Dad's costume for the cables to go through. At one point, when the crew was out of earshot, Dad bent down to whisper to me.

"Kell, I need you to go find me a pair of wire cutters. Quick."

"Okay," I said. "Are they in your dressing room?"

"No. Run over to the prop department, ask one of the guys to give you a pair. Tell them they're needed on the set. Hurry!"

I scurried off to the prop department and announced that I needed a pair of wire cutters. The man shrugged and gave me some from his toolbox. I ran back and handed them to Dad, and he slipped them into the deep front pocket of his pants.

"What's with the wire cutters, Dad?"

"Well, see how tight they have me hooked into this thing?" He pulled on the strap of the harness. "You think any of these people are going to hang around and get me out of this if there's an earthquake or a fire? I'll be left hanging up there while everyone runs for their lives!" He patted the wire cutters in his pocket.

"Good plan, Dad," I said.

Later, when Dad was in the air performing the sketch, I could see the imprint of the wire cutters through his pants pocket. As far as I know, I was the only person in on Dad's emergency escape plan.

When I wasn't hanging out on-set with my dad, I loved going in the makeup room to watch the cast getting their hair and faces made up for the show. The countertops were strewn with boxes and tubes full of makeup in every color of the rainbow. The show used a lot of wigs, both women's and men's, all kept on white foam heads lined up on a shelf. I also ventured into the wardrobe room to see what costumes the legendary designer, Bob Mackie, and his team had laid out.

CBS was so big that it could accommodate the production of multiple shows at one time. *The Sonny and Cher Show* studio was just across the hall from *The Carol Burnett Show*, and in the studio next door, the sitcom *Three's Company* was being taped. This meant that some of the biggest stars on television were all working under the same roof. I loved sneaking over to the other studio across the hall to watch Cher as she rehearsed musical numbers and sketches with her cast. With her tall, lean physique, waist-length black hair, and baritone voice, Cher was unlike anyone else I'd ever seen. I'd slip into the dressing room and gaze at the racks holding her glittery, colorful costumes. Each dress or pantsuit was paired with a matching headdress, all hand-embellished with sequins, feathers, and rhinestones by a team of seamstresses. Bob Mackie, who would later inspire my career in fashion, designed Cher's fantastic costumes. Bob had his hands full doing all the costumes for the two biggest variety shows on television.

Sonny and Cher's daughter Chastity, who later transitioned to their son Chas, was often at the studio. She was part of our ragtag gang that prowled the complex while all of our parents worked. It was always fun to visit the studio of *Three's Company*, one of the most popular sitcoms on television. The show's star, John Ritter, was one of my favorite people at CBS. I would hang out in the makeup room while the stylists readied him for the show, and he'd let me raid the candy bowl on the counter. Suzanne Somers and Joyce DeWitt, who played John's roommates on the show, would also be getting their hair and makeup done. I loved watching the stylist curl and tease Suzanne's long blonde hair into the bombshell look that her character Chrissy was famous for. Sometimes John would ask me if I wanted my hair and makeup done, and I'd say, "Yes, please!" He would let me sit in his high director's chair while the makeup artist did her work.

Even though the CBS studio complex was a maze of fun and distraction, I always made sure to be back on-set when *The Carol Burnett Show* went into rehearsal. Dad loved the spontaneous comedy style that he and his cast mates created together. He was famous for taking a sketch in an unexpected direction that would leave the cast struggling to keep their faces straight.

Dad liked to have props for his character to use during a sketch. The studio employed a talented team of designers and craftsmen who would make anything the cast dreamed up, but Dad sometimes chose to work on his own props at home in order to keep his cast mates in the dark. He was skilled at carpentry and made all kinds of things in the little garage workshop at our house. One of my favorite things to do was to help Dad out in the shop when he was working on one of these surprise props for an upcoming show.

One day Dad came home very excited. He had an idea for an upcoming sketch with Harvey Korman. Dad was always out to "get" Harvey during their performances together. The two loved to play off each other in ways that only heightened the hilarity of whatever situation they found themselves in. It was a sort of game to see if they could crack the other one up during a performance, and Dad went through great lengths to surprise Harvey with unexpected twists during a sketch.

In this sketch, Dad and Harvey play butlers tasked with opening a mansion's imposing front door when the bell rings. But, as always in a comedic situation, a problem arises, thus creating havoc, which leads to hilarity. Dad decided to use the doorknob—a single knob placed in the center of the door, like you sometimes see in grand, old houses—as his key prop. He had an idea in mind for this special doorknob, one that Harvey wouldn't be aware of until he walked onto the set during the taping.

At Dad's instruction, the art department made an oversized doorknob about eight inches in diameter, almost the size of a dinner plate. Once the carpenters had finished, Dad brought the doorknob home to paint it. That night in the garage workshop, armed with paintbrushes, Dad and I bent over the wooden doorknob and coated it with a bronze-colored paint. It looked like a real doorknob—just much bigger.

The day of the sketch arrived, and Dad arranged for the carpenters to install the giant doorknob onto the front door a few minutes before they started taping. As the cameras rolled and the studio audience looked on, Dad's butler character tries to open the door when the doorbell rings, but it's too large for his gloved hand to grasp. No matter how hard he tries, it won't turn. Finally, he calls to the other butler for help, and out walks Harvey. At this point, Dad has hoisted himself up onto the doorknob and is straddling it, his two feet planted against the door, swinging from side to side in an attempt to make it turn. At the sight of Dad hanging on the doorknob, Harvey is dumbstruck. He struggles to stay in character, but you can see the tiny muscles of his face fighting to keep from breaking into laughter. By now, the studio audience is screaming with laughter as Harvey, now stopped mid-stride, his eyes squeezed shut, attempts not to crack up.

There were other props I helped Dad construct over the years, and I loved having a chance to contribute, in my small way, to his vision as a comedic artist. Having spent so many years on the set of *The Carol Burnett Show* and other projects Dad worked on, I grew up with a unique view of how television and movies come to life. I watched the crew create sets from wood and paint and makeup artists transform the cast into fantastic characters. I spent hours studying the costume team while they contemplated fabrics and wigs, watching the seamstresses hand-sew individual beads onto Cher's Bob Mackie gowns. All of those experiences forged my love of creativity into a career as a costume designer when I grew up.

This part of me is also a gift from Dad, as he helped me to understand that the magic of transformation isn't always in front of the camera. It comes from behind it, too.

Chapter 5

Dad's work on *The Carol Burnett Show* was a comedic alchemy of spontaneous creativity and physical humor. And our home life followed the same formula. Dad believed that every day was an opportunity to reinvent a seemingly trivial task into something epic. Although he worked very long hours at the studio and no one would have blamed him for wanting some quiet time over the weekend, watching television all day wasn't Dad's way of relaxation. No matter what his schedule, he always made time for all of us kids—individually and as a group.

Dad had always been a creator. He grew up helping his father build things in their basement workshop, making shelves for Magi's kitchen or a birdhouse for the backyard. There was very little the two couldn't make, or fix, on their own. Even when he was an adult, with enough money to pay other people to do these things, Dad still loved working on projects for our home. When he hunkered down to make something, my brothers and I would stop whatever we were doing and run to join him.

One of Dad's favorite places to go was Builder's Emporium, a huge store where you could buy wood, tools, and other items you might need for a home project. My brothers and I would race up and down the aisles helping Dad gather the supplies, then help him lash everything to the roof of our station wagon for the wobbly trip back home. Over the years we assisted him in building platforms for the treehouse, racks to hold our skis, and shelves for the house.

One of Dad's most ambitious projects came to life when he decided that our family room needed a proper stage for performances. The room had a half-moon-shaped alcove filled with windows that stuck out from the side of the house—the perfect spot. Dad built a full-size elevated stage in this space, complete with rows of theater lights and a sound system, and plenty of room in front for audience seating. Once we added a drum kit, several guitars, and some microphone stands, the stage was set for impromptu rock-and-roll concerts, puppet shows, or karaoke sessions.

Every year the beloved movie classic *The Wizard of Oz* would be played on network television. These were the days before people had instant access to any movie or show they wanted to watch with the push of a button. The movie only aired once a year, so watching it was an exciting and much-anticipated event.

One year Dad decided that we would have a family viewing party of *The Wizard of Oz*. He put our largest television up on the family room stage while my brothers and I set up chairs in front of it. To make the room dark like a real movie theater, we taped tinfoil on all the windows to block any light. Dad made a small "box office" with a window outside the family room, with a turnstile made from a cut-off broom handle in the doorway that swung open and closed. Dad painted red stripes on brown paper lunch bags for popcorn. He also made individual tickets that would be sold through the box office and were required for entry to the movie.

That evening we lined up at the box office to buy our tickets, using a few pennies or some Monopoly money. Tim, who was the usher, looked at the seat number on each ticket and led everyone to the appropriate chair. I worked from the makeshift snack bar scooping hot buttered popcorn into the striped bags while Jamie handed out cans of soda.

Dad flicked the lights to signal that it was time for the movie to start. Everyone scuttled around to find their seats, whispering and giggling in anticipation. Once the audience was seated, Dad switched off all the lights. In the dark, cool room with everyone munching on their bags of popcorn, it felt like we were at an actual movie theater! We all settled back, waiting to be transported into Dorothy's Technicolor world of twisters, witches, and the Emerald City.

About halfway through the movie I got up and left the theater to visit the bathroom. When I came back down the hall to the family room, Dad was waiting by the turnstile. I started to slide past him, but he held the broom handle down so I couldn't lift it.

"Ticket, please!" he said in a brisk, polite voice.

I smirked up at him. "Very funny."

But when I tried to move past the fake turnstile, he held it firmly in place. "Miss, I need to see your ticket."

"Come on, Dad." Looking around him at the screen, I could see that the part where the flying monkeys carry the Cowardly Lion away was coming up. "You're making me miss the movie!"

"Miss," Dad repeated with a smile, "I'll need to see your ticket in order to let you in."

I felt around in both pockets, but there was no ticket.

"I must have left it on my seat," I said. "Come on, Dad—it's me. Kelly. You know I had a ticket because you sold me one before the movie started!" I couldn't believe he was holding me up. His only daughter!

"All right, miss," Dad said, giving me a stern look. "I'll let you in this time. But next time remember your ticket stub so there's proof that you had it. Okay?" Then he smiled and turned the broom-handle turnstile to let me through.

I sprinted past and back into my seat, where I was just in time for the flying monkey attack. Later, when the lights came on, I found my ticket crumpled up under my seat.

Dad's gentle but firm teasing with me over the ticket wasn't just a joke. Although we kids had a lot of freedom in our daily lives and our parents never hovered, we were still expected to have a sense of personal responsibility for our actions. The lesson I learned with the lost movie ticket was that you had to be accountable. Dad, of course, knew that I had a ticket for the movie. The happy sphere in which my family existed was safe and trusting, but the real world wouldn't be so forgiving. Dad wanted us to be ready for it.

Dad's creative energy didn't stop at homemade movie theaters. He never hesitated to enlist us kids when something needed to be done around the house, and he always made even the most mundane chore an adventure.

One day Mom told him that the guesthouse was in dire need of a new coat of paint, and she made it clear that she wanted the job done soon. Dad quickly saw an opportunity to accomplish the task and have some fun, too. He herded all six of us in the car for a trip to Builder's Emporium to buy paint and other supplies. Back home, he gave each of us a new pair of painting overalls and a white painter's hat. Then every kid got his or her very own gallon of white paint and paintbrush. Once he'd fetched his Super 8 camera, it was time for the work to begin.

With a signal from Dad, we attacked the poor guesthouse like a tribe of wild banshees, slapping as much paint on each other and ourselves as we did the house. Tim tried to carry his bucket up a ladder and ended up spilling paint on Jamie's head in the process. Little Seann, who was probably about five years old, quickly abandoned his paintbrush and tried rubbing the paint on with his tiny hand. The whole time Dad stood back filming us with the camera. When Mom came out and saw what was going on, she screamed so loud I'm sure the people two streets away heard it. But even she couldn't be mad for too long—who could be? We were just kids, trying our hardest to get that guesthouse painted. And having the time of our lives.

The year that Mom turned forty, Dad planned a surprise party for her at the house. Mom's birthday was on Christmas Eve, and she had always said she felt cheated about not having a "real" birthday, where the focus was all on her. Dad was determined to make her fortieth birthday an exception.

The party was scheduled for the weekend before Christmas so as not to interfere with the guests' holiday plans. We kids helped decorate the towering Christmas tree in the front foyer, climbing the stairs to hang ornaments along the top branches. All that was left was to place the golden star on the top of the tree, but we couldn't find it.

"Where the hell is that thing?" Dad was looking through all the empty ornament boxes.

"The cat probably ate it," I said.

"Never mind," Dad said. "I'll think of something."

Later that day, I walked into Dad's office, where he was sitting at his desk unraveling toilet paper from the roll.

"What are you doing, Dad?" I asked.

"Making something. Go run and get me some glue, Pal."

I raced to fetch the glue and watched as Dad attached two eight-by-ten headshots of himself on either side of the empty cardboard roll. When the glue dried, I followed him to the top of the spiral staircase.

Dad leaned over the rail and slid the tube over the top of the tree. Then we went back down the stairs and looked up, our heads tilted back. There was Dad's eight-by-ten face, grinning down from the top of our beautiful Christmas tree.

"I don't get it," I said.

"We needed a star for the tree, right?" Dad said. "Well, there it is. A star on top of the tree."

I rolled my eyes. "Funny, Dad."

No matter how much we whined and begged, Dad was firm that Mom's birthday party was for adults only. We were allowed to help him decorate the living room with party streamers and balloons, but once the guests started to arrive we had to get upstairs and stay out of sight.

After a few minutes, we slipped back out of our rooms and crept out to the top of the staircase, where our twenty-five-foot-tall Christmas tree stood in a blaze of lights and ornaments, the top almost grazing the high ceiling. From our perch we sat in a row and peered through the banister rails, enjoying a full view of the guests coming through the front door and heading to the living room beyond.

Everyone mingled around the catered buffet and sipped drinks from the bar. A beautiful two-tiered cake sat on a round table surrounded by flowers. We kids had all been promised a slice if we behaved and stayed out of sight. People took their drinks and drifted in and out of the open patio doors, where sparkling lights hung from the trees. A large fire crackled in the living room fireplace. It looked like a very elegant birthday party, but anyone who knew my dad had to know that *some* kind of catch was in the works.

Mom didn't dance much anymore—with six kids and a household to run, there was no time—but she always loved doing it whenever she had a chance. Just as the guests were into their second or third round of drinks, Dad stood up and called for everyone to gather around. At his signal, three professional dancers wearing matching costumes and tap shoes burst into the room and took their positions in the center of the floor.

"Dear friends!" Dad announced. "Thank you all so much for coming to celebrate the fortieth birthday of my beautiful wife. As many of you know, Mary Anne is a very talented dancer, so I couldn't think of anything better to give her for this special birthday than ... all of her friends tap-dancing along with her!" He turned as two waiters entered the room, carrying boxes full of tap shoes. "There's enough tap shoes for everyone. Find a pair that fits and join us on the dance floor for a Mary Anne birthday tap extravaganza!"

Some of the guests nearly spit out their drinks in surprise as the choreographer cued up a record on the turntable. They were going to tap-dance? Dad went around, encouraging those who were hesitant and also catching anyone trying to sneak off into the backyard. It was impossible to say no to Dad, so even those claiming two left feet put on some tap shoes and took their place on the floor.

Dad lined everyone up in rows with Mom up in front between her best friend Edwina Anderson and Carol Burnett. Then the professional dancers walked everyone through a simple tap routine, repeating it until even the most uncoordinated of the group had caught on. A lively song came bursting out of the speakers and the whole room began to tap-dance together, slowly. Some people tapped on the wrong beat or turned left when they were supposed to turn right. Others collided into each other's arms, nearly falling down from laughter.

I can still see the scene as I viewed it from between the banister railings: That whole roomful of people in their sparkling party clothes, tap-dancing, with Mom and Dad right there in the center. The guests sang along to the songs and laughed as they tapped and whirled across the polished wood floor. The caterers came out of the kitchen and gathered in the foyer to watch. The sound of fifty pairs of tap shoes against the floor rang through the house.

Mom looked beautiful, dancing in her chic black mini dress with her silky red hair piled high at the back of her head. Her face was beaming as she tilted her head back and forth with the rhythm of the music. We all knew she was thrilled with Dad's birthday surprise, paying homage to the dancer's talent he so admired in her. It was a moment of sheer happiness and love for both Mom and Dad, celebrating each other and the life they'd made together.

In six years, their marriage would come to an end, but on that perfect night I saw just how much my parents meant to each other.

Chapter 6

Not many people can say that their mother is their father's godmother, but I can. It's just one of the many odd little stories that pepper Conway family history.

Religion played little, if any, role in Dad's life when he was growing up. Our grandmother Magi did have him baptized in the local Romanian Orthodox church when he was a baby, probably just to be on the safe side. But although they may have attended church on Christmas and Easter, to keep a toe in the holy water, the family wasn't religious. Despite their ambivalence toward structured religion, Magi and Papa raised my dad to live every step of his life with honesty, integrity, and kindness.

I'm pretty sure Dad would have been happy to raise his six kids with the same relaxed spiritual style and thus have our Sunday mornings free to do what we liked. But Mom was a different story. The Dalton family were tough, hard-drinking, but highly pious Irish-Catholics, and only being flat on your back sick in bed could excuse you from missing Mass. Grandfather and Grandmother Dalton might drink and scream at each other all night long, but both would be sitting straight-backed in the pew come Sunday morning. Mom inherited her parents' disciplined faith—along with some of the tendency for screaming, too—but fortunately, not the drinking part. So every Sunday, she always made sure that the Conway family was lined up in a row of eight at the Our Lady of Grace Catholic Church in Encino.

Dad's conversion to Catholicism was, naturally, a humorous tale. While in college, he'd dated a young woman who was a practicing Catholic. As the relationship became more serious, the woman encouraged my father to convert to her religion. I have no doubt that Dad was probably more interested in impressing his girlfriend than in finding spiritual salvation, but he went ahead and met with a priest. On the day of his conversion, a small group of their college friends went along to the church as witnesses. One was Mary Anne Dalton, my mother.

The priest went through all of the holy motions of transforming Dad into a brand-new Catholic boy. But when he got to the question of who would stand as Dad's godmother, a prolonged silence fell. Dad hadn't thought about that one.

"Can you be my godmother?" he asked his girlfriend.

The priest gave a polite cough. "I don't think that's a good idea," he said. "What if your relationship moves to marriage? A wife should not be her own husband's godmother."

The priest had a point. That would be very weird indeed to have your wife as your godmother. They had reached an impasse when my mother stepped up. "I'll be Tim's godmother," she said.

And that's how Mom became the sanctified godmother to the man she would marry just a few years later.

Every Sunday, Dad would put on a nice suit and drive his godmother and their six children to church. We would sit in a row with Mom on one end and Dad on the other to keep an eye on us during the long, boring Mass. My brothers would tug at the collars of their button-up shirts, and I would twist uncomfortably in my stiff, starchy dress that I could hardly wait to tear off the moment we returned home. Each of us would struggle to behave like good little church kids as we went through the motions of standing to sing, sitting to listen, and hunkering down on our knees to pray. Over and over again.

Remaining quiet for an entire hour was difficult for the Conways even under the best of circumstances—Dad included. If we started fussing or whispering, Mom would reach over and clench the offender's arm with an astonishingly hard grip. Her sharp, manicured hands would dig into your flesh to let you know that she meant business. One painful squeeze from Mom was usually all it took to scare us into obedience while the priest droned on from the pulpit.

On Palm Sunday, the church handed out individual palm branches before the Mass. My mother, foreseeing a palm frond sword fight, confiscated the palms from us kids and handed them to Dad for safekeeping when we sat down in the pew. I was sitting next to Dad, and a few minutes into the Mass, I noticed that he was doing something with one of the palms. While I watched, Dad quietly split a few fronds and braided them, forming a circle tied with a knot. He took my hand and tied it around my wrist, never once looking away from the priest.

While I admired my new bracelet, Dad tore off another few fronds and braided them, adding little decorative twists for panache. Then, very slowly, so as not to attract my mom's attention, he slid his arm over the back of the pew and put the "necklace" around my neck. By now, my brothers had noticed, and they all leaned over to get a better look across the pew. Dad was halfway through making the palm ring that would complete my collection when Mom glanced over and saw what he was doing.

"Are you *kidding* me?" she mouthed. It was in the middle of the Mass, so that's all she could do. But once we were in the car, Mary Anne's rage exploded.

"What the *fuck* were you thinking?" she yelled at Dad. "Sitting there *right in front of the priest* making jewelry out of the palms on Palm Sunday? It's fucking blasphemy!"

"Mom!" I yelled. "You shouldn't be saying the 'F' word when we're not even out of the church parking lot!"

I wore my Palm Sunday "jewels" to Du-par's, the restaurant we always went to after church. If they had been made from diamonds and gold, I wouldn't have been any prouder. Dad and I smiled conspiratorially at each other as we ate our pancakes and eggs. The fun had been worth the trouble we were now in, but we made sure to avoid Mom for the remainder of the day.

I started attending Encino Elementary School when I was nine. The school was just one block away from our house, so I could walk there and even come back home for lunch.

One day the teacher assigned each student an American president on which to write a report. We would then give a presentation on our president to the rest of the class. My president was Franklin D. Roosevelt.

When I got home and told my dad about the report, he immediately perked up.

"Roosevelt? Okay, we have to get you a suit."

"A suit?" I said. "Why?"

"You can't be President Roosevelt without a suit."

I realized that Dad was going to do what he did best: He would help me make something as mundane as a school report on a president into a real production.

Dad gave me one of his old suits—with the legs pinned up—and a bow tie. He found a pipe that Papa had left behind after one of our grandparents' visits. Dressed in my baggy suit, with the pipe dangling from the corner of my mouth, I resembled a Little Rascals character more than an actual president. Dad looked me over thoughtfully. I could tell he still wasn't entirely satisfied with my transformation.

The day before I was to give my presentation, Dad came home and walked through the front door pushing a wheelchair.

"What on earth, Tim?" Mom yelled as we kids raced down the stairs.

"It's FDR's wheelchair!" said Dad. "Kelly, tell your mom and your brothers why your President Roosevelt needs a wheelchair."

"Because he was a paralyzed at age thirty-nine after a long illness!" I piped up. "But he didn't want people seeing him in a wheelchair, so he tried not to let anyone photograph him in it."

"Exactly!" Dad crowed. "So, it's only appropriate for Kelly's FDR to have a wheelchair."

My brother Patrick sat in the chair while Tim and Jamie pushed him around the foyer in circles.

"Hey!" I yelled, running to shove Patrick out of the chair. "I'm Roosevelt, and that's *my* wheelchair!"

Mom stood with her hands on her hips. "You are saying that she is going to take the wheelchair with her to *school?*"

"Sure," said Dad. "I'll take her tomorrow."

Mom sighed and watched helplessly while we kids took turns pushing each other around the house in our new toy.

The next morning I put on my FDR suit, settled into the wheelchair with my book bag and lunchbox in my lap, and Dad pushed me down the block to Encino Elementary.

"Knock 'em dead, President," he said, and with a quick kiss good-bye, he was out the door.

When it was my turn to present, I wheeled up to the front of the room and gave the class my report on President Franklin D. Roosevelt. I'm pretty sure I got an A on the assignment.

After the last bell rang, I sat outside, slumped in the wheelchair, waiting for Dad to appear. When he didn't come, I went back in and called the house from the office.

"Dad," I said when he answered the phone. "Where are you?"

"I'm at home, Kell. Doing some work stuff. How did your report go today?"

"It was great. But I need you to come to push me back. In the wheelchair, remember?"

"Is the wheelchair working all right?" Dad asked.

"Yes!" I said. "But I'm done with it now. So can you just come get me?"

There was a pause on the other end of the line. "Well, if you have a perfectly functioning wheelchair at your disposal, then you don't really need anyone to push it. I think that you can probably make the one-block trip home just fine on your own. See you soon!"

Since I usually walked to and from school every day, this wasn't really a hardship. You have to consider that these were the days when parents didn't do everything for their children, or fret about them going places on their own. Kids could walk—or roll—a block home from school all by themselves, and no one thought a thing about it.

So what else could an American president faced with such a challenge do? I pushed the chair back outside, sat down with my metal Mighty Mouse lunchbox on my lap, and started to roll myself home along the sidewalk. I'm sure the sight of a fourth-grade girl wearing a suit and mustache while chugging along in a wheelchair was quite strange to the people driving by. When I wheeled up the driveway, Dad was waiting at the front door for me, laughing so hard that tears came to his eyes.

Franklin D. Roosevelt wasn't the only school costume that Dad had a hand in helping me create. For many years Cher had been my idol. Getting to see her in person at the CBS studios on Thursdays was always the highlight of my week. I studied her walk, her laugh, and her dance moves. I wanted to *be* her.

One year for the seventh-grade talent show, I decided that I would lip-sync to the popular Sonny and Cher hit, "I Got You, Babe." Dad suggested that since the song was a duet, it only made sense that I should dress up as both Cher and Sonny.

We found a sparkly jumpsuit with a funky jacket, and Dad sat down in his workshop to make me a long wig out of black yarn. During my performance, I wore the wig while lip-syncing to the Cher parts, and when it was Sonny's turn to sing, I turned from the audience, ripped off the wig, held up a mustache clipped to a clothespin to my lip, and swung back around to continue the song. Since Sonny and Cher alternated the lyrics back and forth, I had to do this whirlwind transformation several times. I can't remember if I won the talent show, or even placed, but Dad's creative flourishes to my costume made it a memorable performance.

Around this age, I had started taking gymnastics classes. We'd always been a highly active family, and Dad's passion for hockey and Mom's love of skiing made natural athletes out of each of us kids. I eagerly joined my brothers in baseball games on the lawn and hockey on our tennis court, but gymnastics was the sport I loved the most.

In the late 1970s, there was no bigger star than Romanian gymnast Nadia Comaneci. Nadia had become a worldwide sensation when, at fourteen, she became the first gymnast to win a perfect ten score at the 1976 Olympic Games.

I felt a deep kinship with Nadia because I also had Romanian heritage through my grandmother, Magi. Nadia's posters adorned my bedroom walls, and I collected any magazine or article that mentioned her. If I couldn't be Cher, then I desperately wanted to be Nadia. I bought a white leotard with yellow and blue stripes like the one she always wore and tied my hair in a high ponytail with red yarn ribbon, the same way she styled hers. Dad made me a gym bag in the red, yellow, and blue Romanian colors, just like Nadia carried when she went to competitions. Whenever she was competing on TV, I'd sit close to the screen, studying her gymnastic moves and trying to replicate them myself. Dad even built me a balance beam—albeit just a few inches off the floor, since he knew my balancing skills were a bit less advanced than Nadia's were.

One day I put on my white leotard, adjusted my Nadia ponytail, and went outside to practice. In the center of our large front lawn, I waved to the imaginary crowd, turning right and left, and then took my position for a floor routine. Going through the moves, I imagined that instead of bushes and trees there were grandstands full of cheering fans surrounding me, whooping with delight as I whirled into a cartwheel with a somersault over the grass. I twisted my body into a roundoff back handspring as the judges sat awed with their mouths agape. These feats of astounding ability were lightened by some artistic prancing and "jazz hands" before I swung around at the end of the lawn, preparing for my grand finale.

This was the moment that could make or break my gold medal dreams. After a second of fixed concentration, I bounded across the grass to complete a double back handspring that ended with me landing on my butt instead of my feet. But no problem, I was up in a flash and the crowd took to their feet, roaring. I stood with my back arched and arms up, savoring the ecstasy of my Olympic victory!

Suddenly I heard the sound of clapping—real clapping—coming from the house. I looked up and there was Dad, leaning out of his bedroom window. He'd watched my entire routine and was now cheering with his hands held high over his head.

"Amaaaaazing, Kell!" he hollered. "That was the best gymnastics routine I have ever seen in my life!"

My chest filled with pride. "Really?"

"Absolutely!" he yelled back. "I give it a ten-ten-TEN!"

"Thanks, Dad!" I called, waving to him with both hands over my head—just like Nadia waved to her fans. Dad continued to applaud as I turned in a triumphant circle, drinking in the adoration of my one-person audience.

That was Dad. Always my number-one fan.

Chapter 7

ACCORDING TO PEOPLE WHO STUDY THESE KINDS OF THINGS, THE NUMber of siblings a person has—and where they fall in the birth order—can strongly influence their personality. I wonder what a psychologist would have to say about my role as the eldest child and only girl of six children. Perhaps they would point to my independent streak and my need to take charge in most situations as a classic "oldest child" trait. Maybe they would nod knowingly at my tendency to be the savior, and my constant desire to make everything right, for everyone to be happy.

After I was born, my younger brothers followed in rapid succession—five boys in seven years. My childhood was like being a single piece in a complex puzzle. No matter how much those pieces jostled around, our lives were never complete until we'd all fit back together again.

Although sometimes locking the parts into a picture of domestic happiness could be a little rough.

My parents loved to tell the story about my reaction when my infant brother Seann, the last of the six, came home from the hospital. At that point, I already had four younger brothers, and I wanted a sister more than anything. Even at age eight, I understood the fundamental laws of statistics: If you tossed a penny enough times and got heads, tails would always turn up after a few tries. I told everyone who would listen that Mom would finally be bringing home my baby sister—my future best friend and fellow she-warrior to battle against the boy tribe. Surely, after so many heads, my penny would land tails up this time.

It was August of 1970, and the summer heat created blurry waves over the valley floor. In the shade of a small birch tree in front of our small house in Tarzana, my brothers and I sat waiting. Perched in a row of foldout chairs, we kept our eyes fastened on the winding road that led up to our driveway. Our grandparents, Magi and Papa, in town to look after us while Mom had the baby, kept close watch from their seats on the porch. Whenever a car would approach, Timmy and I would gasp and grip the armrests to hoist up for a better look.

"It's them!" Timmy shouted, pointing. "It's them!"

"No, Timmy," I scolded. "That car is blue. That's not them."

"Come sit inside for a while," Magi called, fanning herself with a magazine. "You kids are going to get sunstroke sitting out there with no shade."

But I didn't budge. Nothing was going to make me miss the arrival of my new baby sister, not even the oppressive summer heat.

It was midafternoon when a familiar beige station wagon made its way up the hill toward the house. In an instant, my brothers and I were out of our seats, racing to meet it in the driveway.

Dad stepped out of the car and met us with a big hug. We peered around him to the passenger seat where Mom sat holding a tiny bundle. Dad went over and opened the door to gently help Mom out of the car as Magi and Papa came over from the house and joined us.

I pushed through the crowd to look at the tiny, wrinkled face of the newest Conway baby. It stared back at me fiercely, wrapped in a light blue blanket.

"Meet Seann," Dad said. "Your new baby brother."

Brother? The word fell on me like a ton of bricks. I'd wished harder than anything for a sister, even praying to God before bed, and I'd never once doubted that a baby girl would be my reward.

While everyone else fussed over Seann, I stood in shock. Another boy. Another *brother*.

Everyone began to make their way up to the house. Numb with fury, I bent down and took a fist full of gravel in my hand.

"No!" I screamed, hurling the pebbles toward the group. "It's supposed to be a *girl*! Take him away!"

The gravel landed harmlessly short of hitting baby Seann, but everyone stared at me as though I was possessed.

"Kelly Conway!" Magi said. "What in God's name is wrong with you, child?"

I spun around and ran into the house.

Sulking behind my closed bedroom door, I listened as the rest of the family gathered in the living room, laughing and fussing over the new baby. After a few minutes, I went out and stood in the doorway, watching.

Magi was sitting on the sofa with Seann in her arms, and she looked up.

"Kelly," she said with a gentle smile. "Come see your new little brother."

I went and sat on the arm of the sofa next to her.

"You know what?" she whispered. "I think he looks exactly like you did when you were a baby."

That got my interest. I peered down at the little face, studying his rosebud lips and the fuzz of golden hair covering his head. He *was* really cute. Seann's eyes swiveled around and then fixed straight into mine, and in that very second, I knew I would love him. And I did. Even if he hadn't been the sister that I'd so hoped for.

———

As I got older I realized that there was something special about being Dad's only daughter. We had a unique bond that grew stronger as the years went by, and although I was just as tough as my brothers and loved sports, Dad was protective of me. Even when I became an adult, Dad always knew where I was. I never stopped being his little girl.

The day I started first grade at Our Lady of Grace Catholic School, I was seven years old and terrified. As Dad drove me to school that morning, he kept looking over at me and asking if I was okay. When we arrived, the school looked enormous and scary. Dad walked me to my classroom, met the teacher, and helped me find my desk. I remember sitting there miserably as he looked back from the door and mouthed "Good-bye."

The morning quickly progressed, and my anxiety faded as the teacher busied us with tasks and art projects. Little did I know that Dad was still outside the school. After leaving me in the classroom, he couldn't bring himself to head home. My sad little face was burned into his mind, and all he could do was drive around the block, over and over, worrying.

A short while later, the teacher led us outside to the playground for recess. I was still feeling shy around my new classmates, so I found a corner of the yard and began pushing the dirt into little piles and shapes. I was so absorbed that I didn't even notice when the teacher called the class to go back inside. When I looked up a few minutes later, everyone was gone, and I was alone. I didn't know which door led back into the school, and I was terrified that the teacher would be angry with me. Standing in the middle of the playground, I burst into tears.

Dad had just made another circle around the block when he spotted me from the street. He pulled the car over, ran to the fence surrounding the playground, and pulled me over it. As I sobbed into his shoulder, Dad cursed the neglectful school.

"That does it," he said. "You're done."

We got in the car and drove straight home. I resumed first grade at another school where Dad was assured that I would not be abandoned in the playground.

My dad was the kind of father who saw value in education beyond the confines of a classroom. He'd been a passionate fan of horse racing all his life, so he felt it was quite logical that we kids could learn valuable lessons from the stands of Santa Anita. Sometimes, when he had a rare weekday off from work, he'd pick up me and my brothers from school in the middle of the day and off we'd go to the track, where we'd sit in Dad's box eating hot dogs as he explained the statistical art of horse betting.

The floors of the stands and lobby were littered with discarded betting tickets, and my brothers and I would run around picking them up and stuffing them into an empty garbage bag that we'd begged off of the snack-bar workers. We just knew that some distracted racetrack regular had accidentally thrown out a million-dollar ticket, and with enough effort, we'd be lucky enough to find it.

As soon as we got home, we would spread the tickets out on the floor and examine each one against the racing program that listed the wins for that day. Most of the tickets were worthless, but sometimes we'd find one with an uncashed $2 or $5 winner. Once we'd gathered up the winning tickets, Dad would take them back to the track to cash them in for us. It was incredibly exciting to think of all the money that other people had just thrown away like it was trash.

One evening after Dad had taken us to the track, Tim, Patrick, Corey, and I were busy sorting through our piles of tickets on the living room floor.

Mom walked in and glanced over at us. "What are you doing?" she asked.

My brothers and I fell silent. "We're checking tickets, Mom," I said, trying to sound casual.

"I can see that," Mom said. "Where did you get them?"

"From the floor," Tim said.

"And from the trash cans, too," Patrick added helpfully.

Mom put her hands on her hips and frowned at us. "And *where* was this floor and these trash cans that you got these tickets from?"

The jig was up. "At the track," I confessed.

"Tim Conway!" Mom yelled. "Get in here!"

When Dad walked in and saw us with the tickets, he went a little pale.

"Tell me you didn't pull these kids out of school and take them to the racetrack." Mom was furious.

"What are they going to learn in school they can't learn at the track?" Dad asked.

"What are you talking about?" Mom snapped.

Dad turned to Corey, who was about eight. "Corey, if a horse goes off at three-to-five in the sixth race, and you have two dollars on it to win, what does that pay?"

We all looked at Corey, and he stared back, knowing the pressure was on him to prove Dad right. He bit his lower lip and squinted his eyes in concentration. You could have heard a pin drop. "Umm," Corey said after a moment, "three dollars and twenty cents?"

Dad turned to Mom with a huge grin. "See? Every single race is a math problem. You think they'd learn that kind of math in school?"

Mom was still angry at Dad for taking us out of school, but even she was impressed with Corey's skills.

After that, while Dad still let us play hooky from school to accompany him to the track from time to time, we were careful to hide our tickets from Mom.

Dad wasn't trying to turn us into school-skipping, track-betting juvenile delinquents. He just wanted us to make the most of our daily lives. The only limit was our imagination.

But sometimes, things went a bit awry.

One hot Saturday afternoon, when my brothers and I were bored and whining, Dad had an idea. He set to work attaching the end of a steel cable to the top edge of the patio wall. The six of us followed, handing him tools and pelting him with questions. Dad stretched the line across the patio's length, over the pool, and then across the yard, where he fastened the other end to the cinder-block wall that encircled our property. Then he looped additional pieces of wire to the line and secured them to short metal bars that hung down, to make handles.

Voilà! A homemade zipline.

A riot ensued as we fought over who would be the first to ride it, but I won the honor. Dad helped me climb to the top of the ladder by the patio wall and gave me the handles. The zipline was on a slight downward angle so that when you jumped off the ladder, you would slide down the wire and build speed until you got to the pool. At this point, Dad instructed, we were to let go of the handles and fall into the water.

With a push, I was off, my hair flying behind me as I flew through the air across the patio. When I reached the center of the pool, I released my hands and plunged into the cool water. It was exhilarating. I clambered out of the pool as my brother Tim climbed up the ladder for his turn.

All the brothers had their ride on the zipline until it was little Seann's turn. Dad held Seann until he had gripped the handles tight and then gave him a gentle push off the ladder. While the rest of us cheered, Seann sailed over our heads and toward the pool. And kept going. He'd forgotten that he was supposed to let go over the water. In just seconds he had glided out over the lawn, rapidly gaining speed as he neared the concrete wall at the end.

Dad sprinted faster than I'd ever seen him, with the rest of us at his heels, yelling, "Seann, let go! Let go!"

But Seann held on.

His flight ended when he smacked against the wall and fell a few feet to the ground. Fortunately, Dad had propped up a lounge cushion against the wall as a bumper, so the impact wasn't too hard when he hit.

When we reached Seann, he was sitting on the ground, looking a little dazed, but he was fine.

A shriek pierced the air. It was Mom, barreling toward us in her bathrobe. She had heard the yelling and had watched with horror from a window as her youngest child went flying past on a runaway zipline.

She took Seann up in her arms, and although he'd been just fine a few moments before, he now burst into tears.

"Tim Conway!" she screamed. "Are you seriously trying to kill our children?"

Nobody got a second ride on the zipline.

—◆—

As the family grew, my parents hired a housekeeper to help keep an eye on us kids. This allowed Mom some freedom to have a life beyond that of a harried mother of six. One of her lifelong passions was playing bridge. Mom became so good at this card game that she advanced to the level of Life Master. Her expertise qualified her to play in advanced tournaments all over the country. With our trusted housekeeper, Yolanda, and later, Araceli, she was able to leave town for a few days at a time to try her skills against some of the best bridge players in the world.

My brothers and I always loved having the house to ourselves with only the housekeeper to watch us. We always missed our mom and were happy when she returned, but in her absence we found that we could push the rules and be as wild and carefree as we wanted.

Mom had subdued good taste in a city where women often dressed in flashy styles that were decades too young for them. Mom would never think of leaving the house without a matching outfit and lipstick, her purse the same shade as her shoes. Matching was a sort of religion to my mother. The decor of our entire house was carefully color-coordinated down to the smallest detail, and she insisted that the family car, and even our dog, match the palette, too. Whenever the family had to go someplace that required more formal attire than jeans and T-shirts, every one of us wore the same color. Lined up in our matching outfits, we looked like a 1970s Southern California version of the von Trapp family.

Mom loved snow skiing, and we took regular family trips to Mammoth Mountain. Dad wasn't as much of a ski bum as Mom, so he was the one who would spend the day on the easy hills with the boys, giving Mom the freedom to tackle the bigger hills on her own. I was just as crazy about skiing as Mom, so I'd be out all day, tagging along behind her. My brothers were often not as enthusiastic. One of them was always sick, sleepy, or just wanted to stay in the warm coziness of the room, watching television. And because these were the days before cell phones, Dad needed a way for the boys who stayed back at the hotel to signal if they needed him.

The Mammoth Mountain Inn was at the base of the resort near the beginner chairlift, so you could see the balconies when you were riding up. Dad tied a pair of one of my brother's underwear onto the end of a ski pole to make a sort of flag. If there was a problem in the room, one of the boys could hoist the "flag" out the window so Dad could see it from the chairlift. He'd get off at the top of the hill and ski back down to the Inn to take care of whatever issue had arisen.

Toward the end of the school year, as summer approached, a new kind of excitement built up in the house. Every day my brothers and I would run and look at the calendar that hung in our kitchen, taking turns counting the number of days that remained before a much-anticipated date in early June. I do not doubt that both of our parents looked forward to this happy day as much as we kids, because it marked the start of six weeks blissfully free of children.

This June date was when our parents would herd all six of us kids on a plane and drop us off to spend the summer with our beloved grandparents, Magi and Papa. The day we left for Chagrin Falls, Ohio, couldn't come fast enough.

Chapter 8

OUR DEPARTURE FOR MAGI AND PAPA'S MIGHT BE A FULL THREE WEEKS away, but my brothers and I would already have our bags packed and ready to go. Mom circulated among us, curating the contents of our suitcases and summarily rejecting or approving articles of clothing, swimsuits, and toys. Summer visits to Ohio meant long afternoons at the community pool, delicious meals served up by Magi, and the delight of having both of our grandparents to ourselves all day and night. Magi and Papa dedicated every moment to our comfort and entertainment, and we drank up the undivided attention.

The day we flew out was always a new level of chaos in a house already familiar with pandemonium. Suitcases were lined at the door, ready to be loaded into the van waiting to drive us to the airport, with last-minute dashes back upstairs for some forgotten item. Mom would lay out the matching color-coordinated shirts and jeans that she'd picked for us to wear.

Over the many summers that we made the journey to Ohio, Mom and Dad tried several strategies to monitor the six of us during the four-hour flight. At first, our parents thought that seating three of us in two rows, with Mom sitting in the seat across the aisle of one row and Dad in the other, would enable them to keep us under control. But cruising at thirty-five thousand feet while strapped into a small seat next to one's brothers made pinching, arm-twisting, and ear-poking irresistible. This resulted in quite a bit of whining, screeching, and even some tears, so our parents tried a different tactic.

The six of us were seated in different rows on the next trip, with a parent stationed catty-corner at either end. The rationale was that if we were not directly next to one another, we would not be able to engage in airplane blanket fort-building and spitball launching. This theory quickly dissolved as soon as the plane hit cruising altitude, and one of my brothers lobbed shredded pieces of paper torn from the airline magazine at the head of the brother sitting in front of him. The victim let out a shrill cry of rage and twisted around to seize the leg of the offender, pinching it hard enough to evoke an ear-splitting shriek. Heads all over the plane would swivel around as Mom raced up the aisle and whisper-screamed details of the punishment she'd be doling out once we were back on the ground. This kept the peace for a short while, but eventually, one of us would figure out a new way to torment the sibling sitting in front or behind.

One favorite pastime made special use of the complimentary headsets given out to passengers so they could listen to the in-flight entertainment system. We used the headphones for something much more amusing. We found that when you put them in your ears and had a sibling blow or speak into the other end, the sound was amplified through the earphones. It's a miracle no eardrums were burst during this activity, although inevitably someone would blow too hard, and the kid on the other end would screech in pain.

Mom spent the trip getting up and down to break up fights. Dad did his best to keep us distracted by handing out coloring books and snacks from across the aisle—after he'd confiscated the headphones and tied them into knots.

On a later trip to Cleveland, our parents foolishly convinced themselves that we were now old enough to sit on our own back in Coach while they enjoyed the sanctity of First Class. Maybe they thought their presence made our behavior worse and that if they were out of sight, we kids would ride out the flight looking out the window or quietly reading.

How wrong they were.

Instead of fighting amongst ourselves, my brothers and I joined forces to torment our parents from afar. We would send the hapless flight attendants into First Class with handwritten ransom notes: "Send back exactly six chocolate-chip cookies, or we will throw Seann out the escape hatch." Or we'd take turns getting up from our seats to confront our parents about some complaint or other. Each time we'd get sent immediately back to our seats, but just as Mom and Dad had started on their second complimentary glass of champagne, another kid would push through the First Class drapes to report on who was not behaving back in Coach.

Despite Mom's threats, once we'd landed in Cleveland, most of the in-flight naughtiness was forgiven because our parents knew salvation was close at hand. Magi and Papa would be right there to greet us at the gate, where they'd almost be toppled over from the full force of six small bodies hitting them at once.

Located about an hour's drive east of Cleveland, Chagrin Falls was and still is graced with the family-centered attributes that make it a classic American small town. The Chagrin River flows through the tree-lined terrain and tumbles into a wide, picturesque waterfall, giving the town its name. The streets are lined with handsome brick buildings and restored Victorian homes, with small diners, ice-cream parlors, and other small-town institutions tucked along the main street. The Popcorn Shop, a much-beloved establishment that produced different flavors of fresh popcorn, homemade fudge, and candy, was always a favorite place. This was the town where our grandparents had raised Dad from the day he was born, and he always loved returning to it.

Magi and Papa's century-old house was in a leafy neighborhood close to the center of town. Their neighbors were hardworking and proud people who maintained their lawns and gardens with meticulous care. Our grandparents had a big garden where Papa grew tomatoes, carrots, cucumbers, and other delicious things for Magi to use in her cooking. I loved racing along the rows with an old wicker basket, ducking and searching for vegetables ripe enough to pick. Before our arrival, Papa would have patiently oiled each of the six small bicycles he kept for us in his garage.

The house was small, and the two guestrooms on the ground floor would never have held all six kids, so Papa remodeled part of the upstairs into a kind of dormitory. He made six bedframes with simple wooden headboards that we were allowed to decorate however we liked. The boys would put up stickers and glue funny pictures from comic books on theirs, while I used colored markers to draw the famous "birds in a row" logo of the popular television show, *The Partridge Family*, on mine. The dormitory was next door to Papa and Magi's room, and how they got any sleep when the six of us were there, I'll never know.

Mom and Dad would stay a couple of nights to visit with our grandparents and see some old family friends. Many of the visitors were the parents of Dad's childhood friends and had watched him grow up. They would bring plates of home-baked cookies and cakes, and the adults would sit on the front porch reminiscing while my brothers and I rode our bikes up and down the street getting reacquainted with our summer friends. My best buddy was Molly, who lived in the house behind Magi and Papa's. It was fun to have another girl to play with, and Molly was often my co-fighter in mock battles against my brothers and their friends.

I think everyone was relieved when Mom and Dad kissed us all goodbye and flew back to California a few days later. Now Magi and Papa had us all to themselves and could spoil us as they pleased. Every day Papa would haul the lot of us down to Chagrin High School, which during the summer months would open its three enormous pools to the community. We would swim and splash for hours while Papa watched from a blanket spread out on the grass, his ever-present pipe dangling from his mouth. Around noon, we'd all pile back into the car in our wet bathing suits and go home to the lunch that Magi had prepared. After our meal, Papa would drive us back to the pool for the rest of the day.

At night we would run barefoot over the darkened lawn with little nets to catch fireflies, which we'd collect in a jar closed by a lid with air holes Papa had punched using a nail. Then we would fall asleep while the bugs flickered softly from their jars on the night tables. Sometimes someone would open the jar during the night and release all the fireflies into the room, and we'd have to run around catching them. In the morning, we would carry the jars outside and release our captives back into the yard.

Magi spent most of her time in the kitchen preparing the many delicious meals we'd eat during our stay. There was always a homemade sheet cake for dessert, chocolate with white frosting, or lemon with Cool Whip. My brothers and I could finish off an entire sheet cake in one sitting, even after a full dinner. And the best part was that no one was there to tell us we'd had enough; with our grandparents, no wish went unfulfilled.

Magi and Papa spoiled us, but my brothers and I loved being with them so much that we were much better-behaved in Ohio than we were back home in California. Papa was a gentle and quiet man with a natural ability to keep us all in control. He would take us fishing along the Chagrin riverbanks, patiently baiting and re-baiting the hooks of six fishing poles for hours. On a rainy day, we would gather in his garage workshop and help him build a birdhouse or a small bench. In the evening, exhausted from the long day, we'd lie on blankets on the floor and watch our grandparents' small television until it was time to head up to the dorm for bed.

While we kids spent the long, happy days of summer in Ohio, Mom and Dad would be back in California, savoring their respite from being parents of six. *The Carol Burnett Show*, like most of the network series, would take the summer off, and sometimes Dad would spend part of the break making a movie or a television special. It gave my parents time to enjoy the rare tranquility of an empty house and the freedom to hop on a plane for a quick trip to Hawaii with some of the show's cast and crew.

One summer at Magi and Papa's, when I was about twelve, Magi told us that our dad was coming to visit for a few days. This seemed a little strange because Dad and Mom usually flew out to Chagrin Falls at the end of the summer, but we kids were delighted that he would join in the swimming and fishing fun with us. The day that Dad arrived, Papa took Tim and me to the Cleveland Airport to pick him up. Back then, you could go right up to the gate and meet people as they walked off the plane. Papa was very quiet as we watched for Dad to emerge off the jetway. When we spotted him, Tim and I ran over and jumped into his arms. Dad gave us a quick, tight hug, then stood and embraced Papa for what seemed like a very long time.

We were walking down the corridor to the airport parking area when Dad suddenly stopped. He staggered to a cigarette vending machine and leaned over it, sobbing into his arms. Tim and I were stunned. We'd never seen our dad cry before and didn't know what to do. I ran over and hugged Dad's waist as tight as I could, and Papa and Tim followed. All four of us stood there embracing until Dad calmed down and wiped his eyes. Then we walked silently out to the car and drove back to Chagrin Falls.

Dad slept in one of the downstairs bedrooms, and Magi brought him a cup of hot chocolate and toast, just like she did for us every morning. During his visit, Dad spent a lot of time sleeping and talking with Magi and Papa. About a week later, he hugged us all good-bye and flew back to California.

Years later, my mother told me that Dad had experienced a nervous breakdown. The stress of Hollywood could be intense, and when it caught up with him, he'd returned to the place where he'd always felt safe and loved. Fortunately, Dad got through that difficult period and resumed his career without any further issues. But until Mom told me what had happened, I never realized just how vulnerable my dad could be.

Years later, when I was about twenty years old, Dad called and asked me to come over to his house. When I arrived, Mom was there with all the boys. When Dad walked in, I could tell by the look on his face that something terrible had occurred. With his face in his hands, he told us that Papa had died. He had walked out of the kitchen to his garage and had suffered a stroke. Magi found him lying in the driveway. He was seventy-four years old, and had been healthy his entire life. There had been no indication that anything was wrong.

Papa's death was the first time anyone close to me had died, and I was devastated. Seeing how upset my dad was made me think back to that day years ago at the Cleveland airport when he had collapsed, sobbing, on top of the cigarette machine.

Magi lived another eight years after Papa passed away. Magi and Papa gave my brothers and me some of the best times of our lives, and their loving influence made us the people we are today. I was truly blessed with the best grandparents anyone could ever hope for.

Chapter 9

BY THE MID-1970S MY DAD FELT LIKE HE WAS THE LUCKIEST MAN IN the world. He had a lovely wife, enough kids to form an impromptu baseball game, and a job putting his comedic talent to work with people he adored. *The Carol Burnett Show* was loved by millions of fans who faithfully tuned in every week. The kind of star-quality camaraderie required to grow—and retain—an audience in the highly competitive world of network TV couldn't be faked. Even if you had the biggest names in Hollywood together in one show, it would flop if there was no chemistry between the players. Fortunately, *The Carol Burnett Show* cast had loads of creative charisma. It returned season after season as fans continued to tune in, eager to see what Dad, Carol, Harvey, Vicki, and the rest of the cast would do next.

Most of Mom and Dad's social circle consisted of the show's cast and crew, along with friends who worked in other areas of show business. Dad had many great friendships, but his longest, and probably closest, was with Ernie Anderson. Ernie, who passed away in 1997, is still regarded today as one of the most legendary television announcers in the industry.

Dad and Ernie's friendship began back in Cleveland when both were starting out in their careers. Ernie was a radio DJ at WHK, the same station where Dad was also working, and the two bonded immediately. Ernie, who possessed a razor-sharp wit, sometimes had trouble keeping his mouth shut. After he mouthed off to one of WHK's station owners and got himself fired, Dad, who refused to work without his best friend, quit too.

Dad and Ernie were both hired by Cleveland's WJW-TV, where their interview show, *Ernie's Place*, was seen by the visiting Rose Marie. When Dad decided to move to California to follow his dreams, Ernie did, too.

Once he landed in Los Angeles, Ernie got a few small acting jobs, but he found his true calling when he started doing voice-overs and announcing for major broadcast shows and news programs. By the early 1970s, Ernie Anderson had become the most recognizable and sought-after voice in television. Many people who watched network television in the 1970s and '80s would instantly recognize Ernie's voice as he introduced television shows, such as his iconic "Coming up next, on *The Loooooove Boat!*" Hollywood, it seemed, loved Dad and Ernie as much as they loved each other.

Ernie and his pretty wife, Edwina, and their kids Kate, Paul, Amanda, and Elizabeth, were regular guests for barbecues and pool parties at our home. Paul, known as Paul Thomas Anderson, would become the celebrated director of highly esteemed movies such as *Boogie Nights*, *There Will Be Blood*, and *The Master*. The name of his critically acclaimed film, *Magnolia*, which starred Tom Cruise and Philip Seymour Hoffman, was the name of the street our family lived on. Paul named the lead character in *Boogie Nights*, Dirk Diggler, after a character from Dad and Ernie's old radio show back in Cleveland. The Dirk Diggler that Dad portrayed on the radio show was as far as you could get from the Dirk Diggler in *Boogie Nights*, but Dad thought it was hilarious.

Other close friends in my parents' group were Carol Burnett and her husband, Joe Hamilton, who often came over with their kids, Carrie, Jodie, and Erin. Carol's assistant, Charlene, and her husband Roger Beatty brought along their baby daughter, Jackie, and sometimes Karen and Colleen, his daughters from his first marriage. Harvey Korman and his wife, Donna, would come with their kids, Maria and Christopher. Tom Eagan, a television producer, his wife, Joan, and their five kids were regulars at our house, too. Weekends at the Conway home would be a kind of "Who's Who" of television, except everyone was wearing shorts and bathing suits instead of designer gowns and tuxedos, and there were lots of kids running around. My parents' group lived unpretentious and family-oriented lives in a city known for decadence. They were all very successful, but there was little Hollywood glamour or drama that many people associated with the entertainment world.

The actor McLean Stevenson, who is best known for playing Lieutenant Colonel Henry Blake on the television show *M*A*S*H*, was another close friend of my parents. I remember McLean as a kind and funny man who would occasionally pick me up from school and take me for ice cream if Mom and Dad were busy. All the kids would gather around and stare when McLean, one of the biggest television stars of the day, pulled into the school parking lot in his convertible sports car. It was much more exciting than being picked up by Mom in her beige station wagon.

Two of Mom's younger brothers, Wally and Dan, had moved out to Los Angeles from Detroit. The pair formed a folk-rock group, the Dalton Boys, and got to work playing gigs around town. Their songs usually had very silly lyrics, and watching both of my animated uncles with their flame-red hair sing them was always fun. Later, Dan made a good living writing jingles for commercials, and Wally found a career as an actor and a songwriter. My uncles and their families were regulars at our house, and I loved being around all of them.

When Dad had a break from work, my parents and their group would sometimes leave the kids behind and take "adults-only" beach or golf vacations. They loved Hawaii so much that Dad, Ernie, and Carol all bought a four-plex condominium together. Carol and her family took up the top two units, and the Conways and Andersons had the two below. When *The Carol Burnett Show* was invited to open the newly built Sydney Opera House, Mom and some other spouses joined the cast and crew for the long journey down to Australia. Magi and Papa drove from Ohio to stay with us kids while Mom and Dad were on the trip, which almost made up for our disappointment at not getting to go along.

When *The Carol Burnett Show* took a break during the summer, Dad used the time away from the show to work on other projects, like movies or television specials. My brothers and I had just returned from our visit with Magi and Papa when Dad was wrapping up the Disney movie *The Apple Dumpling Gang*. Set in California during the Gold Rush era, Dad and comedic actor Don Knotts played a lovably inept outlaw duo who help rescue a pack of orphans. We kids were sometimes allowed to visit Dad on the Disney lot when he was working. Although we were all used to being behind the scenes on Hollywood productions, this one was different because there were horses standing on the set and actors dressed in Western-style costumes. Since the Disney lot wasn't "our" studio, like the CBS lot where *The Carol Burnett Show* was taped, my brothers and I knew we had to be well behaved, or there would be no more visits to the set.

——〜———

Dad worked hard throughout the year, but he always made time for his kids. As Dad's only daughter, I cherished the times we spent together away from the boys. Sometimes he and I would spend a few hours wandering around the hardware store together, a favorite Saturday activity that we both enjoyed. Dad had a real knack for listening to my adolescent problems, and when it was needed, gave honest advice that never felt overly critical.

I remember when I was about fourteen and had just returned from spending the summer in Chagrin Falls. As usual, my brothers and I had spent weeks eating huge portions of the rich, delicious food Magi served. Like many grandmothers, Magi showed her love through food and would cook three full meals a day for us, with snacks in between. The food was so tasty and plentiful that I would take second helpings even when I was full. And no meal was complete without dessert: Jell-O with Cool Whip after lunch or a cake slathered with rich frosting after dinner. Then there were the weekly visits to the Popcorn Shop, where my brothers and I would stuff ourselves with bags of warm caramel corn. Although I had been very active bicycle riding and swimming, adolescence was creeping up on me, and I wasn't burning off the calories that I was consuming. When I got off the plane back home, I was at least ten pounds heavier.

Later that week, Dad and I went out to get groceries. Mom was away on a tennis trip with some of her girlfriends in San Diego, so we were in charge of meal planning and shopping for the family. But when we got to the store, Dad walked right by the carts and went over to the meat counter. He began picking up plastic-wrapped chicken and beef packages, examining each label before handing them to me.

"Dad," I piped up, "shouldn't we get a cart?"

Dad was still busy looking through the cooler. "No, just hold them."

The packages were cold against my bare arms, and I shifted uncomfortably as Dad placed another on top of what I was already holding.

"Why are we getting all this meat?" I asked. There had been no talk of a party or barbecue.

Dad didn't answer. He counted silently on his fingers and then held out his hands with the fingers splayed out.

"What's this?" he asked.

"Umm, ten?" I guessed.

"Right. And see those packages you're holding?"

I nodded.

"Well, that is almost exactly ten pounds of meat."

I looked at him blankly.

"It's kind of tough carrying around ten extra pounds of meat, right?"

I looked down at the packages and then back up at him. The frozen meat was getting heavy, and I had to shift them so they wouldn't fall.

"Kell," Dad said. "Life is hard enough without having to carry around extra weight. When you left for Ohio a few months ago, you were trim and healthy. But thanks to your grandmother's wonderful cakes and cookies, I'd say you gained about, oh, ten pounds?" He smiled kindly. "Well, that's the same weight as all that meat you're holding."

He was right. The waist of my pants *had* become uncomfortably tight.

"What should I do?" I asked.

"It's simple," he said, taking the packages out of my arms and placing them back into the freezer. "You just need to go back to the healthy things you usually eat. How about we start now?"

We got a cart at the front of the store and walked down the aisles, picking up different packages to discuss whether they were healthy. When we left, we had two bags full of vegetables, whole grains, lean meat—and not one box of cookies.

Some people might think it was mean of Dad to point out that I'd put on some adolescent pudge. But my father had a stocky build and had always struggled to keep his own weight down. He understood firsthand that developing good eating habits early in life was essential to staying healthy. I'm sure it wasn't easy for Dad to talk to me about my weight, but he wanted the best for me, both physically and emotionally. It was one of the many loving and honest lessons my father taught my brothers and me as we were growing up.

And Dad was right: Once I went back to my regular eating habits, those ten pounds came right off.

Chapter 10

THE YEAR I STARTED HIGH SCHOOL, MY PARENTS BOUGHT A CUTE CONvertible Volkswagen bug so that Mom would have something a little more fun to drive than the family station wagon. Since I was close to turning sixteen, I would be able to use the car once I'd earned my driver's license. Until then, I still had to rely on my mother to get around to practices and dates with friends. But on the weekends, when my friends and I wanted to go to the beach, we often couldn't find anyone to drive us there, so we would take the bus.

There was a bus stop on Ventura Boulevard a few blocks from my house. Three transfers and about an hour later, the bus would deposit us at Santa Monica Beach. The area of the beach around Guard Station 12 was the designated spot where all of our friends hung out. After spreading our towels and tuning the transistor radio to our favorite station, we could look forward to a great day of socializing, getting too much sun, and swimming in the cold Pacific water.

One Saturday morning, I passed through the kitchen on my way out to catch the bus for the beach. Mom and Dad were sitting at the table, drinking their coffee and reading the newspaper. Just as I was about to step out the door, Mom stopped me.

"Whoa, whoa, whoa. Back it up." She pointed at my duffel bag, crammed with towels, lotions, and my mini transistor radio. "You better have sunscreen in there."

Much to Mom's credit, in an age when the attitude was that you could never be "too tan," she was a strong advocate of sunscreen. Mom would hold my brothers in a headlock in order to smear white zinc across their noses if she had to. But despite her attempts, the six of us still tanned dark brown almost year-round. As I grew into my teens, I wanted to be as tan as I could get. My friends and I believed that a deep, dark tan was nonnegotiable for a true California girl.

With an indignant snort, I pulled out a bottle of Coppertone SPF 15. Mom scanned the bottle, nodded her assent, and I raced out of the house to catch the bus.

Once we'd arrived at the beach, I settled back on my towel and withdrew the bottle of sunscreen from my bag. Except what poured into my palm wasn't pasty white sunscreen. Instead, it was silky, sweet-smelling oil. I had emptied the SPF 15 bottle of its contents and replaced it with Johnson's Baby Oil, the summertime concoction beloved by sun-worshippers everywhere. I made sure to rub the clear oil over every inch of my body before laying back to soak in the sun. Everyone knew that if you wanted a deep, dark tan, baby oil was the best way to get it. And though she may have raised an eyebrow as my skin became browner over the summer weeks, Mom was none the wiser.

My weekend trips to the beach required more than just baby oil masquerading as sunscreen. I needed bus fare, money for snacks, and trips to the Galleria Mall with my friends to shop for bathing suits. Since Mom tended to be tightfisted with cash, I began to pester Dad for pocket money on a weekly basis. When I'd come begging to him for another twenty dollars, Dad knew it was time for a father-daughter discussion about economics.

Turns out he had a business opportunity for me.

"You know, Kell," he said, "money doesn't just grow on trees."

"Yeah, Dad, I know that." I tried not to show my impatience. "But can I just have, like, ten bucks? They raised the bus fare, you know. And I have to have some money to get something to eat. You don't want me to get hungry, do you?"

Dad folded his arms and looked thoughtful. "I've been thinking about it, and I have a great idea for you to make some money of your own."

"Okay," I said suspiciously.

"Now, hear me out. What if you were to go buy some of those little rolls we like, whip up some tuna salad, egg salad, and chicken salad, and make up a whole bunch of sandwiches?"

I rolled my eyes so hard it hurt my head.

"Then," Dad continued, getting excited, "you slide each sandwich into a plastic baggie, get some stickers made up that say 'Malibu Beach Buns,' and slap them on the bags. Then get the big cooler we have in the garage, throw a little ice in the bottom, load up your buns, and you're in business."

I stared at him in horror.

"When you get to the beach, you can sell those buns for, oh, I'm guessing, a buck apiece? I bet people would buy them up like crazy. And if you sold about twenty of them, after you accounted for the cost of the bread and tuna fish, you'd make back a nice little profit. Plenty of pocket money for a girl who just needs bus fare for the beach."

I kept waiting for Dad to smile, to show he was joking, and pull out his wallet. But he didn't. In retrospect, the idea was a clever one, but to an extremely self-conscious teenager, the thought of peddling Malibu Beach Buns on Santa Monica Beach was mortifying.

"Oh my God, Dad," I stammered. "As if! First of all, they'd never let me on the bus with such a big, grody cooler, and even if they did, I'd be like so embarrassed in front of my friends." I took a deep, Valley Girl–style breath and continued my outrage. "Gag me, Dad! I mean, this is such a bad idea." Remembering that my friends were waiting at the bus stop, I changed tactics and smiled sweetly. "Please, Daddy, can we talk about this when I get home later?"

Dad broke out in a grin. He gave me some money, and off I went to the beach.

But he'd made his point, and I did end up getting a job a few days each week after school at a boutique where I wrapped gifts in the back room. I still hit Dad up for money from time to time, but it felt good to be earning my own.

When I turned sixteen and got my driver's license, Dad patiently sat through hours of lurching driving lessons on our driveway in the Volkswagen Bug, teaching me how to drive a stick shift. I loved the freedom driving the car gave me, and acted as the family chauffeur, shuttling my five brothers back and forth to their practices and tutoring sessions. Mom loved it, too, because in a way I became her personal assistant, cheerfully picking up my brothers and running errands whenever she needed anything. On the road with the top down and the radio blaring, my sense of newfound freedom was exhilarating.

While I was pretty much allowed to come and go as I pleased, there were a few rules Dad set down about driving the car. One was that I had to promise him I wouldn't drive on the 405, LA's notorious multilane freeway that wound across the city. Usually, this wasn't a problem, except when I wanted to drive my friends to the beach. Taking the 405 from the Valley could zip you right over to Santa Monica Beach in about twenty minutes. The long way on regular streets, with all the traffic lights and slower speed limits, could take as long as an hour.

I didn't usually defy my father's wishes, but the first time I took the car to the beach, I picked up all my friends and we drove right up the 405 ramp. Once I'd entered the freeway, I pushed on the gas, but the car refused to go any faster than forty miles per hour. Cars going twice our speed loomed up behind and swerved around us, horns blaring and people shaking their fists.

"Kelly!" one of my friends shrieked over the wind. "You have to go faster!"

"I'm trying!" I yelled, mashing my foot down on the accelerator. "It won't go any faster!"

Cars continued to swerve around us. Someone leaned out their window when they passed and screamed, "The speed limit is fifty-five, you idiot!"

The next exit off the 405 couldn't come fast enough. Finally, off the freeway and out of danger, I pulled over and sat for a minute until I'd calmed down enough to resume driving. After that, I took the long way to the beach and never said anything to Dad about the car.

Many years later, Dad and I were reminiscing about old times, and the Volkswagen Bug came up.

"Okay, Dad," I said. "Confession time. Remember when I first started driving the car, and you told me I wasn't *ever* allowed to drive it on the 405? Well, I did, once." I continued to tell him the story about driving on the freeway and the car not going any faster than forty miles an hour.

I hadn't even finished when Dad burst out laughing. He laughed so hard that he bent over double and had to take a few moments to catch his breath when he finally stopped.

"Dad," I demanded. "Why is that so funny?"

"Kell," Dad said with a grin, "when you started driving that car, I had a speed governor put on it, so it would *never* go above forty miles an hour, no matter how hard you pushed on the accelerator. That's why I told you never to take the thing on the freeway in the first place!"

When I started attending Birmingham High School, I had one goal: I was determined to make the cheerleading squad. All those years of gymnastics, swimming, and competing with my brothers had made me a sports fanatic. Instead of rock stars or movie actors, I had posters of famous athletes on my wall. My beloved gymnasts hung alongside Terry Bradshaw, quarterback for the Pittsburgh Steelers, and Marcel Dionne of the LA Kings hockey team. Cheerleading would combine all of my favorite things—high-energy dance moves, loud singing, and football—into one activity.

More than anything, I longed to lead the crowds in cheering on the Birmingham Braves as they fought for dominance. The Braves were highly ranked during the years I was in school, so the stands were always packed and rowdy during the Friday-night games.

I practiced my cheers as I walked around the house and nearly drove my entire family crazy. I was determined to be prepared and not miss a single beat. On the day of tryouts I did my best, but it seemed to me that the other girls kicked higher, sang louder, and *looked* better than me. I was unconvinced that all of my hard practice would pay off.

Later that week, the tryout results were posted on the bulletin board outside the gym. All the girls who had tried out were crowded around, searching for their names. I read over the junior varsity list twice, but the name "Kelly Conway" wasn't there. I had failed.

Just then, my friend Vicki screamed. "Oh my God, Kelly—you made it!"

"No, I didn't," I said. "My name's not on the list."

"Yes, it is," Vicki insisted. "It's right here. On the *varsity* list!"

Varsity? Usually only juniors and seniors made varsity, and I was still a sophomore. I leaned in to look at the board. And there it was, my name listed on the varsity list.

That year I jumped, screamed, and danced with my team every Friday night. I loved the adrenaline of the cool night air rushing over the field as the band played loudly and the crowd cheered from the stands.

Since *The Carol Burnett Show* taped on Friday evenings, Dad could only attend the games early in the season before the show resumed production. I was thrilled when he watched me perform with the varsity squad during the season's first game. Afterwards, I found Mom and Dad among the throngs of people streaming off the bleachers.

"Dad!" I yelled. "What did you think? How did I do? How's my hair?"

"You were great, Kell," Dad answered. "But, honestly, it was hard for me to concentrate on the game. That PA system is terrible! I could hardly make out what the announcer was saying with all that static. I couldn't tell what down it was or anything. It was impossible to follow the game at all. But yes, honey, you were terrific!"

He was right. The field's old sound system was pretty terrible.

Dad wasn't the type to sit around and do nothing when he saw a problem. Later that week, he ordered a brand-new PA system for the field and donated it to my high school. After it was installed, the sound-quality difference was amazing; you could hear everything that the announcer said all the way to the top of the bleachers. It made the games much more enjoyable for everyone.

A week or so later, I was sitting in algebra class. Looking down at my desk, I noticed some graffiti scrawled on it: "Tim Conway Bought Kelly's Varsity Spot."

My face burned red, and I quickly slid my notebook over the words. At first, I was angry, but then doubt began to come over me. What if it was true? Had Dad, in some way, been responsible for my making the varsity cheer squad? It was a mortifying—and shameful—thought.

As soon as Dad got home from work that night, I confronted him.

"Dad, did you have anything to do with me making varsity?" I asked. "Tell me the truth."

Dad stared at me. "What the heck are you talking about, Kelly?"

I was trembling, and tears were forming in my eyes. "Someone said you *bought* my cheerleading spot."

Dad shook his head in disbelief, and I suddenly knew the truth.

Of course Dad would never "buy" a privilege for me or any of his kids. As a celebrity, Dad was offered special treatment. This always bothered him. If the tables were full at a restaurant, the manager would sometimes recognize Dad and offer to seat us ahead of other people. But Dad would never accept. He always insisted on being treated the same as everyone else.

Tearfully, I told Dad about the graffiti on the desk.

"Kelly," Dad said, "for one, you know I would never do something like that. And two, you *earned* that place on the squad all by yourself. You worked hard for weeks, every day, and you went and performed your best, and it worked out. There will always be people who say mean things because they are jealous. You can't let them get to you." He tipped my chin up to his face. "Okay?"

I never found out who had written that on the desk, and after my talk with Dad, it didn't matter. My spot on the squad had been earned on merit alone. Even if I hadn't made the cut, Dad would never have used his fame or influence to give me an unfair advantage. Every ounce of success we earned in our lives would come by determination and sheer hard work. Just as he had done.

Chapter 11

Mom and Dad were two very different personalities, and their parenting styles started to diverge even more as my brothers and I grew up. Looking back, I can see that their contrasting attitudes about raising us created friction in their relationship. When we were all little kids, Mom's loud and sometimes abrasive mothering was the same tactic that a lion tamer might use with a ring full of unruly lion cubs. She could also be affectionate, and none of us ever doubted Mom's fierce love for us, but we all grew up knowing that her short temper could explode without warning.

On the other end of that spectrum was Dad. I wouldn't say he spoiled us or excused bad behavior, but his approach was completely different from Mom's. I don't think I ever heard my father yell at us in anger my entire life. Where Mom was always ready to deliver a good spanking when she deemed it a necessary punishment, our father never did. Dad's method was to talk through a situation, the way two adults might diplomatically come up with a solution to a problem. If one of us misbehaved, Dad would sit us down and calmly work through *why* we'd acted out and then coax us to explain why that action was wrong. Together, we'd decide how we could appease the person we'd harmed. The latter usually entailed simply telling the sibling we'd offended that we were sorry. Dad's tactic worked beautifully. By thinking and talking through our misdeed, we would understand the actions that had led to it, accept the guilt for the outcome, and still feel good at resolving it fairly.

I'd always been close to my mother, but we clashed more as I became a teenager. I'm sure many daughters feel this way, but sometimes it seemed that nothing I did was good enough for Mom. I'd always earned high grades, but even the occasional C in a subject I struggled with could make her furious. I remember being driven to tears after being severely admonished over getting a single C on my report card, despite the rest of my grades being all A's and B's. Her contempt made me feel worthless and stupid.

When Dad saw the same report card, he praised me for the good grades. Then he asked if I had any ideas that could help me do better in the class for which I'd received the C. Dad made me feel empowered about what I'd accomplished while also giving suggestions on how I could improve. He also tried to reason with Mom.

"Look, Mary Anne—just because she got a C in algebra doesn't mean she's destined for failure." He turned to me. "Kelly, can you name the Seven Dwarfs?"

I began to name them off, trying not to laugh. "Happy, Sleepy, Grumpy . . . umm, Bashful, Sneezy, Dopey . . . and Doc!"

"Yes!" Dad yelled. "You are correct. Now, you're at Santa Anita, and you have a great feeling about the three horse in the sixth. You've got five bucks in your pocket. What do you say when you get to the betting window?"

I calculated in my head for a moment. "Sixth race, five dollars to win on the three."

"Exactly! That's my girl." Dad put his arm around me. "See, Mary Anne? The kid's fine. Leave her alone."

Mom rolled her eyes to the ceiling. "Seven Dwarfs, my ass," she said. "Kelly, you just make sure you study twice as hard this semester so that your algebra grade goes *up*."

Being the only daughter in the family created other issues for me. My mother expected me to help out with chores that my brothers were *never* asked to do, such as ironing or washing dishes. We had live-in help, but there was always dirty laundry waiting or crumbs to vacuum. It wasn't that I minded helping out with household tasks, but it bothered me that my brothers were not required to pitch in just because they were boys. I recall many afternoons of folding an endless pile of clean laundry while my carefree brothers—many old enough to at least help with minor chores—splashed in the pool or lay around watching television. But Mom rarely asked them to do anything other than taking the garbage out occasionally.

By the time I was in middle school, I had begun to challenge Mom's strict authority. We argued about the usual teenage things: curfew times, where I went with my girlfriends, and the amount of time I spent on the phone. Our family spent a few weeks each summer visiting my mother's family in their small Canadian town on the shores of Lake Erie, and I'd made some friends there that I liked to call. These were the days when long-distance calls were expensive, and talking a few hours a week could run up a substantial phone bill. But as a typical teenager, I didn't think about the dollars adding up as I chatted for hours on the phone with my Canadian friends.

One day, Mom burst into my room and thrust a phone bill in my face.

"Do you see this, Kelly?" she screamed. "It's over two hundred dollars in long-distance calls to Canada. What the fuck is wrong with you?"

Dad came running in from the other end of the house. "What the hell is going on?"

"I'll tell you what's going on. Your daughter here has racked up two hundred dollars in long-distance calls." Mom hurled the bill at me, and it fluttered to the floor. "She has absolutely *no* sense of responsibility. She's a spoiled brat. A simpleminded, spoiled brat!"

By this time, I was sobbing, partly in shock from Mom's surprise attack and partly from shame at having wasted so much money on phone calls. I just hadn't realized how expensive they were.

"She's not an idiot." Dad picked up the phone bill from the floor and looked at it. "But Kell, this is no good."

"I'm sorry!" I cried. "Dad, I didn't mean to do it."

"You have no sense about money at all!" Mom yelled. "What, you think it just rains down from the sky? You are going to pay back every single dime of this bill."

"All right, Mary Anne," Dad said. "Take it easy. There's no need to get hysterical." He turned to me. "Kelly, how much money do you have on you?"

At the time, I didn't have a job, and I only had about fifteen dollars in my purse. Certainly not enough to pay the bill, and I admitted it.

"Okay," Dad said. "Get your shoes on and grab your purse. We leave in ten minutes."

"To go where, exactly?" Mom demanded.

"To Santa Anita. We're going to place some bets with Kelly's fifteen bucks and try to win enough to pay some of that phone bill."

Mom narrowed her eyes. "Oh, really? And if she doesn't win two hundred dollars, then what? Tim, I want her to pay this bill herself."

"She will!" Dad said. "Look, if she doesn't win enough at the track, then we'll figure out another way for her to pay it."

Mom sighed as I jumped up to get ready. A day at the racetrack with just my dad was one of my favorite things, and maybe I'd get lucky on the right horse.

I can't remember exactly how much my fifteen dollars won me that day at Santa Anita, but it was enough to cover a portion of the phone bill. And like Dad promised Mom, I worked off the rest by cleaning the kitchen and hosing down the patio for a few weekends. Mom was satisfied that I'd paid my debt, and from then on, I kept my long-distance phone calls short.

———

I had little routines built into my daily life that took on powerful importance in my imagination. One was that I had to kiss both Mom and Dad good-bye every single morning, without fail. Even when I was a teenager, I was convinced that something bad might happen if I ever skipped this ritual, almost like a "don't step on a crack" superstition.

One morning, I made the usual stop in my parents' bedroom to kiss them good-bye before I left for school. As they did most mornings, Mom and Dad were sitting in bed, drinking coffee and reading the newspaper. I dipped down to give Dad his kiss and then circled the bed to do the same for Mom.

"Wait a minute," Mom said as she looked up from the paper. "What the *fuck* are you wearing?"

I looked down. I had on jeans and a tube top—the same type of clothing many girls my age would be wearing to school on a hot day.

"Mom," I said. "Everyone dresses like this."

"You mean everyone dresses like a tramp?"

"Mom!" I looked over at Dad. "Dad! Tell Mom I don't look like a tramp!"

Dad put down his paper and sighed. "Come on, Mary Anne . . . relax."

"You really are okay with our daughter going to school looking like this?" Mom snapped. "Well, I'm not."

"No," Dad said. "I agree with you. I don't think that what she's wearing is appropriate for school. But we don't need to have a meltdown over it." He climbed out of bed. "Come on, Kelly, let's go look in your closet and see what else you have in there."

In tears, I followed Dad back to my bedroom. He opened the closet and started rifling through it. "Let's see. How about something with some sleeves on it. This shirt is nice." He held up a striped T-shirt.

I took the shirt. "Mom said I looked trampy."

Dad pulled me into a hug and kissed the top of my head. "Kell, I don't think you look trampy. But don't you think a tube top is more appropriate for the beach?"

I nodded, wiping the tears off my face.

"Now, go put that shirt on and show your mother, so she doesn't explode through the roof."

And just like that, everything was okay again.

Although Mom frequently hurt me with her harsh criticism, I now realize that having six kids and a household to manage created a lot of stress for her. Dad was a wonderful and highly engaged father, but he also had the luxury of going to work every day, where there were no unruly children. Mom had her bridge games and her Friday nights out with the CBS crowd, but seven days a week she was stuck with six small children. She had to scream just to be heard above the noise we made. I didn't realize it at the time, being so caught up in my teenage world of cheerleading, school, and hanging out with my friends, but this pressure weighed heavily on both of my parents.

One evening the whole family was preparing to leave for dinner at our favorite pizza place. When it was time to go, my brothers and I were still milling around, getting dressed. Mom was already in the car, waiting for all of us. When minutes went by and we didn't come out, she started to lay on the horn. Finally, we all ran down one by one and piled into the car, bracing for a severe chastising for our tardiness.

But Mom didn't say a word. She put the car in gear and started to drive off.

"Mom, wait," I said. "Isn't Dad coming?"

Mom didn't answer. She stopped the car halfway down the driveway. Then she bent her head forward on the steering wheel and burst into sobs while the six of us sat mute with shock. True, we sometimes drove Mom to tears with our bad behavior, but this was far more serious. For a couple of minutes, we waited as Mom cried, her mascara trailing in dark streaks down the side of her face. Dad never came out of the house.

Finally, Mom stopped crying. She took a tissue from her purse and looked in the rearview mirror as she wiped her face clean. Then without a word, she shifted the car into gear and we drove off to dinner, leaving Dad behind.

It was the first sign of what had formerly been unimaginable to my brothers and me: My parents' eighteen-year marriage wasn't so rock-solid after all.

Chapter 12

ONE EVENING NOT LONG AFTER THE NIGHT THAT MOM HAD CRIED IN the car, my parents summoned all my brothers and me into the living room. Magi and Papa, who were visiting from Chagrin Falls, sat on the sofa with sad expressions on their faces.

"Kids," Dad said, "we need to talk to you about something." He took a deep breath. "Your mother and I love you all very, very much. But we have decided not to be married anymore."

Tim, Jamie, and I looked at each other in shock. Patrick stared down at his hands. Corey and Seann, who were still pretty young, just looked confused.

I was the first to break the silence. "You guys are getting a *divorce?*" Even Corey and Seann knew what the word meant, but it was a term none of us had ever dreamed would be connected to our parents.

"Yes," Mom answered. "We're getting divorced. But we're going to do everything to help you kids keep your lives as normal as possible."

"Normal?" I shot back. "What could possibly be normal if you get divorced?"

My thoughts were racing, trying to sort out the logistics of a new world where my parents weren't married. I was in a happy place in my junior year of high school, with cheerleading, a busy social life, and the promise of adulthood still safely in the future but close enough to anticipate. So much was evolving each day, but Mom and Dad together formed the foundation I had always believed would never shift.

"Kell," said Dad, reaching out to squeeze my knee. "I know it's a shock, but everything will be fine."

I stood up. "How can it be fine? What am I supposed to do when something happens at school, and I need to talk to both of you? Do I have to go to one house and then the other? That is completely selfish. You guys are just being selfish!"

A few days later, Dad moved into Carol and Joe's beach house until he could find a place to buy or rent. I don't recall a specific day that my father moved out of our home. I'm sure he waited until we kids were at school to take the few belongings he wanted over to his new place.

Dad would pick all of us up for visits whenever he could. At first, it was strange to see him in a place that wasn't our family home, but he kept the six of us busy with days on the beach, takeout dinners, and board game marathons. And despite their differences, both of my parents made their split an amicable one, sparing their children the misery that is so common in divorce. In the settlement, Dad gave Mom her due for the many years she'd been his wife and raised his six children; she would keep the Magnolia house and have enough money to live a very comfortable life.

Not wanting to intrude by staying at Carol and Joe's beach house for too long, Dad took up temporary residence at the Westwood Marquis Hotel. Since it wasn't far from the Valley, I would drive over every day after school or cheerleading practice and wait for Dad to return from work. I must have made a sad sight, sitting in the hotel hallway against Dad's door, surrounded by my schoolbooks. As soon as he came out of the elevator, I sprang to my feet and met him with a big hug, sometimes in tears.

We'd order room service and soon I'd be chattering on happily, telling him all about my day. For a few magical hours, it would feel like nothing had changed, but then I'd have to gather my things and head home, leaving Dad waving good-bye from his hotel room door as I walked down the hall in tears.

While he looked for a house to buy, Dad rented a one-bedroom condominium right on Carbon Beach in Malibu. The first weekend he moved there, Mom called him to make plans for all of us kids to spend the weekend. He hadn't been able to have all six of us at the hotel, but now that he had his condo, Mom assumed we'd be able to stay with him. I was sitting in the kitchen during the call, and it soon became clear that Dad wasn't quite ready to have his six children come for a weekend visit. He told Mom the place was too small and that he needed a little more time to settle in. And to be honest, as much as he missed all of us, I'm sure Dad was looking forward to enjoying his newly single status at his new beachside bachelor pad. Carbon Beach was—and is still today—known as the beach to see and be seen.

But Dad should have known better.

"I don't give a fuck if you're not ready for them," Mom snapped. "The kids are home from school, they are going to have a snack, I'm going to put them all in the car, and they will be at your place by 4:15. Good-bye!"

And a few hours later, there we were, all six of us with our duffel bags, standing at the door of Dad's condo.

Fortunately, Dad was able to rent an adjoining unit so that there was enough room for us to sleep when we visited on the weekends. About six months later, he bought a house back in Encino, a short distance away from our family home. It was so close that we could ride our bikes over.

Dad immediately put his carpentry skills to work customizing the house to his liking. Gone was the tailored, matching decor and neutral colors that my mother favored. Instead, Dad went for an old-fashioned English pub look, with a large oak bar and antique metal signs. He installed a tournament-sized billiards table on one side of the main room on a raised platform, with a brass rail around it. On the walls were the things Dad loved: photos of us kids, an address plaque of his childhood home that he had made in high school shop class, and pictures of racehorses, including some he owned. Dad's lifelong dream of racing horses hadn't resulted in him crossing the finish line on top of one, but he'd been able to purchase a couple. One favorite, named Bossy Knickers, he owned in partnership with Harvey Korman and Ernie Anderson, though all three men claimed she cost them more than she'd ever earned them.

My brothers and I loved staying at Dad's house. We spent hours playing pool, darts, or on one of the full-sized arcade games Dad had installed in the game room. Dad bought a pair of antique slot machines that he stocked with quarters, and if we pulled enough on the heavy brass handles, sometimes a stream of them would pour out into our hands, accompanied by ringing bells and flashing lights.

Splitting our time between two households required some adjustment. The first time we spent the night with Dad, none of us had thought to bring a toothbrush. The next morning, with the six of us crammed into the tiny car, we christened my VW Bug the "Bad Breath Mobile" on the drive back to Mom's house. I'm not sure how Mom felt being alone in that big, quiet house the first night we spent away from her, but she soon began to enjoy the freedom of split-custody.

With Dad now living close by we were able to see him almost every day. My younger brothers could bike back and forth between the two homes, spending a few hours after school with Dad before pedaling back to Mom's house. Weekends were usually spent at Dad's place, indulging in late nights of billiards tournaments and video games. We loved the lazy mornings when Dad would stand flipping pancakes until the stack towered a foot high on the plate. It was a laid-back and comfortable atmosphere, one that the six of us kids might have taken for granted.

When my third brother Jamie was born, Mom and Dad had employed a full-time housekeeper. We kids were used to leaving our dirty dishes on the table after a meal without a second thought because Mom or the housekeeper would pick them up. I don't think Dad ever realized how spoiled we were until he got his house—without a housekeeper—and began having us over regularly. He was dismayed to see that after every meal we'd all push back from the table and race off, leaving the dirty dishes behind.

"Hey, guys," Dad said one day as we finished our hamburgers. "After dinner, I want you each to take your plate and cup to the kitchen, rinse them off, and put them into the dishwasher. Tim and Kell, I'll need you to help the little ones carry their dishes. But Seann can at least carry his cup, right, bud?" Seann nodded between gulps of milk. "Can you all do that?"

"Sure, Dad."

The Dukes of Hazzard was about to come on TV, so we got the table cleared quickly.

But old habits die hard. The next night after dinner, Dad found the table littered with dirty plates again, after we'd all forgotten our promise and scrambled off to watch *Fantasy Island*.

"Excuse me," Dad said, standing in front of the TV set. "But I think you all forgot something?" We looked up at him blankly. "Your dirty dishes, maybe?"

Groaning, we got up and shuffled back to the table.

Dad was sure that we'd remember next time. He was wrong. After the next dinner at Dad's, we all excused ourselves from the table and went off to play video games, again leaving our plates sitting on the table.

When it was time for bed, I brushed my teeth and got into my pajamas. It was pretty late, and after a busy day of swimming at the beach and playing video games with my brothers, I was exhausted. I pulled back the blankets on my bed and prepared to climb in.

Under the covers lay my dirty dish, fork, and knife. There was barbecue sauce sticking to my crisp, clean sheets along with a couple of greasy potato chunks. I let out a high-pitched screech.

In the bed across the room, Tim pulled back his covers. "What the heck!" he yelled. Apparently, dirty dishes had found their way into his bed, too.

In the room next door, we heard our brother Patrick let out a howl. The dirty dish bandit had struck again.

Dad suddenly appeared and leaned against the doorway. He was smiling.

"Dad!" I wailed, holding up a dirty plate. "Someone put these in my bed. My sheets are all disgusting!"

"Mine too!" Tim said.

Dad's jaw dropped in mock outrage. "How on *earth* could those dirty dishes have gotten inside your nice clean beds, all the way from the dining room table?"

Tim, Patrick, and I looked at each other.

"Well," Dad said, "I guess you better hurry and get those sheets stripped off and get them in the washing machine before that barbecue sauce sets in." He yawned and glanced at his watch. "Gosh, it's so late, too. Those sheets won't be clean and dry for another hour, at least."

We were tired and grumpy during the next hour while we washed the sheets and waited for them to dry. Dad's dirty lesson hit the target, because we never forgot to clear our dirty dishes from the table again.

Mom and Dad kept up their part of the bargain to make their separation as easy on us as possible, but I was still struggling with the idea that my parents would never be together again. At home, Mom was briskly moving on with her life, filling her days with tennis, shopping, and bridge games. I grew to dislike being around the house when my mother was hosting a bridge tournament, the ladies squinting at their cards through cigarette smoke for hours on end.

There were more changes to come for Dad. After 11 seasons and 279 episodes, *The Carol Burnett Show* taped its final program in 1978. The show had run continuously since 1967, and Carol was ready for a break and a chance to do something new. She and her husband Joe, who had been the show's executive producer from the start, wanted it to end on a high point. It was a hard decision for Carol, and she wept when she broke the news to Dad, but he understood the reasons for her decision.

When he wrote the last sketch that he and Carol performed together for the final episode, it was classic Tim Conway and Carol Burnett: two supremely talented, funny people saying good-bye to their fans, and each other, after many great years together. There was hardly a dry eye left in the studio when they wrapped, and everyone from the live audience to the cast and crew spent the rest of the evening hugging and congratulating each other.

Television was changing, and the era of variety shows was coming to an end, soon replaced by the sitcoms and cop shows that dominated the 1980s. I know Dad and the rest of *The Carol Burnett Show* felt proud they had been one of the best in the field for so many years. Even when you watch it today, apart from the fashion and hairstyles, the show's material still plays as fresh and relevant. Such was the magic that Dad, Carol, Harvey, Vicki, Lyle, and all the other cast and crew who worked on the show were able to create together, and it remains timeless.

While Dad would go on to more successful projects in his long career, he once said that when *The Carol Burnett Show* ended, a part of his heart went with it.

Chapter 13

DAD HAD BEEN VERY GENEROUS WITH MOM IN THEIR DIVORCE SETTLE-
ment, giving her not only the house on Magnolia but also a substantial
monthly alimony payment. Later, Dad said that he'd given her most of his
savings because he knew that he could still work and make more money.
They agreed to split custody of us kids, and Dad had Mom agree that
she would not move any of the children outside of Los Angeles until my
youngest brother, Seann, had graduated from high school. He wanted
to make sure that we always lived close enough to him that he could be
involved in our lives as much as possible. A few years later, Dad would
reluctantly release Mom from this promise, which he regretted for the
rest of his life.

Corey was barely twelve and Seann ten when our parents divorced.
They became very close to our housekeeper Araceli, who we called Ali.
Ali was calm and reassuring, and she never lost her temper. Ali gave the
boys the comforting and dependable presence they needed during those
years. They were close to our mother, too, but she was busy trying to figure
out her own life as a new divorcée, with a calendar full of bridge games,
tennis, and the constant redecorating of the house.

Now that I could drive and was busy with school and my friends, I
wasn't around the house as much. When I would leave, Corey and Seann
would run after me, wanting to know where I was going and when I
would be back. I'd give them hugs and promise not to be gone for very
long. Sometimes I would even cut short my time with friends to get back
home early. Being so young during a divorce surely affected my youngest
brothers much more than it did me or the other boys, who were already
in their teens.

The divorce was a hard blow for Mom. For nearly twenty years, her entire identity had revolved around being the wife of Tim Conway and mother to his six children. Mom's social life was primarily television industry people, from the Friday-night tapings of *The Carol Burnett Show* to the weekend trips my parents would take with other couples in the business. When they split, that social life mostly disappeared for Mom. Whether it was fair or not, Dad was the link to all those people through his work. It must have been a very lonely time for Mom, being suddenly cut off from the social world that had been a part of her life for so long.

The stigma of divorce bothered Mom, too. Although it was becoming more common by the late 1970s, there was still a lot of shame attached to it—especially for women. As a devout Catholic who faithfully attended Mass every Sunday, she must have felt a lot of guilt in breaking one of the central tenets of her faith. Mom worried about what the neighbors and people in our community would think, too. After the divorce was final, Mom made me and my brothers swear we wouldn't tell our friends because they might tell their parents. My best friend at the time, Vicki Ueberroth, lived on our street, and I remember feeling so awkward at having to keep this secret from her and her parents, who I loved. Everyone knew that Dad had moved out and they probably figured divorce was in the cards. But because I had promised Mom, I wasn't allowed to provide any clarity to the situation.

When I felt sad, I often turned to Mr. Ramirez, the beloved athletic director at my high school, who also managed my cheerleading squad. Mr. Ramirez was the warm, open, and honest touchstone that every teenager should have in his or her life. He was part uncle and part friend, and never failed to offer honest advice and a shoulder to cry on when needed. Mr. Ramirez would sit and listen as I fretted over my woes—boyfriends, school, and my now-divorced parents. Looking back on it now, I see that my life was pretty great even with its flaws, but when seen through my teenage lens, I often felt on the precipice of disaster. Mr. Ramirez, bless his beautiful soul, would talk me off the ledge every time.

I needed this support when Dad started to date. While my dad was the first to joke about his lack of screen-idol looks, he was handsome in his way. With boatloads of charisma and considerable success in television,

Dad probably could have had his pick of dates. But in reality, Dad only dated a few people while he was single.

His priority was always us kids, and he was careful not to have his lady friends stay over on the nights we spent with him. We did meet some of the women he dated over dinner or walks on the beach. What my brothers thought of these ladies, they kept to themselves as boys typically do, but I let my feelings be known. Although my mother seemed to be doing fine on her own, I felt protective of her. And I was jealous, too. There had never been any other women in Dad's life except for Mom and me, and I'd always been secure, knowing that I was the favorite. These new women, eager to please my father and desperate to be accepted by us kids, were a threat to that stability.

One lady Dad casually dated for a while was a former beauty queen who had made a career in sports broadcasting. Tim and I referred to her as "Miss America," and indeed, she was tall, blonde, and beautiful. I disliked her immediately. It was all on my part—Miss America was a lovely person with a great career, not some gold digger looking to latch on to my father. But it didn't matter how nice she was because I was determined that my dad would remain single.

Miss America traveled a lot for her job, so she and Dad usually only saw each occasionally. One time she came to have dinner with us at Dad's before flying out for an assignment. Miss America wasn't familiar with Encino, and when it was time for her to leave to go to the airport, Dad asked me to drive my car to the freeway ramp so she could follow me. I cheerfully hopped into the Bug and, with Miss America behind me in her rental car, drove the half-mile to the freeway. I pointed out the window to the ramp and watched her wave back in response as she drove up it.

Later, she called Dad and told him that she had almost missed her flight because she had taken the entrance ramp going north on the freeway instead of south. It had taken her an hour to figure out she was going the wrong way, maneuver across six lanes of bumper-to-bumper Los Angeles traffic to exit, and then get back on going the right way to the airport.

When Dad questioned me about it, I denied everything.

"Dad!" I yelled. "I drove her right to the freeway, just like you asked. How can I help it if she was stupid enough to go up the wrong ramp?"

I'm not sure if my scheme had anything to do with it, but Dad and Miss America eventually stopped dating.

Some of my friends had divorced parents, and I knew I was lucky because Mom and Dad had worked hard to make their split an amicable one. Many of these friends also bitterly complained about their new stepparents. I was grateful that Dad was still single and hoped he would remain so for a long time. Sharing my dad with my mother had been one thing; sharing him with a stranger would be another. I loved being the main girl in Dad's life, and wasn't going to give up that distinction without a fight.

Once when I was at his house the phone rang and I answered it.

A cheerful-sounding lady was on the other end. "Hi, is this Kelly?"

"Yes."

"Oh, *hi*, Kelly! I've heard so much about you. Your dad told me you were in cheerleading! He said you made varsity your sophomore year? That's amazing! How did you manage that?"

"Just like Carnegie Hall," I said.

"Excuse me?"

"Practice, practice, practice."

"Oh, how funny! Is your dad home?"

"Yes, he's home." *Click.* I hung up the phone.

"Umm, Kell," Dad said later that day. "Have you noticed anything weird with the telephone lately?"

I shrugged. "I don't think so, Dad. Why?"

"Well, a friend of mine said she called, but the person, a young lady, hung up on her. Any idea of what could have happened?"

"Gosh, Dad, I have no idea. Maybe squirrels chewed the phone wires?"

"Squirrels, huh?"

"Yeah, Dad. You know squirrels do that, right?"

"I know one squirrel that could be guilty." And he'd give me a wry smile because although I'd been rude, he couldn't help himself.

Although Mom and Dad's amicable divorce didn't leave much for the gossip magazines and tabloids to speculate on, that didn't stop them from trying. Shortly after Dad moved out, Mom had a hysterectomy and had to spend almost three weeks in bed. She was a very active woman, but the surgery was complicated and the recovery long. One day, a big bouquet arrived at the house. I was sitting on her bed when she opened the note and read it. I remember it went something like this: "Hello, Mary Anne! Hope you're feeling better very soon. If you want to talk about anything, I'm always here." The note was signed by a woman who was a reporter for the *National Enquirer*.

The flowers went straight in the trash.

Another time, Dad came over to the house. When he walked into the kitchen, he found the housekeeper sitting with a strange woman. After some quizzing, the woman admitted that she was a reporter and had been sent over to our house specifically because she spoke Spanish.

I have never in my life seen my father so angry. He firmly took the reporter by the arm and escorted her off the property, telling her that if she ever came back, he would call the police. The housekeeper, who hadn't realized the woman's true identity, was mortified. Dad wasn't mad at her, but he made sure that everyone in the house knew to be on the lookout for gossip-seeking intruders.

Realizing there was no dirt for them to dig, no more reporters came snooping around. It was the first time in our lives there had been any tabloid interest in Dad and his family. Until the divorce, the Conway family had been so "normal" that we hadn't merited much media attention.

Although I didn't know it at the time, the hurt and anger I felt over my parents' divorce would be nothing compared to what I would experience years later, when I would find myself fighting for my dad's very life.

Chapter 14

DESPITE THE CHANGE MY PARENTS' DIVORCE HAD CAUSED IN OUR LIVES, I was determined to make my senior year as fun and normal as possible. My weekdays were busy with school, cheer practice, and driving my younger brothers to their various hockey games and baseball practices. Weekends were split among my friends and spending time with Dad.

Newly divorced, Mom decided she was going to have some fun, too. With proceeds from the divorce settlement, she immediately purchased two vacation homes. One was a cabin at a ski resort on Big Bear, just an hour's drive from Los Angeles. I was delighted because my love of skiing had become a genuine passion, and now that I could drive, the cabin was accessible for my friends and me on weekends. Mom also bought a cottage in the small fishing village of Erieau on the Canadian side of Lake Erie, where her family had vacationed for generations. My brothers and I would spend a few weeks every summer at the lake, meeting up with our friends we'd known for years. We would swim in the lake all day and build bonfires on the beach at night, roasting marshmallows and sneaking bottles of beer from our parents' refrigerators. There were dances at the yacht club and sailing lessons, and some of my youthful rites of passage took place on that sandy shore.

Mom and Dad continued to make good on their promise to raise us together and respect one another as their lives went in different directions. Dad still stopped by the house from time to time, and their conversations were usually short but friendly. Despite her lingering hurt at the demise of their marriage, I know Mom tried to keep their relationship as positive as possible.

When the Emmys came around later that year, Dad asked me if I wanted to go with him to the awards ceremony. The movie *10* had recently come out, and I was inspired by the cornrow braids that the star,

Bo Derek, had worn in it. I figured that if I had my hair braided in the same style, I wouldn't have to worry about keeping a brush in my small cocktail purse. The day before the Emmys, Mom took me to a salon where my long hair was woven into tiny braids from scalp to tips, each secured with white beads. I felt very chic with my new braids and loved how the beads looked with my outfit.

When Dad arrived in a stretch limo to pick me up for the Emmys, I raced down the steps just as he stepped out of the car. He looked at me, and a confused smile froze on his face. "Umm, what is on your head?"

"They're braids, Dad. And beads!" I swung my head so that the beads clacked against each other. "This hairstyle is, like, really popular now."

Dad looked over at Mom, who was standing with her arms crossed. She shrugged.

"All right, Bo Diddley," Dad said. "Get in the car."

"Oh my God, Dad!" I yelled. "It's Bo *Derek*!"

I don't remember much else about that evening, but Dad and I laughed about my "Bo Diddley" braids and beads for years afterward.

The night of homecoming my boyfriend, Greg, picked me up for dinner before the parade and the dance. I descended the curved stairs in my trendy black satin jumpsuit. Mom was exasperated that I didn't wear a fancy dress, but I knew it would be a long night and I wanted to comfortable. Dad filmed with his new video camera while my brothers goofed off and made faces behind me. Greg was taking me to dinner at Moonshadows, a popular restaurant on the beach in Malibu. We'd enjoy our very adult, romantic dinner watching the Pacific waves crash under the restaurant's panoramic windows, and then drive back over the hill to the Valley in time for the homecoming ceremonies.

It seemed like everyone else in LA had decided to eat at Moonshadows that same night, and it took a long time for our food to come out.

Just then, the waiter hurried over. "Are you Kelly?" he asked.

"Yes," I answered.

"You have a phone call at the host stand."

At first, I was alarmed, thinking that there had been some accident with my parents or brothers. But when I got to the phone, it was Mr. Ramirez.

"Kelly!" he said. "You need to get those dinners to go and get to the stadium as soon as possible."

"Uh, okay. Why?"

"Never mind why. Just get here as soon as you can."

Greg and I had our fancy dinner boxed up and ate in the car on the drive back. By the time we arrived at the stadium, the band had already launched into their homecoming ceremony repertoire. As we hurried to take our place in the stands, I saw Mr. Ramirez running toward me, looking very excited. He took my arm and pulled me through the crowds standing on the edge of the field.

"What's going on?" I yelled over the noise, trying to keep up with him in my high heels. Glancing up at the bleachers, I saw Mom and Dad, with my brothers, sitting in the crowd.

Mr. Ramirez turned and started fixing my hair, which had become disheveled in the wind during the ride from Malibu. "What's going on?" I demanded.

He frowned and dabbed at a dribble of cocktail sauce on the collar of my jumpsuit. "You're the homecoming queen. That's what's going on. Now get up there!"

"I'm *what*?"

Mr. Ramirez gave me a little push, and I walked out on the field toward the raised dais where the rest of the homecoming court were already waiting. The band burst into another rousing song. I mounted the stage and stood next to the homecoming king as someone placed a tiara on my head and a satin band across my shoulder.

I was in complete shock; it had never crossed my mind that I might be homecoming queen.

After the ceremony, my parents found me in the crowd. Dad chuckled and reached up to straighten my crown. "What kind of homecoming queen is late for her own coronation?" He gave me a big hug. "I'm really proud of you, Kell. Even though they made that poor band play the school fight song five times in a row while they tried to locate you."

Although Mom and Dad were sitting together the night I was crowned homecoming queen, my high school graduation ceremony would be very different.

The morning of my graduation, Mom had brusquely informed me that she and Patrick, Corey, Jamie, and Seann would sit together during the event, while Dad and Tim would sit in another area. It was clear that she was angry with Dad but didn't say anything more, and I was so busy trying to get dressed that I didn't press for information. This day represented the beginning of a whole new chapter in my life, and I'd been looking forward to it all year. But I'd never imagined that when Mom and Dad watched me take that first symbolic step into adulthood, they would be sitting apart. I sat among my fellow graduates, a glorious California sun shining down on our blue-capped heads, feeling more disappointed than excited.

Really, Mom and Dad? I thought as I gazed at the crowds of people sitting in the stands. *An hour-and-a-half event, and you two couldn't even pull it together just for me?*

It wasn't until later that I learned what had caused the crack in my parents' delicate post-divorce relationship. Dad had a new girlfriend, and she was someone all of us had known for years. She was also someone that Mom had considered a very close friend.

Charlene Beatty had been part of my parents' social circle ever since Dad started working on *The Carol Burnett Show*. She worked as Carol's personal secretary and had been married to Roger Beatty, a writer and associate director for the show. They had a daughter, Jackie, who was four years younger than my brother Seann. For over a decade, Charlene, Roger, and Jackie were regular guests at our house for swimming and dinner parties. When *The Carol Burnett Show* went to Australia, little Jackie had stayed with us and we'd all helped our housekeeper look after her while our parents were away.

Charlene and Roger had divorced not long after my parents split. Around the time of my graduation, I'd noticed that Charlene was coming around to visit Dad. Sometimes I would stop by his house and find Charlene and Jackie hanging out there. At first, I didn't think much of it because Charlene had been a close friend of Dad's for years. But gradually, it became clear that there was more to the relationship than just friendship, and once the news was out, Charlene and Jackie were at Dad's house almost every weekend.

Although I was initially surprised at this new development in Dad's romantic life, I wasn't opposed to it. If Dad had to be with anyone, then Charlene was a great option. My brothers and I already knew her and Jackie very well. She understood how important we were to our father, and there was none of the awkwardness that came with trying to accept a stranger into our tight-knit group. By choosing someone we already knew and liked, Dad made his transition from single back to a committed relationship nearly seamless.

My mother, however, didn't quite see it that way. She felt betrayed by Charlene. When they were still married, Mom and Dad would take vacations to Hawaii with Charlene and her then-husband Roger, Carol and Joe, and other couples from *The Carol Burnett Show* group. When Charlene gave birth to Jackie, Mom and Dad were among the first friends to see the baby. And, although it wasn't deliberate, Dad's new relationship with Charlene further helped to alienate my mom from the social circle she'd been a part of for so many years. Mom was probably also embarrassed that she'd been one of the last to know about it.

It didn't help matters when Dad announced his graduation gift for me: a trip to England and Italy. Carol was scheduled to appear on *The Muppet Show* in London, and I would be going along with Carol's daughter Erin and Charlene. It was a magical trip from start to finish. We flew on the *Concorde* to London and spent a few days touring the city. I remember—me, a Valley girl who was no stranger to big malls—being awestruck by the lavish, multilevel Harrods department store, with its enormous crystal chandeliers and elaborate window displays. But for me, the highlight of the trip was when Erin and I visited Jim Henson's studio where the show's artists created the Muppets, and we were allowed to make our own Muppet to take home.

Charlene and I then flew to Italy, where we stayed at the famous Villa d'Este resort on Lake Como. Dad and Charlene had friends who lived in the area, so our days were spent waterskiing on the impossibly blue waters of Lake Como and wandering through the villa's manicured gardens graced with statues and fountains. It was the first time Charlene and I had spent time alone together, and I felt almost guilty about how much fun I had with her. She was loud, funny, always up for anything, and very different from my more-reserved mother. She let me sip wine at dinner with the adults. It was like being with a cool aunt.

When summer was over, I started classes at Pierce Junior College, just a short drive from home. Although I had been a high school overachiever in sports, socializing, and cheerleading, my grades were another story. I always assumed I'd go on to the University of Southern California to continue my cheerleading career. Mr. Ramirez was a passionate alumnus, and he believed that my place was among the university's esteemed Song Girls, the elite squad who cheered at the USC football games. But before USC would accept me, I had to get my grades up a few notches, so junior college would be next destination before I could aim for Song Girl glory.

I worked hard to get good grades in junior college, and after a year, I transferred to USC. I wasn't exactly sure what I wanted to do as a career, but since I'd grown up in the entertainment business, I thought it made sense to major in film. The school was close to home but I chose to live in a dorm on campus. Since I'd lost a year while attending junior college, I was eager to assimilate into USC life, and decided that joining a sorority would help. But as the months went by, I began to realize that being a USC student, something I'd dreamt about for so long, wasn't as fulfilling as I'd imagined it would be.

In the 1980s, a particular style of student dominated USC's campus. Even growing up in the Valley hadn't prepared me for the onslaught of preppiness, both in looks and attitude. It was like all the girls competed to see who could "out-prep" the other, with big bows in their hair, pearl necklaces, and white flats. Even the boys were in on the game, sporting whale-printed shorts and tasseled loafers worn without socks. I preferred a more-casual style for trekking across campus with an armload of books, and instead opted for simple shorts and T-shirts with flip-flops on my feet. It seemed that my fellow students were obsessed with class and money, to the point where I realized that many of them were simply snobs.

The final straw came one night when I was running late for dinner at my sorority house. At Monday-night dinners—which were mandatory, whether you were hungry or not—all the girls were expected to wear white dresses. That particular evening I was late returning from a study session and went ripping through my closet to find a white dress. Realizing I didn't have a clean one available, I dug through my laundry basket to retrieve a dress that was wrinkled but otherwise okay. I hung it in the bathroom while I showered to steam out the creases, then yanked it on and ran out the door. Sitting at the table surrounded by a hundred other young women in their white dresses, I wondered what the hell I was doing there. Shortly afterward, I quit the sorority.

Ever since making the varsity squad by sophomore year in high school, cheerleading had been the course I'd expected to continue through college. Mr. Ramirez's dream for me to be a USC Song Girl was just within reach, and with a little effort, I'd be cheering at all the big college games in no time.

Except my heart wasn't in it anymore. Another passion had taken its place.

Chapter 15

I'd been taking advantage of my access to Mom's cabin in Big Bear and was spending more and more time driving up there to ski. First, it was just weekends. Then I began to go up for a night or two during the week, which meant I was also skipping classes. By my second year at USC, I'd already become so disillusioned with college that I didn't care how many classes I missed. I didn't really like USC, and skiing had become my escape.

I'd make up my mind that it was time to sit down and tell my parents I wanted to leave USC, but then I'd think about how disappointed they'd be and would put it off. Weeks went by like this, and soon I was spending more time skiing and less time in class. When the spring semester came around, I had stopped attending classes altogether.

One day, my mother opened the heating bill for the cabin. She noticed it was much higher than it should have been, since she believed it was only being used on the weekends.

"Kelly," said Mom when I stopped by the Magnolia house one day. She held out the bill. "Can you explain this?"

In a torrent of guilty tears, I confessed that I'd quit attending classes at USC. My parents were rightfully furious that I hadn't told them of my plans until after they had paid for the next semester, and to this day, I still feel terrible about the wasted money. Mom agreed to let me stay at the cottage in Big Bear, as long as I paid all the bills myself. Which meant I would have to get a job.

I signed up for ski instructor courses at Snow Summit in Big Bear Lake, and upon completion, was hired as an instructor. It was exciting to be among the few women instructors among throngs of gorgeous young men. I became fast friends with Kristin, who was from Colorado, and two other girls, Yvonne and Rose, who were also working at the resort. We spent our days teaching skiing and nights partying with our fellow instructors, where my fake ID came in handy at the local bars, since I was still only twenty. The season went by in a happy blur of crisp mountain days on the slopes and nights hanging out at après-ski happy hours and hot-tub parties.

For two years, I lived in Big Bear during the ski season. During the summer, Kristin and I rented an apartment in Huntington Beach. I got a job at a swimsuit boutique in Newport Beach and spent my off days at the beach. I was having a wonderful time, but Mom kept urging me to go back to college. She had worked hard to put herself through college when education wasn't considered a priority for women. The thought of her only daughter becoming a career beach-and-ski bum mortified her.

"Kelly!" she screamed after I'd blown off her attempt to talk to me about my future. "You're going to regret this. You won't think it's so cute when you're forty years old, too tan, living on happy hour, and lounging on the beach all summer!" Although part of me could have happily continued my carefree lifestyle, I knew she was right. It was time to get serious about what I would do for the rest of my life.

I had always been fascinated by the behind-the-scenes side of the entertainment business. All the hours I'd spent watching Bob Mackie work on Carol Burnett and Cher's magnificent costumes had left a powerful impression on me. I decided to follow my dad into show business, on the other side of the camera, as a costume designer. There were many design colleges to choose from, and some were in Los Angeles, but going someplace far away from home appealed to me.

I chose the Academy of Design in Toronto, Canada, about as far away from Southern California as you can get without crossing an ocean. Also, many of my old friends from Erieau lived near the city. And it was worlds apart in so many other ways, too. Mom came out for a few weeks to help me settle into my tiny downtown apartment just a short walk from school. Those weeks with just Mom and me were some of the best times we'd ever spent together. Without the distraction of the rest of the family, we could fully enjoy each other's company. We spent days exploring the city, eating dumplings in Toronto's Chinatown, and browsing the shopping district.

When she finally flew home, I was sad to see her go, knowing I wouldn't see any of my family until Christmas break.

But being so far away from Dad was the hardest of all. We talked almost every day on the phone, and I'd tell him about my classes and the friends I was making, and he would fill me in on what was happening back at home. If I weren't home he would leave rambling, funny messages on my answering machine about something my brothers had done, or even what he'd eaten for lunch that day. I'd walk around my apartment, listening to his voice and cracking up as the message went on for several minutes. His relationship with Charlene was getting more serious. Initially, I felt a flare of jealousy, anxious that Charlene and her daughter, Jackie, might be taking my place in Dad's affections.

"All right, Dad," I said after he'd told me about something fun that he and Charlene had done together. "That's great, but I'm still you're favorite girl, right?"

"Kell," he replied, suddenly serious. "You will *always* be my favorite girl."

Since Dad was taking some time off from work, he could indulge in his passion for horse racing. Part of this had to do with Charlene, who had grown up the daughter of a New York City bookie and loved horse racing nearly as much as Dad did. My mother had never been very interested in the sport, so now that Dad had a partner who was horse-crazy, too, he could spend as much time and money at the track as he liked. With Charlene's encouragement, he bought a few horses and worked closely with the trainers to develop them. Although he'd later admit that his investments never paid out, Dad loved being a part of horse racing, and it brought him a tremendous amount of joy.

He also found a way to give back to the sport he loved. Since most jockeys were appallingly underpaid, Dad supported organizations that raised money for their retirement and medical bills. Ever since he had been a boy, he'd admired the dedication that jockeys gave to their racing careers, even though only a small percentage made a good living from it. When Dad learned that there was no endowment for helping ill or injured riders, he decided to start one with some fellow racing enthusiasts. Everyone wanted to name the fund after Dad, but he refused and instead suggested naming it in honor of Don MacBeth, a well-known rider who had died of cancer at age thirty-seven. Within a few years, the Don MacBeth Memorial Jockey Fund provided support for more than two thousand riders all over the country.

At one benefit for the fund, Dad agreed to ride in a race against the famous jockey Laffit Pincay for a televised event hosted by Dick Van Patten. Dad had always wanted to be a jockey, and in a way, this opportunity fulfilled his lifelong dream. For weeks he worked with a trainer, doing laps around the track on a retired racehorse to prepare. He had colorful jockey silks made to wear during the race.

On race day, Dad lined his horse up next to Laffit in the starting box in front of a full crowd watching from the stands. The cameras rolled as the starting shot went off, and both horses lunged onto the track. Dad's horse was neck and neck with Laffit's horse for a while, until Dad lightly tapped his horse on its flank with his whip. The feel of the whip must have reminded the old horse of his racetrack glory days because he shot ahead. With Dad clinging on for dear life, they thundered around the track and crossed the finish line. And kept going. The cameras whipped around to follow the action, and the spectators jumped to their feet, cheering. Dad clapped both arms around the horse's neck and hung on. Man and beast were coming into the last stretch of their *second* lap when an outrider caught up with them. The outrider grabbed the horse's reins, slowing them to a walk. Dad and his runaway steed were led to the winner's circle, where he received a trophy to a full standing ovation. Dad donated his appearance fee to the jockeys' organization—and could hardly walk for the rest of the week after his wild ride.

Back in Toronto, listening to Dad tell stories like this over the phone made me roll on the floor with laughter. It also helped keep me from being so homesick. Where USC had left me feeling like an outsider, at design school, I fit right in, just being myself. My classmates were from all backgrounds, ages, and ethnicities, and being a part of so much diverse creativity made me see the world in a new light.

I became friends with another student, a very stylish woman named Margitta, who was a few years older than me. One day when Margitta and I were having a coffee between classes, I mentioned that I wanted to attend Toronto's Maple Leaf hockey games. The Maple Leafs were a legendary team, revered like rock stars to their hometown fans in the 1980s, and getting a ticket to a game was nearly impossible. I was a huge LA Kings hockey fan, but the Maple Leafs were a close second.

"You like hockey?" Margitta said, surprised.

"I love hockey!" I said. "My brothers and I played hockey all the time when we were growing up. And if I could get to see a Maple Leaf home game, my brothers would be *so* jealous."

"Well, no problem," Margitta said. "You can come with me to the game on Saturday night."

"No way!" I said. "You have tickets?"

"Yes, I have tickets." She smiled and raised an eyebrow. "I don't think I've ever mentioned it, but Börje Salming is my husband."

I nearly fell off my chair. Börje Salming was ice hockey royalty. His nickname, "The King," summed up the Swedish defenseman's dominance in the game.

The night of the Maple Leaf game, I found myself following Margitta down the long arena steps to where the VIP boxes lined the ice. Just inches away from the action, we watched as players slammed each other into the glass in front of our seats. The crowd was wild with enthusiasm, and I don't think I've ever experienced a hockey game that was so close up and charged with emotion.

Living in Toronto made it easy for me to visit our lake cottage during school breaks. In the warmer months, I would board a train from Toronto, and a few hours later I'd step onto the platform where one of my uncles would pick me up from the station. A lot of the cousins and friends that I had known since childhood still lived in the area, so there was always someone fun to hang out with.

One boy I'd known since childhood, Patrick O'Brien, had become a kind of summer boyfriend when we were both in our teens. Ever since I could remember, he and his family shared a lake cottage with his cousins just down the beach from ours. Pat was funny and sweet, insanely handsome, with golden sun streaks in his brown hair and a bright smile. We would stay in touch by writing letters back and forth after we'd both gone back home when summer was over. Although being apart most of the year kept us from becoming a serious couple, we had a genuine love for one another that I knew would last a lifetime. Pat was the first person I contacted whenever I went back to the lake.

I was back at school in Toronto one night when the phone rang. It was my friend Colleen, Pat's sister, sobbing. She had terrible news. Pat and some friends had been driving home from a party when the driver lost control of the car, and it went tumbling off the road. Pat had been rushed to the hospital and was in a coma. The prognosis, Colleen said, did not look good.

When I hung up the phone, I was so numb with shock that I couldn't even cry. I couldn't get it through my head that Pat, so vibrant and strong, was lying in a hospital in a coma, fighting for his life. My first call was to Mom, and as soon as she picked up, I broke down and wept so hard I could barely speak. Mom got on the next plane from Los Angeles and arrived in Toronto the following day.

We rented a car and Mom drove five hours to the Windsor hospital while I cried nonstop in the passenger seat. Mom had known Pat's family for years, and she wanted to be there for them, too. The family had already experienced tragedy years earlier when Pat's younger sister, Anne Marie, had died in a bicycle accident. Everyone was gathered at the hospital when we arrived, and as soon as Pat's mother stood up to embrace me, I fell into heaving sobs. While I calmed down, Mom went in to see Pat, but after just a couple of minutes, she joined us back in the hall.

Later, she told me what happened.

"I was sitting there, Kelly, just holding Pat's hand and talking to him. I told him that we'd driven nonstop to see him and that you were talking to his mom and sister, but you would be in to see him any second. Just then, the machines surrounding his bed started pulsing fast and beeping, and the nurse came over to check him. She said his vital signs were surging and asked me to leave the room because she needed to call the doctor."

The doctor didn't want anyone to visit Pat after that. My last good-bye to my longtime sweetheart was through the tinted glass that looked into his hospital room. All I could see was his head of tousled, sun-streaked brown hair against the pillow; the breathing tubes concealed most of his face. Pat died a day later.

For three weeks, Mom stayed with me in Toronto as we both processed our grief. I didn't attend classes during this period. At the end of those weeks, I knew it was time to get myself together and go on with my life.

I felt aching loneliness as I watched Mom drive away in a cab to the airport. Part of me wanted to jump in and fly home with her. I was alone in a foreign city and utterly heartbroken. But I was committed to finishing school no matter how hard it was going to be to start living again.

Chapter 16

ONE DAY DURING MY LAST YEAR AT COLLEGE DAD CALLED WITH SOME news.

"Guess what?" he said when I answered.

"What?"

"Charlene and I are getting married."

"Oh, wow, Dad. That's great!"

I meant it. I knew that Dad and Charlene were very much in love, and they had so much in common. I felt fortunate that if my dad was going to be married to anyone else, it would be to Charlene, a person I had known since I was a child, and who I liked so much. I felt a quick stab of sadness for my mother, but my next thought quickly eclipsed it.

"So, when's the wedding? Are you doing something big, or just friends and family? Formal, casual? And what should I wear?"

"There's not going to be a wedding," Dad replied with a laugh. "Just a trip to the courthouse."

"Have you told Mom?" I ventured.

"Not yet. She's my next call. I wanted you to be the first to know. It means a lot to Charlene and me that you're happy for us, Kell."

I knew that Dad didn't want to have a big, fancy wedding because it would only hurt my mother even more. Dad and Charlene got married at the Los Angeles courthouse, with just a couple of friends standing by to witness. Then they all went to the racetrack to celebrate.

Shortly after Dad and Charlene got married, Mom called with some news of her own. She was selling our house on Magnolia. Tim and Patrick had moved out after graduating from high school, and the house was just too big for Mom and my three younger brothers, who still lived with her. I was devastated about losing my childhood home, but Mom was ready to make a new start and leave behind the place that held so many memories.

What Mom told me next was a complete surprise. She announced that she would be moving to Steamboat Springs, Colorado. I knew that Mom had been very unhappy in Los Angeles since the divorce. Most of the friends that she'd had over the years had been through Dad's work. And now that Dad and Charlene were married, and a lot of those same people had been friends with Charlene for a long time, there was no room in the social circle for Mom. She was eager to close the door on California and start life over in a new place, where she wouldn't just be known as Tim Conway's ex-wife.

On Christmas break, Mom had flown my brothers and me out with her for a visit to Steamboat Springs, which was then a small ranching town nestled among breathtaking snowcapped mountains. We spent a week skiing and soaking in the area's famous hot mineral springs. After the break, we all flew back to Los Angeles so we kids could spend the rest of Christmas with Dad. While we were with Dad, Mom flew right back to Steamboat Springs. A few days later, she bought a house there.

When Mom returned to Los Angeles, flush with excitement about the move, she immediately launched into sorting and packing our house's contents. I spent the last few days of Christmas break boxing up my belongings from my old room. My old stuffed animals, trophies from gymnastics meets, and all other remnants of my childhood were banished to brown moving boxes and destined for storage. Packing up a household of six children is not easy, and hurt as much, if not more, than the divorce.

The day before I flew back to Toronto, I wandered outside to the pool, where tinfoil trophies had been presented for the biggest splash, and across the lawn, over which Seann had flown on a zipline years ago. In the branches overhead were the old treehouses Dad had built for us, their boards warped and faded from the sun, where Tim and I had lobbed water balloons down on the heads of our unwitting younger brothers.

Dad arrived to take me to the airport and we packed my things into his car. As we pulled out of the driveway, I turned to look back at the house one last time.

"Hey, Pal," Dad said. "What's with the tears?"

"It's just so sad. Our whole lives are in that house, and now it's going to belong to someone else. It's just strange to think about Mom moving away."

Another thought came to me. "What about the boys?" I asked. "I thought you and Mom had an agreement that none of the kids who were still living at home would leave Los Angeles?"

Corey and Seann still lived at home, and Mom had said that she would be taking them with her to live in Steamboat Springs.

Dad's face darkened a little. "I'm still working on that, Kell. It's a tough situation."

"But wasn't it part of the custody agreement?"

"Yes, that was the agreement we'd made." I could tell I'd hit a nerve. "As I said," Dad continued with a heavy sigh, "it's a *very* complicated situation."

I later found out that Dad had asked Mom not to take the boys to live so far away from him. But she was determined to go, and Dad didn't want to push the matter. I know that he still felt guilty about the divorce, and he was aware that Mom was not happy in Los Angeles. Also, he didn't want to drag the boys through any sort of legal battle. He let them go, but he later said it was a decision he regretted for the rest of his life.

I flew back to Toronto and finished up my final year of school. For our graduation, all the fashion design students created a line of clothing and presented them in a real fashion show, with professional models walking the runway. I was thrilled to see the collection that I'd designed finally spring to life from my sketchpad, and, after so many hours of hard work, actually being worn by real people. We students ran around backstage before the show snipping loose threads, changing out accessories, and adjusting hems until our first model stepped out on the catwalk. Dad wasn't able to attend, but Mom did. Watching from backstage, I could see the pride on Mom's face as my collection made its debut.

After graduation, I decided to spend a year with Mom and my brothers in Steamboat Springs. There was plenty of room in Mom's large, log cabin–style house, and it was right in the downtown area close to the restaurants, bars, and shops. I got a job working as a cocktail waitress at a place called The Tugboat, and spent my days skiing with Mom. We had become so much closer once I'd left home for college, and what had been a sometimes combative relationship when I was a teenager had grown into a real friendship. I realized just how much fun my mom could be, and her delight in finally living a life of her own was infectious.

Mom had always had a good head for business, and when she bought a clothing boutique on Steamboat Springs's main street, I was able to put my fashion degree to use, helping her run it. We would fly to New York or Chicago on buying trips, going from one shop to the next to examine all the latest collections. There were some hit-or-miss decisions, as sometimes the things that Mom and I thought were fabulous didn't quite appeal to the "plaid and flannel" shoppers back in Steamboat Springs. We quickly learned that Ralph Lauren worked while Norma Kamali didn't. But to me, it was never a total loss, because the clothes that didn't sell often ended up in my closet.

After a year in Steamboat Springs, I began to miss the hustle and excitement of Los Angeles. It was time for me to get back and start a career. Dad had bought two condos as an investment, and I lived in one while my brother Tim lived in the other. Both of us paid full rent just like any other tenant would. Tim was also interested in going into the entertainment business as a production assistant on television and movie projects. I thought between Tim and Dad, making connections would be easy.

But it was actually Mom's brother, my uncle Wally, who gave me the phone number for Bobbie Mannix, one of the top stylists in the industry. He knew Bobbie because they both frequented the same coffee shop and had become casual friends over the years. It was only because Bobbie liked Uncle Wally that she had agreed to even meet me. Being hired by Bobbie kicked off my career, and I'm still thankful to my uncle for helping me get my foot in the door.

When I called Bobbie the first time introducing myself, she talked so fast that I misunderstood her. When we hung up, I thought she'd asked me to come to her studio. But when I showed up the next day and gave the receptionist my name, she looked surprised.

The studio was crammed with racks of clothes and boxes of accessories. Assistants dashed back and forth, answering phones, sorting wardrobe by style, or steaming wrinkles out of fabric. There was a sense of urgency and purpose in the air, and I knew right away that I wanted to be part of it.

Bobbie came into the room and looked me up and down.

"Who are you?" she asked.

"I'm Kelly!" I piped nervously. "Kelly Conway. We talked on the phone yesterday?"

Bobbie nodded slowly, looking confused.

"And you told me to stop by to see you?" I added.

"No!" Bobbie rolled her eyes. "I told you to *call* me."

I felt my face redden. The assistants had all stopped what they were doing to listen.

I started to apologize, but Bobbie interrupted me. "Since you're here, I can put you to work," she said, grabbing a bag filled with clothes and thrusting it into my arms. "Here, take these back to Macy's." She picked up another bag and handed that one to me, too. "And these need to go back to Sears. Receipts are stapled to the bag. Be sure to bring back the return receipts and give them to my sister Debbie. Got it? Good. Now off you go."

I went on to work as Bobbie Mannix's assistant for six years, and could not have had a better mentor. Bobbie had styled some of the most iconic films of the 1970s, including the cult classic *The Warriors* about street gangs in New York City, and *Xanadu*, the fantasy musical starring Olivia Newton-John which kicked off an instant fad for flowy, off-the-shoulder dresses paired with leg warmers and roller skates. Bobbie was a pioneer for modern fashion styling and she taught me more in one year than I'd learned in all my years at design college.

In between movie projects, Bobbie's team styled a lot of television commercials, and my days were filled with running around town to various department stores and costume rental places with a list of sizes for the actors. Sometimes I had to find multiple outfits for kids, men, and women, then take them all back to the studio where Bobbie would pore over the selections, swapping out tops and pants and throwing anything that didn't work back into the bag to be returned. You would never believe how much thought and effort went into which jeans or T-shirt a child should wear in a breakfast cereal commercial. We would haul all the costumes to the set during the shoot, along with irons, steamers, and a sewing kit, ready to jump in if the director requested a change or an actor wrinkled their clothes.

As a costume designer, you try to prepare for any whim or emergency that might arise on-set. Sometimes good old-fashioned improvisation is required to get the job done. I was on a shoot where the director decided he wanted the actors to wear different-colored socks than what I had brought with me. We were too far away for me to run to a store, and minutes wasted can cost thousands of dollars in production. So I grabbed some cash, ran to a nearby house on the street where we were shooting, and knocked on the door.

"Hi," I said when the lady answered the door. "I'm working on the commercial shoot down the road, and this is probably going to be the craziest thing anyone has ever asked you. But do you have a pair of blue socks I can buy from you?" I held up a pair of twenty-dollar bills to show I was serious. No one ever turned me away empty-handed.

I got my first solo job by accident, when the stylist that I was supposed to assist on a music video shoot got too busy to do it and handed it over to me. The video was for Tom Petty's song "Free Fallin'," a big production with multiple locations and lots of actors to dress. It was a lot to handle on my own, but I was excited about making all of the creative decisions instead of just assisting like usual. The costumes ran the gamut from 1950s dresses to LA punk styles, so I went to vintage clothing stores and hip boutiques all over town to find the perfect looks for the shoot.

The video looked great, with the same actresses who appeared so sweet in their 1950s skirts morphing into sexy punk princesses prowling Ventura Boulevard. But in my eagerness to choose the best costumes, I had gone way over budget. When I turned in my receipts, the company producing the video hit the roof. I called Dad, crying, convinced that my reputation was ruined and that I'd never get another job styling again.

"Kell," Dad said. "You think you're the first person in this town to go a little over budget? Please. Because of you, that video turned about exactly the way they wanted. Just use this as a lesson for the next time."

"But the production company is so pissed off at me!" I said. "What if they never hire me again?"

"Stop with the what-ifs," Dad scolded. "Tell them you will work some extra hours to make up for it. Kell, you're great at what you do. You're reliable, creative, and hardworking, so they will want you again. It's not 'show *friends*,' it's 'show business.' You have to keep that in mind, and try not to take things so personally." He laughed. "Or trust me, it will kill you."

Dad was right, of course. It was another lesson for me, and one I never forgot.

I now realized that a director's vision often goes far beyond the boundaries of the budget. A stylist's job is figuring out a way for the two to meet halfway so that in the end, everyone is happy. It's a fast-paced job that requires long days and early call times, and there's no end of emergencies requiring immediate intervention. The night before a shoot, I can never sleep because I'm too busy mentally inventorying everything I need to bring for the job. But it was, and still is, the perfect job for me in so many ways, and I have loved every moment of it.

Chapter 17

AFTER TAKING A FEW YEARS OFF, DAD JUMPED RIGHT BACK INTO WORK, and soon he was as busy as he'd ever been. There were countless appearances on talk and variety shows, guest spots on television series, and lots of comedy specials. He co-starred in the 1980 movie *The Private Eyes* with his friend Don Knotts, a spoof based on the Sherlock Holmes mysteries. Dad loved working with Don, who he considered one of the nicest—and funniest—people in show business.

In 1983, Dad signed on to star in a comedy television series called *Ace Crawford, Private Eye.* The series only lasted five episodes before CBS pulled it. Dad always said he was never comfortable heading a show and that he did his best work when he was in a support role. Dad thrived when his humor was part of a group effort, and when the comedic ball bounced from one person to the next he was at the top of his game. On his own, Dad felt a little awkward and even shy. Nonetheless, he had a great attitude about his failed solo adventures. At that time, thirteen episodes was the minimum number that a network would produce for a new show. Dad joked that the show would be axed long before it aired thirteen episodes whenever he was the top billed star. He even got a vanity license plate for his car that read "13 WKS" to honor that distinction.

In 1986 Dad wrote and co-starred in a comedy movie centered around horse racing called *The Longshot.* Cast with his friends Harvey Korman, Jonathan Winters, Ted Wass, and Jack Weston, the film is about a group of racetrack regulars who are perpetually down on their luck until they devise a scheme that could pay out big. The movie was set at the Santa Anita racetrack, and I spent a lot of my free time hanging out there with Dad and the crew. The costume designer even let me help her out, which was an excellent opportunity for me to learn a lot about full-scale movie production. I was around the set so much that Dad decided to write a small role in the movie for me as a program seller. I only had a couple of lines, but it was great fun.

The Longshot did not go on to be a critical smash, but Dad loved making a movie about horse racing, and he got to work with some of his good friends. He even wrote a rap song for the opening titles, which he sang with a young, up-and-coming LA rap star named Ice-T.

Although I was still working as an assistant for Bobbie Mannix, I began to get more styling gigs of my own. It was a great time to be in costume design because of the sheer number of jobs available. The television commercial industry was booming, and these clients usually had huge budgets for their shoots. Sometimes the entire production would come to a halt because the director realized the actor's blue shirt blended in with the blue wallpaper. I would rush off to the wardrobe trailer to grab more choices while the rest of the production waited.

Busy times were usually seasonal, so you'd have a few months of twelve-hour days working without a break, and then a few months where the work was more sporadic. During the slower times, I would head up to the mountains to ski or, during the summer, fly to Canada to stay with Mom at the lake cottage.

I also did wardrobe for a lot of music videos. They could be exciting to work on, although budgets were often stingy, with very tight shooting schedules. We'd work from six a.m. until six a.m. the following day without a break. Still, the energy on a music video shoot was a lot of fun and I usually enjoyed myself, even if I was exhausted by the time it wrapped.

I was required to sew for my job, and if I had some alterations to work on, I'd carry them over to Dad's house and he would help me. Dad had been taught to sew as a young boy by his mother, Magi, and he was very good at it. Even as an adult, he'd sit happily at his sewing machine, making slipcovers and curtains for the house. Dad loved plaid, and he decorated his home office with drapes and a matching slipcovered sofa in green tartan-plaid. Later, he got ambitious and decided to make a sports jacket using one from his closet as a pattern. He spent hours working on the jacket, sewing in the lining and cutting the lapels, but this task proved to be beyond his skill set. Still, Dad wore his homemade jacket and proudly told everyone that he'd made it himself.

One day he went to retrieve the jacket from the dry cleaners. The man behind the counter, who was used to Dad bringing in finely tailored clothes, shook his head gravely as he handed the jacket over.

"Mr. Conway," the man said. "I don't know how to say this, but whoever made this jacket for you didn't know what they were doing."

"Really?" Dad said. "Is it that bad?"

"Yes!" The man replied. "Look here, the shoulder seams are crooked, and the lining is a complete mess! You should really demand your money back."

Dad was crestfallen, but the dry cleaner's criticism of his work only made him more resolved to improve his skills. He made another jacket and took it to the dry cleaner's. Again, the man commented on the shoddy workmanship of the coat. Undaunted, Dad got right to work on another jacket. He was determined to produce a jacket well-made enough that the dry cleaner wouldn't comment on it. Finally, after the fourth jacket, the dry cleaner simply handed it over without saying a word. Dad was thrilled.

Between his tailoring and slip-covering gigs, Dad continued to work in television. He also appeared in some commercials because it was great money for a few days of work. I worked as a stylist for a few of them. I remember one shoot for Contac cold medicine, where he and Harvey played television news announcers. Harvey's character is trying to deliver the news while Dad sneezes and sniffles loudly next to him. The director had given Dad and Harvey leeway to ad-lib the dialogue, and I remember they were on fire and having so much fun with it. Even the crew was laughing.

After a while, the director stopped them. "Can you guys maybe, umm, be a little *less* funny?"

Dad and Harvey stared at him.

"I mean, we want you to be funny, of course," the director said. "But you know, it's a cold medicine, so the client doesn't want it to be too funny."

The cameras rolled, and Dad and Harvey continued with their banter. Of course, they were hilarious, and once again, the crew could hardly contain their laughter.

"Stop," the director called. "Look, I love what you guys are doing. I personally wouldn't change a thing. But the client may have an issue with it being this funny."

Harvey lowered his head and put his face in his hands. It was probably the first time in either of their careers when someone asked them to be less funny.

"Why did you hire *us* to do this commercial if you don't want it to be funny? Why didn't you hire *him*?" Dad pointed at the sound guy. "Hey, Harvey, think you could dial down the funny a bit? It's a cold medicine we're talking about here. Stop being so damn funny." The entire set, including the director, burst out laughing. The shoot continued, and the result was just funny enough to please the client. But not *too* funny, as Dad and Harvey would go on to joke with each other.

Dad was friends with Johnny Carson and would often appear as a guest on *The Tonight Show*. Typically, comic actors would perform a stand-up routine before heading over to join Johnny on the couch for a chat. But Dad never liked just standing at a microphone telling jokes. If he didn't have a cast to work off of, he loved props. For an upcoming appearance on *The Tonight Show*, he decided to come up with a comedy sketch. That's where Dorf was born. Dorf, a very, *very* short jockey, was inspired by one of Dad's characters on *The Carol Burnett Show*.

For a *Fantasy Island* spoof on the show, Dad played Hervé Villechaize's role of Tattoo, the dwarf assistant to the island's debonair host. To prepare for the role of Dorf, Dad tried kneeling on the set with his knees bent on top of a pair of shoes. But it didn't look authentic enough for Dad. He had the carpenters cut two holes on a raised platform that he could slide his legs in up to the knees. He then asked me to help him with the shoes, which is where the time I spent at Jim Henson's Muppets Studio paid off. I had learned techniques there that worked great for Dorf's shoes, which had to be cut in the back to fit around Dad's legs at floor level. Once Dad had his legs in the holes and the shoes Velcroed on, he could move his upper body around. Dad added an ill-fitting toupee and a slightly Eastern European accent, and the character of Dorf was complete.

I always loved any chance to work with Dad as a stylist on one of his projects. It was a chance for me to show him that I was now a true professional in the business, and I wanted everything I did to be perfect. On one video shoot, where Dorf appears as a jockey, I tailored the jodhpurs to fit Dad's shortened legs and the backless boots to fit around his knees. The night before the shoot, I steamed the jockey silks and placed them into a clear garment bag, with the helmet, boots, and riding crop hung in a separate bag.

The next morning at the location, I helped Dad get into costume as he stood with his lower legs inside the platform. We all stood back to admire our jockey, Dorf.

"Looks great, Kell," Dad said. "Now, I just need the crop."

The crop? I felt a flutter in my stomach. I didn't recall seeing it when I'd emptied the costume bags.

"It probably fell out in my backseat," I said. While the crew waited, I raced to the car and tore through it, but it wasn't there. Frantically, I retraced all my steps, thinking it must have fallen out of the bag when I carried everything to the set.

There was no sign of it on the ground. At this point, I was fighting back tears. Dad always liked having a prop to use in his sketches, and the Dorf character wielded the riding crop as a kind of comic exclamation point. And here I was, Tim Conway's stupid daughter who couldn't even find it. Everyone was still waiting, so I had to confess that the crop was missing. Although I was embarrassed in front of the crew, disappointing Dad was much worse. There was no time for me to drive anywhere to buy another, so we would have to improvise.

"Okay, let's think about this," Dad said, still encased in his knee-high platform. "Kelly, how can we *make* a riding crop?"

Suddenly, I was laser-focused on the task. I found a tree branch about the right length, then borrowed a roll of black gaffer's tape from a crew member. Once I'd wound tape around the branch, if you didn't look too close, it looked just like a riding crop, with tassels cut on one end. My handmade crop worked fine for the shoot, and you couldn't tell it wasn't real on the video. After that, I never left home before a job without triple-checking all my costumes and supplies.

The branch-and-tape riding crop wasn't the last time I would have to make miracles happen while on-set. Being able to improvise was a valuable skill I inherited from my dad, who had always been a fast-thinking and creative problem solver.

The Dorf videos were a huge success, and Dad went on to make videos about Dorf's fishing, hunting, and baseball adventures. When Dad decided that Dorf needed to make a golfing video, he persuaded legendary golfer Sam Snead to appear in one of the videos, where Dorf pompously attempts to outswing him. Dad liked to refer to Dorf as his special "annuity" because of how many DVDs the character sold.

When I wasn't working, I spent a lot of time with Dad and Charlene. Charlene was an excellent cook, and she loved to host big dinners for friends and family, filling the house with the savory aromas of her classic Italian dishes. Charlene had grown up in New Jersey, the daughter of a large Italian-American family rumored to have ties to the Mafia. Her father was a trumpet player who toured the big band circuit and moonlighted as a bookie. When she graduated secretarial school, Charlene crossed the Hudson over to Manhattan to find work at one of the big television networks. Armed with her street-smart chutzpah, she got herself hired at CBS as a junior secretary. Eventually she was hired as producer Joe Hamilton's secretary when he worked for *The Gary Moore Show*, and there she met and befriended Joe's wife, Carol Burnett. Once *The Carol Burnett Show* was under way, Charlene became Carol's personal secretary and lifelong friend.

Charlene had married Roger Beatty, an associate director and writer on the show, and they had their daughter, Jackie. Dad was good friends with Roger, and the two remained close even after Dad married Charlene, Roger's ex-wife. Charlene also had a good relationship with her two stepdaughters, Karen and Colleen, Roger's daughters from his first marriage. Karen was close to my age and we had known each other since we were kids running around the studio when our parents worked on *The Carol Burnett Show*. Karen and Colleen were regular guests at Dad and

Charlene's house for dinners and holidays, and we all considered them part of the family.

Charlene and Roger's daughter, Jackie, was a teenager when Dad married Charlene. Although we'd known her since she was a baby, Jackie was shy and never seemed fully comfortable around my brothers and me. We always tried to make her feel included, but at family dinners she usually ate quickly and went off to her room. Later, Charlene would accuse us of purposefully ignoring Jackie, which was far from the truth. She just seemed to prefer being by herself or with her friends.

Charlene made Dad very happy, and they had a lot of fun together, going to the racetrack and traveling around the world. I remember thinking how lucky I was that Charlene was my stepmother, out of all the women he could have married.

It's difficult for me to think back on those days when our families blended so harmoniously, knowing now that my happy relationship with Charlene would someday end in so much pain.

Chapter 18

WHILE I WORKED MY WAY THROUGH COMMERCIALS AND MUSIC VIDEOS, Dad began to take his act on the road. There was a big demand for comedy acts around the country, often held at casinos or other large venues, so Harvey and Dad decided to tour together as a double billing. In some of the country's more-remote areas, people would drive for hours to see the show. Dad also played Vegas, sometimes opening for other entertainers and sometimes solo. Dad had never loved doing stand-up comedy; it was hard for him to go out on an empty stage and talk into a microphone. But his discomfort quickly diminished when he saw the enthusiastic response from his audiences. He and Harvey were very popular, and their schedule was filled with appearances at casinos and clubs all over the United States and Canada.

Dad and Harvey had been touring for about a year when I broke up with a boyfriend of two years and was nursing a broken heart. Dad suggested I join them for some of the tour, and getting out of town sounded like precisely the kind of medicine I needed. I packed my bag and headed out to the regional airport, where a private plane waited to fly everyone from Los Angeles to Galveston, where Dad and Harvey were booked to perform at a casino.

Private planes were not the usual transport for Dad, but this was just after the terrorist attacks of 9/11, and commercial flights had not yet resumed full schedules. As we settled onto the plane, the pilot, a handsome British man, stepped back to say hello to Dad and Harvey. His name was Phil, and he had become friendly with the two after piloting them on other trips.

"And who is this?" Phil asked, smiling at me. I realized I was blushing as Dad introduced us. Once we hit cruising altitude, I popped my head into the cockpit and chatted with Phil for the duration of the flight. The longer we talked, the more attracted I was to him. When we got to Galveston, Phil sat with me during Dad and Harvey's show. For the rest of the tour, we were inseparable.

The tour stopped in New York City for a couple of days between shows. With Phil along, Dad, Charlene, Harvey Korman, his wife Debby, and I had a wonderful time. It was close to Christmas, and the streets were strung with sparkling lights and decorations. We walked around all day, shopping, eating, and taking in the sights until our feet ached.

A woman passed us on the sidewalk. I was walking behind our group and saw her eyes fall on Harvey. When she saw Dad, she did a double take and turned to catch up with us.

"Oh my God," she said. "You're Harvey Korman. And you're Tim Conway!"

Dad paused and smiled as he always did when someone recognized him.

"I gotta tell you, Tim," the woman continued in her loud New York accent, "I named my son after you!"

We all laughed appreciatively and started to say good-bye, but the woman wasn't finished.

"No, no, you gotta hear this. I was nine months pregnant, and I didn't think that baby was ever going to come. Then one night, I was sitting on the edge of the bed watching you on television. And you got me laughing so hard that I fell off the bed and my water broke. My baby boy was born a few hours later. And I just had to name him after you!"

By the end of the tour, Phil and I were officially a couple. Dad was thrilled, but Harvey was practically over the moon about it. Harvey thought Phil was the coolest man ever, and we teased him about his "man-crush." When he was in town, Phil joined me for dinners and parties at Dad and Charlene's house. Harvey was always the first to jump up to welcome him with a big hug and hearty slaps on the shoulder.

Phil's job piloting a private plane put him in contact with some very wealthy people. He was such a likable person that many of his passengers became his friends. One family enjoyed Phil's company so much that they insisted he and I join them for a cruise off the coast of Spain on their mega yacht. It was luxurious beyond anything I'd ever experienced. Gourmet, multicourse meals were prepared by a private chef. And the sheets on the bed in our stateroom were the silkiest I'd ever felt. I sometimes missed the lavish breakfast spread that was served each morning on the open deck because sleeping in was so luxurious. When I mentioned how much I loved the sheets to our hostess, she told me where I could buy them. But when I saw how much they cost, I nearly passed out. The price of a single set was more than what I paid for my mortgage each month.

Back home in the real world, I worked one styling job after another, sometimes running from a music video one day to a fast-food commercial the next. Most of the people I styled on these jobs were actors, but I occasionally worked with other famous people. There were music videos with Cheap Trick, Jimmy Buffett, and Sammy Hagar, who was friendly and easygoing. But one of my most memorable assignments was for the country star, Garth Brooks.

The job was for the video shoot of his hit song, "The Red Strokes." In the video, Garth gets lowered into a vat of red paint while wearing a white tuxedo. This meant that I had to purchase twenty-five identical tuxedos that he could change into until they got the shot just right.

On the morning of the shoot, I was staggering from my car with an armload of tuxes when I heard a man's friendly voice call out.

"Excuse me. Can I lend you a hand?"

When I shifted my load to see who was offering to help, I was shocked to realize it was none other than Garth himself standing there.

"Umm, sure!" I gasped.

Meeting famous people usually doesn't faze me one bit, but I was a massive fan of Garth's, and here he was, kindly offering to help me carry stuff from my car.

"I mean, no! I have it, but thank you so much!"

Garth laughed and bent into my car, picking up the rest of the tuxedos. During the shoot, we became instant friends. When the shoot was over, Garth set the beautiful white cowboy hat that he'd worn in the video on my head and told me to keep it. When we were hugging good-bye, unbeknownst to me, Garth slipped the bow tie and cuff links he'd worn in the video into my coat pockets.

Reshoots for the video were scheduled in New York. They could have easily found a stylist locally, but Garth requested me, so the company flew me out for the shoot. We had to dress Garth in the same tuxedo for the reshoot, but no one could find the bow tie and cuff links he'd worn in the previous footage. While I scoured every inch of the wardrobe trailer, the producers ran through stores in the city to see if they could find anything similar.

A few hours later, I put my hands in the pockets of my coat and felt something. It was the bow tie and cuff links, exactly where Garth had put them two weeks earlier, without me knowing. I'd had them with me the entire time. The producers were thrilled, and the cuff links and bow tie were used to complete Garth's outfit for the shoot. When the video shoot wrapped, I didn't get to keep the bow tie and cuff links, but the cowboy hat that Garth placed on my head is still mine.

I worked with Garth again when he appeared in a McDonald's commercial being shot in Century City. While we were working, I mentioned to Garth that my dad was a big fan of his.

"No way," Garth said. "Tim Conway is a fan of *mine*? I'm a huge fan of his!"

Garth told me that he and his family had spent every Saturday watching *The Carol Burnett Show* when he was growing up, and that Dad was his favorite. I asked Dad to come visit us on-set for lunch, and the two men spent the entire time in mutual adoration of each other.

"You're the king of the world!" Dad said to Garth.

"No!" Garth retorted. "*You're* the king of the world. You're Tim Conway!"

"But you're Garth Brooks!" Dad shot back. Watching them banter was delightful, and I think I laughed during the entire lunch.

Another memorable celebrity I worked with was actress Kirstie Alley. The shoot was for a Disney holiday special, and we shot at the Disneyland park after it was closed for the night. I had made a red velvet gown for Kirstie to wear, with Swarovski crystals hand-sewn onto the bodice and down the skirt. When she stepped out of the hair and makeup trailer in the dress, the effect was breathtaking. Kirstie is a strikingly beautiful woman, and every crystal sparkled in the light as though she were a Disney princess come to life.

Kirstie and I chatted while we waited for the crew to finish setting up. Suddenly, she sucked in her breath and pointed to something. I turned and saw the faux mountain peak of the Matterhorn roller coaster rising in the distance, illuminated by spotlights.

"I love that ride!" Kristie said. "I have always loved that ride!"

"The Matterhorn?" I said. "Oh, yeah. It's a great one."

Kirstie clutched my arm. "Kelly, I want to ride it. Now."

"Umm, I don't think that's going to happen." I laughed. "First of all, it's closed. And I think they're almost ready for you."

Kirstie shook her head of voluminous auburn waves. "I don't care. I want to ride it, and I want you to come with me."

It began to dawn on me that she wasn't joking.

"I don't think they can just start up a ride in the middle of the night."

"Oh, yes, they can," Kirstie said. "I am not doing anything until you and I get a ride on the Matterhorn."

She started to walk toward the assistant director, leaving me staring after her. I watched as Kirstie gestured excitedly as they talked, and when I saw her turn and point toward the Matterhorn, I knew she was dead serious.

No one could talk Kirstie out of riding the Matterhorn. Finally, someone made a call, and a couple of the park's maintenance engineers appeared. Kirstie and I giggled as they escorted us up the dark, winding pathway to the Matterhorn. I helped Kirstie pile the folds of her red velvet dress into the toboggan car before climbing in behind her. One of the engineers hit a switch, and off we went, cranking and clicking slowly up the steep track until we hung in the balance at the top. We had a second or two to take in the vast darkness below before the toboggan fell into a near-vertical lunge. Kirstie whooped and raised her arms as we hurtled around hairpin curves and made the final descent into a pool of cold, murky water, drenching both of us. When we climbed out, laughing hysterically, Kirstie's hair was a total mess, and the red velvet dress was splattered with water.

"Okay," Kirstie whispered as we walked back toward Cinderella's castle where the motorhome was parked, "I guess I'd better get serious now. I think the director is going to kill me."

Everyone quickly snapped into professional mode. I ran over to my work kit and found the hair dryer I kept for when clothes got wet. While the makeup artist fixed Kirstie's smudged eyeliner and the hairstylist smoothed her hair back into shiny waves, I carefully dried the long velvet dress and polished each crystal until they sparkled.

"Okay, Miss Matterhorn," the director said with a smile, once we'd gotten Kirstie back to looking like a goddess. "If you're done yodeling, we're ready for you."

I felt a little embarrassed that I'd been part of delaying the shoot, but the thrill of that late-night Matterhorn ride with Kirstie Alley was worth it.

<hr>

When Christmas Eve arrived, Phil accompanied me to Dad and Charlene's annual "Feast of the Seven Fishes" celebration. Over the years, it had grown into a sit-down dinner of forty or more people. We hadn't celebrated Christmas Eve in such a lavish fashion when I was growing up, but many Italians revere it even more than Christmas day. Charlene would spend weeks before the party preparing her wonderful Italian cuisine. In addition to the seven traditional fishes, she made huge trays of eggplant parmesan, roasted veal, and side dishes of every kind. Hanson's Bakery delivered chocolate yule logs, pastries, and a two-foot-high snowman cake.

In true Italian tradition, everyone ate at one long row of tables covered with white cloths and pine wreaths tied with big red bows. As the party grew over the years to include more guests, the line of tables ran out of the dining room, through the hallways, and around corners into other rooms. When the guest list rose to almost sixty people, the table chain went through the open French doors and out onto the patio, where portable heaters were placed to keep those dining al fresco warm in the cool December air. The tables, set with sparkling crystal, silver, and candles, were a beautiful sight.

Some guests came every year without fail, like the Kormans and the Andersons. Carol Burnett and her family usually attended, too. Years later, Paul Anderson brought his wife, the actress Maya Rudolph. At one point, Maya looked around the table in amazement. "I cannot believe," she said, "that I'm sitting at a Christmas Eve dinner with Tim Conway, Harvey Korman, and Carol Burnett."

One of my stepsister Jackie's best friends brought along Kato Kaelin the year that O.J. Simpson was on trial for brutally murdering his wife and another man. Kato, who'd been renting Simpson's pool house when the murder occurred, was a key witness to the case, and the media were hounding him. It was rumored that just talking about the trial with Kato could get you subpoenaed by the court. Charlene and Dad always welcomed any Christmas Eve "orphan" to the party, but they laid down the law to everyone before Kato arrived.

"I don't want to be called as a witness to this trial," Dad said. "So there will not be any discussion about the O.J. trial when Kato arrives. Don't ask him anything about it. Don't even *think* about the trial when he's here."

"That's right," Charlene added. "If I even hear one person mention O.J. at this party, I'm going to throw everyone out on their asses!"

We were all intrigued when Kato showed up, but as promised, no one said a word. Kato was a gracious, engaging guest, and he was probably relieved to have an evening without a single person asking him about O.J.

Christmas Eve of 2004, Phil and I arrived early for the small cocktail hour that Dad and Charlene held for family and close friends before the other guests arrived for dinner. Everyone was sitting and talking when Phil suddenly stood up. He clinked a fork against his glass, and the room quieted down.

"Everyone," Phil said, "I would like to make a toast."

I looked up at Phil in surprise. He had never made any toasts before, even though he'd been my date to numerous family get-togethers.

"I just want to say how much it has meant to me, getting to be part of the Conway family. You have all welcomed me into your lives, and I can't imagine being with a nicer group of people. And Harvey, even though you're not a Conway, same goes to you."

Harvey beamed, raising his glass.

Then Phil turned to me, and I could see sweat beading on his forehead. He sank to one knee.

"Kelly," he said, "I love you so much, and I wanted to ask if you would marry me?"

Everyone gasped, then the room fell completely silent while they waited for my answer.

I was shocked. Phil and I had been together for almost two years, but we'd never discussed marriage. My heart pounded as I looked around at all the happy, expectant faces waiting eagerly for my answer.

"Yes," I squeaked.

The room erupted in cheers as Phil took my left hand and slid a diamond solitaire onto my ring finger. Everyone jumped up to give hugs and congratulations.

Dad was thrilled, but I don't think anyone in the room was happier than Harvey. He was the first to wrap Phil and me in a giant bear hug.

The women gathered around to admire my ring while Charlene brought out more champagne to continue the celebration.

I often think back to the night of this Christmas Eve party, when Dad was the happiest he'd ever been. He was still in the prime of his life. His six children were grown. He had a wife he loved and friends he adored. I remember looking at him across the table, his face bathed in candlelight, laughing with his friends as Charlene brought platter after platter from the kitchen. He was so handsome in his red cashmere holiday sweater, dark pants, and classic Gucci loafers.

At one point, he caught my eye and smiled. There was so much love and pride on his face that I had to blink away tears. I know Dad was happy that I'd found Phil, a man he admired and liked so much, and someone who would take good care of me, just like he had always done. And I loved Phil, so even though his surprise proposal had been a shock, I was sure marrying him was the right thing to do.

I was a lucky girl to have so much.

Chapter 19

My mom loved skiing so much that I thought she would never leave the mountains. But after years of enduring Colorado's brutal winters, Mom was tired of digging her way out of snowbanks whenever she wanted to leave the house. Her cottage on Lake Erie was great in the summer months, but winters there were harsh. She was ready for a change, she told me, preferably someplace that was warm year-round.

Mom often went to visit friends who lived in the little town of Naples, nestled on the Gulf of Mexico off Florida's west coast. After enduring one particularly hard winter in Colorado, she decided she'd had enough snow and moved there. Although she was sad to leave her beloved mountains, her new home offered year-round warm weather, palm trees, and white-sand beaches. People drove their golf carts down the elegant main street lined with cafes, art galleries, and boutiques. The seaside town also had a thriving, tight-knit social scene that appealed to Mom, who still loved her bridge games and tennis matches. Once she'd settled into her new tropical home, she found a Catholic church and resumed her daily Mass routine. She even gave tango dancing lessons to some of her new friends.

A couple of months into 2005, Mom called from Naples with some startling news. She had been diagnosed with bladder cancer. She started chemotherapy treatments immediately. Mom and I talked on the phone every day, and I could tell she was getting weaker.

"Let me come stay with you, Mom," I said. Plans were already in place for me to fly out a few weeks later to join her on the drive back up to the lake cottage in Canada, where she spent the summers.

"No, I'm okay," she insisted. "You're working. I'll be fine for a little longer."

But she wasn't fine.

One day, Mom confessed that she was having trouble hiring someone to help her around the house. The chemo was making her so weak she couldn't do many of the more-strenuous chores herself.

"You can't get anyone around here!" she said. "It's probably because there's so many damned old people in this town, and *everyone* needs assistance!"

"I'm calling to book a flight right now," I replied. "See you tomorrow." Then I hung up so she couldn't try to talk me out of it. After I called my brother Seann, he also booked a flight to Naples.

I was shocked to see how sick Mom was when I got to Naples. The chemo had attacked her strong, athletic body with ruthless efficiency. Each treatment left her more nauseous and exhausted. Even though Mom didn't have much of an appetite, Seann and I prepared all her favorite meals in hopes that she'd be able to get a few bites down.

A couple of days later, we accompanied her to her oncologist appointment. The waiting room was filled with miserable-looking older people. And the doctor, though professional, didn't seem particularly interested in Mom's treatment. I felt that the appointment was rushed, with little discussion of any alternatives. No one here knew Mary Anne as a person; she was just another patient in a very long line of sick people.

At the same time, Dad was on the road with Harvey for some East Coast shows, with Phil as their pilot. They had just finished a show in Jupiter, on the other side of Florida from Naples, when I called Dad after Mom's doctor's appointment.

"Dad, it's really bad," I whispered, so Mom wouldn't hear me in the next room. "Mom's not getting the attention she needs. No one cares here." I started to cry. "She needs to be at Cedars, where Dr. Hekmati can take over."

Dr. Hekmati had been our family physician ever since I was young. We trusted him, and I wanted Mom in his care.

"Is she well enough to fly to California?" Dad asked.

"I really don't think so." There was no way I could safely get Mom, who was continuously nauseous, through an airport and on a five-hour flight where she would have to sit up the whole time.

"What if we came to get her?" Dad said. "We just finished a show in Jupiter. It's only a thirty-minute flight from Naples. I'll let Harvey know, and Phil can make arrangements for us to land in Naples tomorrow."

The next day, Seann and I bundled Mom up and drove her to the regional airport to meet the plane. Dad was the first one off the plane to greet us when it landed. My parents hadn't seen each other for almost twenty years. When Dad leaned down to take Mom's hand and speak to her, tears filled my eyes.

Mom was so weak she couldn't walk, so Phil gently carried her on the plane where we tucked her into a reclining seat. Also on board were Charlene, Harvey and his wife, Debby, and Roger, Charlene's ex-husband. All former friends—and in some cases, ex-spouses—who hadn't been together as a group in decades. It would have been hysterically funny if the situation were not so sad.

Everyone was overcome with emotion, but Harvey had different concerns.

As Phil was going through his preflight checklist, Harvey poked his head into the cockpit.

"Hey, Phil, can I talk to you for a second?" he said.

"Yeah," Phil answered. "What's up?"

"Umm, don't you think we should have Mary Anne's stuff checked out before we take off?"

Phil was confused. "What do you mean, checked out?"

"Well, you know . . . have security look through the bags. Just in case, you know?"

"In case of what?" Phil asked.

"Well, it's just, you don't know Mary Anne like I did. When she and Tim got divorced, it was pretty nasty. Not Tim, of course, but Mary Anne took it hard. She was really pissed!"

"So," Phil said, trying to understand, "your point is?"

"It's just . . ." Harvey struggled to find the right words. "What if she decided, 'Hey, I've got stage four cancer. I'm going to be in a plane with my ex-husband, his second wife and *her* ex-husband, and their asshole friend, Harvey.' So, *kaboom*! She plants a bomb and blows us all up. It's the perfect opportunity, right?"

"Harvey," Phil said slowly, "that would mean she'd also be killing her son and daughter, too."

"Yeah, I know, but—"

"Harvey, get the fuck back to your seat."

Harvey threw up his hands. "Okay, okay. Just forget I said anything."

When Phil recounted this conversation to me later, I burst out laughing. Harvey was known for being charmingly neurotic. He'd always thought everyone was out to get him. After the 9/11 terrorist attacks Harvey had installed a sophisticated alarm system in his home because he was convinced that Osama bin Laden was out to kill him, specifically. And indeed, there were probably times in the past when my mom *had* wanted to kill Harvey, so maybe he had a point.

Seann and I took turns sitting with Mom, holding her hand during the flight home. At one point, I got up to sit next to Dad. Everyone else on the plane was dozing, and the cabin was quiet.

"Thank you, Dad," I said. "For helping Mom. You didn't have to do this. And I know she was kind of difficult at times . . ."

He squeezed my hand. "I'm glad we could help."

I'm still in awe of Dad's kindness toward my mother during that time. And Charlene, too, who was completely supportive of the plan and had been very kind to Mom during the flight. I'm sure that the extra flight back to Los Angeles from Florida was expensive, but Dad hadn't hesitated. He did what he felt was right.

When we landed, an ambulance met the plane and whisked Mom off to Cedars-Sinai Medical Center, where Dr. Arman Hekmati had organized a team of top-tier specialists to examine her. A few days later, she underwent surgery to remove some of the cancerous tissue on her bladder. I felt so relieved that Mom was getting the treatment she needed and that it was all under the watchful eye of Dr. Hekmati.

By the end of the week, Mom was able to walk a little down the hospital corridor, feeling better than she had in weeks. But she was worried about her cat, Sneakers, who was being looked after by a pet sitter back in Naples. Before anyone knew it, Mom had booked a return flight to Florida and was preparing to check out of Cedars-Sinai.

Dr. Hekmati was outraged when he learned Mom was leaving. Like the rest of us, he'd assumed she would continue her treatment in Los Angeles for a while longer. But Mom was determined to get home to Sneakers, and no one was about to stand in her way.

"What?" Dr. Hekmati cried. "A cat called Sneakers? *That* is why she is leaving? It is because of this animal, Sneakers, that your mother gives up the best cancer care in the world?"

My brother Corey flew with Mom back to Florida and helped her get settled in. After finishing the rest of her chemo in Florida, Mom's health seemed to dramatically rally. She was even feeling strong enough to make the long drive back up to Canada by herself, something she'd done every year after moving to Florida. She packed Sneakers in the car and made the two-day trip back to her lake cottage in the village of Erieau. The local Canadian hospital wouldn't take Mom's American insurance, so every week she drove two hours over the border to the Henry Ford Hospital in Detroit for her remaining chemo treatments.

I called Mom every day, and each time we talked, she sounded more energetic, telling me about her plans for the week. She was excited about getting back to the usual things she loved, like playing bridge and sailing with friends on the lake. It began to feel like the cancer was just a bad dream.

I was home one afternoon when I got a call from Mom's friend, Camille Kerr.

"Kelly," Camille said. "You need to come. Your mom's not well." She told me that Mom had passed out on her drive home from Detroit. Fortunately, the car had rolled off the road and stopped in a ditch, so she wasn't injured. But the incident revealed that Mom was once again very sick.

I flew to Canada the next day.

When the doctors performed exploratory surgery, they found that the cancer had spread beyond Mom's bladder into other parts of her body. Chemo and radiation treatments were useless at this point, the doctors said, and would only prolong her suffering. Instead, Mom received heavy doses of medicine that mercifully eased her intense pain. She was too weak to be moved to the hospital in Detroit, so she stayed in the small regional Canadian hospital in Chatham, a half-hour drive from Erieau.

I spent every moment that I could with Mom in her hospital room, sleeping on a small cot next to her bed. Seann flew out to help, and the two of us took turns, one staying with Mom while the other ran out to get food or back to the cottage to shower. Mom grew weaker every day. Her body was so frail now that all her gorgeous muscles built from years of tennis, dancing, and skiing were gone.

One time I was looking out of the window of her hospital room. It was a bright, crisp fall day, and orange and gold leaves were falling from the trees.

"Look, Mom," I said, pulling the drapes back so she could see. "The leaves are beautiful, huh?"

From her bed, Mom gave a long, drawn-out sigh.

"Kelly," she said. "Can you do me a favor?"

"Of course, Mom. Anything!"

"Can you not say 'huh' ever again? You sound like a hillbilly. Just say, 'eh.' That sounds so much better."

"No, problem, Mom," I said with a smile. Clearly, despite her dwindling physical state, a part of Mary Anne was still as strong as ever.

Mom had been sleeping more and more, but neither of us wanted her to be alone. One afternoon I left Seann with Mom at the hospital and headed back to the cottage to take a shower and change. I had just arrived when my phone rang. It was Seann.

"She's gone, Kell," he said, breaking into tears. "Mom just died."

I stayed at the cottage to call my other brothers while Seann waited at the hospital for the funeral home to collect Mom's body. When he got back, we sat down and I poured each of us a drink.

"Mom waited for you to leave before she went, you know," Seann said. "I don't think she wanted to die in front of you."

Mom passed away on October 13, the same date as our brother Tim's birthday. She was seventy-three years old. Tim and his wife, Jen, had just welcomed my niece, Sophia, into the world a week earlier, so it was a bittersweet time of joy for the new baby and sadness over the loss of our mother.

After we gave a toast to Mom, I got to work washing the stacks of dirty dishes and laundry that had piled up since we'd been spending so much time at the hospital. Seann went outside and started raking leaves. It seemed strange to be doing such ordinary things, like household chores, when our mom had died only a couple of hours earlier. But in a way, doing these tasks enabled us to process the reality of her death.

A few days later, the rest of the family, including our other brothers, arrived in Erieau for the memorial. Mom had requested that her body be cremated and the ashes stored in a large beer stein she'd bought in Germany when she had lived there as an Army Special Services dancer.

While we were planning a memorial service at the local Catholic church Mom had attended, my uncle Jerry asked if I wanted to hold the wake in the church's basement.

"Are you kidding?" I said. "Mom would be so mad if we were all sitting around the church basement, eating cookies for her wake."

I had something much more appropriate in mind to serve as a tribute to Mom. The only bar in town, called The Sandbar, was a casual watering hole filled with fishermen and sailors. I knew this would be a more fitting place to celebrate Mom's life.

My brother Tim delivered a touching and funny eulogy at the memorial service. Afterwards, a band of bagpipers met everyone outside the church playing a medley of Irish songs. The bagpipers led us on a foot parade down Erieau's main street that ran along a narrow peninsula, with Lake Erie crashing on one side and the calm waters of the bay on the other. People came out of their houses to wave, and kids rode alongside the parade on bikes they'd decorated with paper streamers, which they sometimes did when there was a funeral. Some people stopped what they were doing to march with us.

When we reached Mom's cottage, we paused while the bagpipers played "Amazing Grace." My brothers and I stood together listening. Then the parade continued down the street to The Sandbar, where everyone in town came to drink, dance, and celebrate our mom. The bar didn't close until the sun was about to rise, and a few of the revelers passed out and ended up spending the night on the hard wooden benches. Mom would have loved every moment of it.

We kept Mom's cottage on Lake Erie for a few years after her death, and I flew out every summer for about a month. But my brothers rarely, if ever, used the cottage, and they wanted to sell it.

I'd always imagined that the cottage would be kept in our family, a familiar place where all of us could gather. My brother Tim and his wife had their new baby girl, and I knew it wouldn't be long before my other brothers also had children of their own. Our many cousins who lived in the area were starting families, too. I envisioned summers on the lake with my nieces and nephews digging in the sand and learning to swim on the same beach where my brothers and I had played when we were little.

But I was the only sibling who spent time at the cottage, and it was expensive and difficult to maintain on my own. After a few years I agreed to let it go, and we sold it to the Wilsons, one of Mom's favorite families in the village.

I still visit Erieau every year to spend time with Erin, Carole, and Bobbie-Jo, all of whom are my childhood best friends and who are like my sisters. Although I am a true California girl, Erieau is in my blood. To me, it will always be one of the happiest places in the world.

Chapter 20

I DIDN'T REALIZE HOW MUCH I MISSED MY DAILY CALLS WITH MOM until she was gone. I would sometimes find myself reaching for the phone to give her a call before remembering that she wouldn't answer. Phil was supportive when we were together, but we were both so busy with our careers that it seemed one of us was rushing out of town just as the other was coming back in. I still had the engagement ring he'd given me at the Christmas Eve party, but the idea of planning a wedding and getting married was far from either of our minds.

The physical stress of working long hours began to exacerbate an old neck injury from a ski accident I'd had years before. At first, I ignored the pain, thinking it would go away on its own with some rest, but it only got worse. I consulted a doctor who recommended an epidural shot injected into my spine to help ease the swelling. A couple of weeks after the injection, I developed a high fever and numbness in my neck. Phil drove me to the hospital, but he had to leave soon after for a flight, and since Dad was out of town, my brother Tim came to be with me. After a quick examination, the doctor ordered an emergency MRI.

The MRI results showed that I had a staph infection in my spine from the epidural injection. The doctor told Tim that I needed surgery that very night or the condition could worsen, leading to paralysis or even death.

I was delirious from the massive dose of medicine they'd given to help lessen the severe pain. When Tim told me that I needed surgery right away, I became hysterical.

"No!" I cried. "I won't have surgery if Dad's not here."

"Kelly," Tim said. "The doctor made it very clear that there's no choice. You have to have it tonight."

"But Dad's not here!" I said tearfully.

"Dad's on his way home right now. Snap out of it, Kelly. If you wait any longer, you may not ever ski again."

You have to hand it to my brother Tim to talk straight when you need it. I agreed to have the surgery, and within an hour, it was under way.

The surgeons removed three of my infected vertebra and put in a plate to hold my spine together. Then I was placed into a medically induced coma for four days so that I wouldn't move while the vertebrae fused onto the plate.

When I woke, the first thing I saw was my father's face, with tears streaming down his cheeks. Charlene was there, too, but all I could look at was Dad.

"I'm here, Pal," Dad said, smoothing my hair. "Everything's okay. And I'm not leaving you."

I burst into sobs. The breathing tube was still in, so I couldn't speak. Someone got me a notepad and a pen. With a shaky hand, I scribbled on the pad.

Dad took the pad back. "Trader Vic's is closing?" he read, puzzled. "Well, yes, honey, it is closing. Very sad. We always loved going to Trader Vic's."

Trader Vic's was a renowned Polynesian-themed restaurant and lounge in Beverly Hills that had recently shut its doors after sixty-five years. For some reason, this was the essential message I needed to convey after being woken from my coma. I motioned for Dad to give me the pad again. When I handed it back, he read the new message out loud: "These fucking nurses won't give me any more fucking pain medication."

"Ah, Doctor," Dad joked. "Can we get Miss Conway *back* into her coma, please?" He turned to Charlene. "I think she went under the knife as Kelly and came back as Mary Anne." Charlene laughed because it really was the kind of thing Mom would have said. Dad kept the note as a memento of my drug-induced personality swap.

Recovery was long and hard, starting with intensive physical therapy to get my damaged spine back into shape. My work as a stylist often required lifting heavy boxes of clothes, being on my feet for twelve hours straight, and a lot of running back and forth. It took six months for me to be strong enough to start working again.

My surgery was a success, and I resumed work as soon as the doctor said it was okay. Phil had been very supportive during my hospitalization and recovery. If he wasn't away on a trip, he was there to help me with whatever I needed. But I was so emotionally spent from the year's events that my heart just wasn't into making the relationship work. I loved Phil, but I needed to concentrate on my own life, and it wasn't fair to keep him waiting. We had a long talk and ultimately decided that going our separate ways would be best for both of us. While we were sad, I don't think anyone was more upset about our breakup than Phil's biggest admirer, Harvey Korman.

Another partnership also came to an end around this time. After a few years of taking their comedy show on the road together, Dad and Harvey stopped touring. Ever since meeting on *The Carol Burnett Show* back in 1967, the two men had been practically inseparable. Dad once quipped about his relationship with Harvey, "With the exception of height and religion, we were the same person." Harvey was tall and Jewish to Dad's short and Catholic, but the differences stopped there. They had an almost psychic quality as a comedy team, improvising plot twists and punch lines with the effortless grace of two people bouncing a ball back and forth. And each made Olympian efforts to crack the other up on camera, with Dad usually the victor.

Like Dad, Harvey was a family man, and although his first marriage had also ended in divorce, he adored his four children. Harvey was a true eccentric. He didn't care about the kind of things other people in Hollywood did. Many of his clothes were ones he'd nabbed from *The Carol Burnett Show* wardrobe, whether they were in style or not. Harvey could also be hilariously outspoken at inappropriate times. Once, he and Dad were sharing a table at a benefit luncheon with elegant actor Cary Grant. When Mr. Grant dropped a bit of salad dressing on the lapel of his tailored suit, Harvey blurted out, "I don't believe it—Cary Grant dribbles too!" Fortunately, the entire table, including Mr. Grant, laughed heartily.

Harvey's cheapness was legendary. When the roof of his car developed a small hole, Harvey solved the problem by taping an LA Dodgers' baseball helmet over it. He could have easily gone out and paid cash for a brand-new luxury car, but that wasn't Harvey's style.

But while Harvey could be a little salty at times, he was incredibly kind and generous to the people he loved. To me, he was almost like another father. I could talk to him about things that I felt funny telling Dad, like what was happening in my love life. So when he passed away in 2008, our entire family was devastated.

Dad liked to say that he did his best work at funerals. He had a knack for memorializing a person in a way that was tender and respectful, but also hilarious. Harvey's memorial was one of Dad's finest moments. He spoke about all the weird and wonderful things that had made Harvey so special. By the end of the service, everyone was laughing through their tears.

After Harvey's death, Dad still traveled some for appearances, but it wasn't the same without Harvey as his tour partner. He kept busy with voice-over work, most famously as Barnacle Boy on the cartoon hit show *SpongeBob SquarePants*, and an occasional guest spot on television shows. In 2008, he won his sixth Emmy for his role in an episode of the hit show *30 Rock*.

Dad was an admitted homebody, but Charlene wanted to travel, so the two took trips to Europe and even went on safari in Africa with another couple they were close with. They came back filled with funny stories about their adventures, and I was glad that Charlene had insisted Dad leave the comfort of home to see the world.

As Dad approached his eighties, he was still very active and independent. All his life, he'd tried to eat a balanced diet, and while Charlene's small frame put on more weight as the years went by, Dad kept his body trim and healthy.

But then he started to forget little things.

At first, we weren't alarmed. There had been a long-standing joke in our family that Dad had had Alzheimer's since he was forty. Dad's brain was a machine in constant motion. He'd be thinking up a new joke, scheming a way to prank Harvey, and figuring the dimensions of a project he was working on, all at once. Dad observed the world through the eyes of a true comic, analyzing the most mundane situations for any glint of humor. With so many simultaneous ideas streaming through his mind, Dad was sometimes lost in his own world.

More worrisome than Dad's forgetfulness was when he began to have trouble keeping balance. He'd always been quick and athletic with a mastery of body language that translated so wonderfully into his comedy routines. Now he would get dizzy even walking across the room, and we were concerned that he would fall and injure himself.

Dr. Hekmati scheduled four days of comprehensive tests for Dad. When the results came in, Dad, Charlene, Tim, and I gathered in his office, all four of us crammed on the single sofa. We waited nervously while Dr. Hekmati gathered the reports on his desk.

Charlene couldn't stand the tension. "Dr. Hekmati," she blurted out. "Does he have the 'A' word?"

Tim leaned over and stared at her. "Dad doesn't have AIDS, Charlene! What the hell are you talking about?"

"I don't mean that!" Charlene snapped. "I mean the other 'A' disease—Alzheimer's!"

Laughing, Dr. Hekmati assured us that Dad did not have Alzheimer's. We all breathed a collective sigh of relief and sank back into the sofa. But with the dreaded A-word ruled out, more tests were needed to determine why Dad was having memory and balance issues.

A few weeks later, the answer came when it was discovered that Dad was suffering from a syndrome called normal pressure hydrocephalus, or NPH. The condition is caused when spinal fluid builds up in the brain cavity and can't flow back out, resulting in damage to the brain. The symptoms—difficulty in walking and dementia—are similar to Alzheimer's and Parkinson's diseases, and become more severe over time. It was not good news.

We immediately consulted a specialist to see what Dad's options were. Carol Burnett's eldest daughter, Carrie, who had died from a brain tumor when she was in her late thirties, had been treated by Dr. Keith Black, a leading surgeon in the Los Angeles area. Dr. Black recommended that Dad have a shunt implanted into his brain that would drain the fluid down a tube into his abdomen.

Despite his health problems Dad was determined to live life with the same vigor he'd always had. He wrote his memoir, *What's So Funny?*, in

2012, and embarked on a multicity book tour to promote it the following year.

Dad was no newbie to the touring scene, but the promotional schedule was challenging for him. In New York, Dad was booked for all the top morning shows and had to be up before dawn to make it to the first appearance. Then he and Charlene would rush to the next show with hardly enough time in between for a bathroom break. Then there were the radio station visits with multiple interviews back to back.

Dad's publicist, Roger Neal, was on hand to make sure that each appearance went as smoothly as possible for Dad. Roger—part troop leader and part pit bull—stepped in when fans on the street got a little too overwhelming and ensured that Dad got the best time slots for his appearances, even if he had to rattle some cages to make it happen. Charlene also did her best to care for Dad, but the nonstop schedule took its toll. Still, Dad was the consummate pro every moment the camera was running. He joked with Kathie Lee Gifford and Hoda Kotb, charmed the studio audiences, and got everyone laughing.

Back home in LA, I checked in with Dad and Charlene every day and worried about his health. The day he appeared on the *Today* show, interviewed by Matt Lauer, I watched anxiously from home. Charlene had mentioned that Dad's memory had worsened due to the stress of the tour, but so far, he'd been able to get through all the interviews without a mishap.

I watched as Dad sat across from Matt, talking about his life and career. He seemed to be doing fine, cracking jokes, and making Matt laugh.

"So," Matt said, "you have a book."

Dad stared blankly at Matt. "There's a book?" he said.

I felt my stomach lurch. *Oh my God*, I thought. He forgot. *Oh my God, please, no. Not on live television!*

A couple of agonizing seconds passed.

Then Dad's face broke into a big grin. "Oh, yeah!" he said. "The book! Well, you know, I haven't read it yet." Matt and the audience burst into laughter.

I nearly collapsed.

The book was a huge success, but everyone was relieved when Dad and Charlene flew home after the tour. He could finally get back to enjoying life again, with plenty of rest and visits from his children and grandchildren. We were sure that with the right care, there would be many more happy years left for him.

I never dreamed those years would soon become a nightmare.

My dad thought he might have a day off.

Dan Conway (Papa), Sophia Murgoi (Magi), and my dad outside the house on Orange Street, Chagrin Falls, Ohio

Papa and Magi

My dad just out of college, 1956

My dad and his parents, Christmas 1951

My mom, "Miss March," in the Bowling Green State University Calendar, 1954

My mom entertaining at the USO Gopp, 1958

Surprised by the loud bagpipes behind her. My mom and dad's wedding day, Windsor Canada, 1961

On the way to their honeymoon

Actor Hugh Reilly,
my dad, and Ernie
Anderson, 1961

My dad, my godmother, Rose Marie, holding me, Papa, and Magi 1963

Topanga Canyon, 1962

My mom's eyes and my dad's hairline

One year old with my mom and dad, June 1963

In my dad's wood shop at our new house, Tarzana, California

The pool at my parents' first apartment on Sherman
Way in Van Nuys, California, 1963

Just starting to walk and already knew who my best
pal was

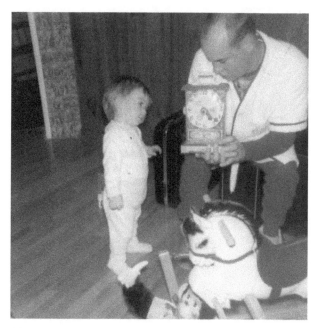

Christmas, 1963

Already curious about the label
of my mom's dress, 1964

Joe Flynn, my dad, and mom, 1963

On the back lot of Universal Studios, 1962. We all went to visit my dad while he was shooting his first television series, *McHales's Navy*. Papa, Magi, my mom, me at three months old, and my dad in costume

Ernest Borgnine holding me at our mom and dad's first apartment in Van Nuys, California

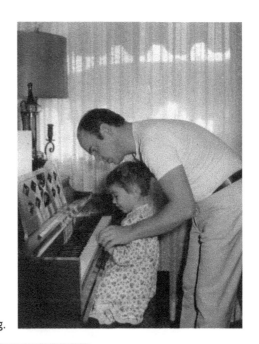

Neither of us knew how to play
the piano, but we had fun trying.

"Tiny Braids of Gold," written by my dad for me when
I was little

My brother Tim Jr. was born October, 1963.

My brother Tim Jr. and I, and still my best pal

Big Bear Lake California, 1964

Cypress Gardens, Florida. We got to meet everyone in the water show that day.
My dad, Tim Jr., me, and my mom, pregnant with Patrick, 1964

Daytona Beach,
Florida

On a tour of the theme park
at Cypress Gardens

Me and Seann at the Magnolia house, 1973

Easter morning, 1971, in Chagrin Falls

Jamie, Patrick, me, and Tim Jr.

The Magnolia house, where we grew up in Encino, California

Chagrin Falls in front of Magi and Papa's house

Chagrin Falls, 1966

Corey was born 1968. That would be my fourth brother in the middle.

My parents met at Bowling Green State University, and they sent us all sweatshirts. Between BGSU and the Cleveland Browns, we were always wearing some combination of orange and brown.

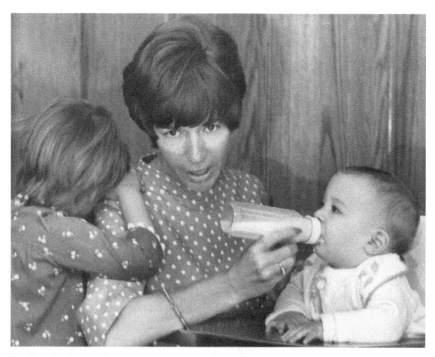

Another brother. Me, my mom, and Jamie, 1967

My mom and Corey, 1971

Seann, 1971

Me on the ground and little Seann

Jamie

Tim Jr.

Patrick

I had the happiest childhood ever.

My dad at our pool house, where all the parties, swim meets, volleyball games, and the best times of our lives took place

Picture of my mom taken by Ernie Anderson, 1969

Saul and Shirley Turtletaub, McLean Stevenson and his wife Carrie, Larry Sands, and Edwina Anderson. July 4, 1972

My mom, 1972

Picture of my mom taken
by Ernie Anderson in the
pool of the Magnolia house
Encino, California, 1969

My mom going to play tennis with a great outfit and a checkbook in hand

Me poolside, 1972

My uncles Jackie, Danny, Tommy, Wally, and Jerry; my mom; and my aunt Peggy at the cottage in Canada, 1986

Tuesday

Backstage at *The Johnny Carson Show*. My dad, me, and his longtime agent and friend Phil Weltman

Typical Sunday in the backyard of our Tarzana home

My mom and Carol Burnett following the choreographer at her 40th birthday tap-dancing surprise party. Fifty guests tap dancing in our living room until 3 a.m. Surprise, Mom!

My mom's 40th birthday tap-dancing surprise party

My dad and
mom at Magi
and Papa's

Our first Seder
dinner at a
friend's house in
Brentwood

Cathy Rigby trying to teach me gymnastics at work one day with my dad

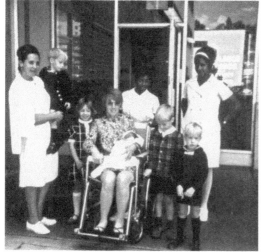

Coming home from the hospital after Corey was born, 1968

Magi teaching Corey to walk, Tarzana house, 1969

The original selfie

It's A Small World ride at Disneyland, 1967. Me, Tim Jr., Patrick, and Jamie in the front. Always dressed the same so my mom could identify us quickly in a big crowd

Me and my mom in the cafeteria, Mammoth Mountain

Ski trips with the circus

My mom taught me how to be a good skier, 1972. At the bar after a hard day of skiing

Me and my mom (when she would actually sit with us) on one of the early trips to Chagrin Falls to see Magi and Papa

Patrick and my mom before the days when they would separate us on the plane

My mom and dad enjoying their summer alone in California while we were
all in Chagrin Falls with Magi and Papa

Tennis camp, 1970

LaCosta resort in Carlsbad, when they needed a break from six wild animals

The Kahala Hilton on Oahu, my dad's favorite place on Earth

My beautiful mom after having six children!

My dad and Ernie Anderson, 1977

The best grandparents in the world

Spoiled with love

Magi teaching Papa and me how to sew

Feeding the ducks at Reseda Park with Magi and Papa

Six Conways, four Andersons, and three Hamiltons on the back of casino owner Bill Harrah's boat, Lake Tahoe, 1976

Lifeguard tower, 18 Santa Monica Beach, 1976

Birmingham High School 1979 cheerleading squad

Spring 1979 cheering
at the Birmingham
Braves baseball game

My first Friday night lights football game

At the condo at Kapalua Bay Hotel on Maui

Carbon Beach Malibu outside my dad's condo, 1977

Kiddieland on the way to CBS to visit my dad

On a cruise to Hawaii for Christmas

Dad and me at the Emmys GETTY IMAGES

On the homecoming queen float, November 1979

Erin Hamilton and me making our own Muppets in London at The Jim Henson Company, 1980

My 21st birthday party at The Palace, Hollywood. The 80s band The Eurythmics played that night just by chance.

My brother Tim and Jen's wedding

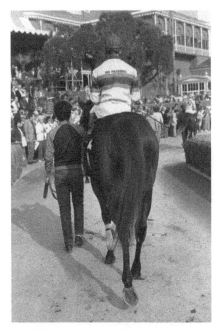

Santa Anita Racetrack. My dad
designed the NO PASSING silks.

My brother on set with my dad, 1974

A scene from the movie *The Longshot* with my dad and me

At the LA Coliseum parking shooting *The Longshot*.
Me, Dad, and Harvey Korman, 1985

The producers of the Ralph Edwards show *This Is Your Life* asked me to reproduce these pajamas we all had when we were kids.

This is how it turned out!

The time when my dad needed a jacket made out of the extra fabric from the walls in his office

Shooting a Contac commercial with my dad and Harvey, the first job I got to work with them as a costume designer

When we saw this, my dad said, "Slightly off. The story of my life."

Me, Tim Jr., and my niece Sophia

My dad and my brother Tim at Santa Anita Racetrack

My brother Tim, his beautiful and funny wife Jennifer, and my incredibly stunning niece and buddy, Sophia

Sophia loved her papa.

My dad . . . father, guidance counselor, security guard, cook, therapist, swim
team coach, family talent night director, chauffeur, bank, secret keeper, homework helper, racetrack handicapping trainer, Tooth Fairy, goalkeeper, photogra-
pher, fort builder, tour guide, doctor, zip line maker, dog catcher, defenseman,
Santa, bicycle fixer, ski repair guy, and the best pal I will ever have

Chapter 21

I LIFTED THE LARGE CAKE BOX FROM MY CAR AND CARRIED IT INTO THE house. It was Christmas 2013, and the walls and doorways were strung with pine branches and red bows as they were every year for Dad and Charlene's big Christmas Eve party.

I followed the savory smells to the kitchen, where Charlene and two helpers were busy preparing food for the party. It was an hour before the guests, all forty of them, were expected to arrive for the annual sit-down dinner celebration.

"Hi, Charlene!" I said. "Here's the cake. It looks amazing." At her request, I'd picked up the huge snowman cake from Hanson's Bakery that had been the centerpiece of the party for years.

Charlene, hunched over the counter chopping herbs, grunted a reply without looking up. I knew the hours leading up to the party could be stressful, so I shrugged off her dismissive greeting.

"Oh," I added, pulling two glass bottles from my grocery bag. "I also grabbed some cranberry juice for Dad. Maybe it will help his UTIs."

Dad had been suffering from recurring urinary tract infections, and I'd always heard that drinking cranberry juice was beneficial.

Charlene stopped chopping and turned to me.

"You know what, Kelly? We're good. We can take care of your dad just fine."

I was startled by her outburst. "I know that, Charlene," I said. "I just thought I'd bring him some fresh cranberry juice."

"Well, okay. But you're not his wife. And this is all under control. Okay?"

"Sure. No problem." I didn't know what else to say.

Dad was sitting in the living room with my brother Tim and a few friends who had arrived early. He looked thin and tired in his red Christmas sweater. After hugging Dad, I sat next to Tim.

"Charlene just bit my head off," I whispered. "Because I brought cranberry juice for Dad!"

Tim nodded gravely. We'd both noticed that Charlene had become less welcoming to us since Dad's health started to decline. She seemed to take our concern for Dad and our questions about his treatments and doctors' appointments as criticism. It was surprising, as we'd never questioned Charlene's dedication to Dad. But he was our father, and Tim and I saw or talked to him almost every day. We just wanted to be aware of everything that affected his well-being.

A while later, I walked back into the kitchen.

"Hey, Charlene," I said, "Corey just called. He's held up on the other side of the Valley, so he won't be here for dinner. But he'll stop by later for dessert."

Charlene slammed a casserole dish onto the counter. "And what about Jamie?"

"Umm, Jamie is having dinner at his girlfriend's parents' house. I'm sorry, I thought he told you."

I couldn't understand why Charlene was so angry. In the past, the Conway Christmas party had always been a relaxed affair, with people coming and going as they hopped from one holiday event to another. Whenever someone arrived mid-meal, extra chairs were pulled up to the table to make room. The spontaneity of guests popping in and out during the night added to the fun. And if someone had another obligation and couldn't attend, there were no hard feelings.

"So, what you're saying is Jamie's not coming," Charlene said. "And Corey will come when he feels like it." She shoved a pan of green beans into the oven and slammed the door. "Fine. Whatever. But I never want to hear you kids say I was keeping you from your father. You're not going to Casey Kasem me!"

"Charlene," I said. "What are you talking about, 'Casey Kasem me'?"

But guests were starting to arrive, and Charlene pushed past me.

Casey Kasem me? The strange phrase spun in my head as I went through the motions of smiling and greeting people as they walked in. Later, I realized what she had meant.

The fight between the beloved radio personality Casey Kasem's adult children from his first family and his second wife, Jean, had been all over the news. Casey was suffering from a Parkinson's-like disease, and his health was in rapid decline. His children from his first marriage, led by daughter Kerri, claimed Jean had not allowed them to see their father and had gone to court to get visitation and medical decision rights. A vicious legal battle ensued. I was shocked that Charlene would even think of comparing our family to such a horrible situation.

By now, the house was full of people. Even though she circulated among the guests, laughing and talking, it was apparent that the strain of hosting the party was taking a toll on Charlene. And I could tell it was hard on Dad, too. Halfway through dinner, he left the table to go lie down upstairs for a while. When I went up to check on him a bit later, I was alarmed to find that he wouldn't wake up.

Someone called 911. When the paramedics arrived, they placed an oxygen mask on Dad and carried him out on a stretcher. The party guests watched, wanting to help but not knowing how. Charlene rode in the ambulance with Dad, and I followed in my car with my friend Beth.

As soon as we reached the ER, I asked to see my dad. The nurse explained that only two people were allowed in the room, and that Charlene and his daughter—Jackie—were in with him.

"*I'm* his daughter," I told the nurse. "Please ask Jackie to step out so I can go see my dad."

When Jackie came out of the room I joined Charlene next to Dad's hospital bed, where the nurses were busy administering IV fluids and checking his vitals.

The doctors said Dad had passed out from dehydration, which was also causing his recurring urinary tract infections. The doctors reminded us that Dad needed to drink a lot of fluids, even if someone had to regularly bring him glasses of water and make sure he drank it all. He stayed in the hospital overnight for IV fluids and observation.

I called every day to check on Dad. Half the time, no one would answer, and Charlene or Jackie would rarely call me back when I left a message. When I did talk to Charlene, she'd crisply remind me that "they had it under control" and make it clear that my help wasn't needed.

Jackie was still living at home with Dad and Charlene even though she was in her mid-forties. She had attended a performing arts college in Pasadena after high school and wanted to be an actor. Charlene didn't want her to work while she pursued her dream, so Jackie never moved out of the house. Later, Charlene admitted that coddling Jackie had been a mistake.

To make it as an actor, you have to spend every day driving all over town to audition for jobs you usually don't get. You have to get up and go to the next audition, regardless. Los Angeles is filled with men and women waiting tables or cleaning pools between trudging to auditions and taking acting lessons. Through a friend, Jackie got a few jobs here and there, acting in commercials, but with a comfortable, rent-free home and all of her bills paid, she may not have had the motivation to sweat it out in the tough world of show business.

Since she was already living with them, Dad and Charlene paid Jackie to be their assistant, running errands and managing the house-keeper. Charlene had stopped driving years before, so Jackie was responsible for taking Dad to doctors' appointments and keeping track of his many prescriptions.

After Dad's trip to the ER on Christmas Eve, he had a follow-up appointment with Dr. Hekmati. I attended, even though I knew Charlene didn't want me to come. Although Dad was feeling better, Dr. Hekmati wanted him to have another MRI as soon as possible to make sure that the dehydration hadn't caused any additional brain damage. "Be sure to make that appointment right away," Dr. Hekmati said after he'd written the referral and handed it to Jackie.

The moment I got home, I called the MRI imaging center and booked Dad an appointment for the very next day. The receptionist said the doctor's referral, which Jackie had taken from Dr. Hekmati, was required before Dad could have the MRI. I tried to call both Charlene and Jackie, but neither answered their phones. I left a message, explaining that I needed the referral from Dr. Hekmati so that Dad could get the MRI the following day. Neither of them called me back. I tried texting them both but still did not hear back.

First thing the next morning I called and texted again. There was no answer. I kept trying for hours to reach them.

Finally, at around two p.m., Charlene picked up the phone. It was only two hours until Dad's MRI appointment. "What's up, Kelly?" she said.

"Hi!" I said, trying to sound normal even though I'd been frantic all day. "I don't know if you got my messages, but I was able to get Dad an MRI appointment today at four. They were booked solid, but the receptionist managed to fit him in. I have to call them right back with the doctor's referral. Is Jackie there? I know Dr. Hekmati gave it to her."

Charlene gave a loud sigh. "Let me go see if she's up."

If she's up? I thought. *It's two o'clock in the afternoon!*

"Hello?" Jackie said groggily.

"Jackie! Did you get my messages? I got Dad an MRI appointment, and it's in two hours. I need the referral Dr. Hekmati gave you!"

"Umm, yeah." I could hear her fumbling like she was digging through her purse. "Let me call you back. It might be in the car."

Fuming, I paced my kitchen floor while I waited. The phone rang twenty minutes later.

"I've looked everywhere," Jackie said. "I have no idea where it is."

I wanted to crawl through the phone line and throttle her neck, but I forced my voice to remain civil.

"Well, okay, that's not good. Let me call Dr. Hekmati's office and see if we can have another one faxed over."

"I'll call—"

"No, Jackie!" I interrupted. "I'll call. You get Dad ready to go."

But it was too late to reach the doctor, and Dad missed the MRI appointment. I made another appointment for a few days later and called the house to tell Charlene.

This time, I barely had time to give her the information when she tore into me.

"You're overstepping your boundaries, Kelly. And if you do it again, it won't go well for you."

I hung up the phone in shock. What had I done to make Charlene so furious at me? I'd never been critical of Charlene's treatment of my father in the twenty-plus years they had been married. I'd often told friends how good she was for him, and that the two were perfect partners. She had always taken such great care of him, breaking his junk food habit of cheeseburgers and donuts. I wasn't trying to usurp Charlene's role as his wife. I only wanted to help.

And, I wondered, what exactly did Charlene mean by *It won't go well for you*? I tried to shrug it off, but her words troubled me.

Dad finally got to his MRI appointment, but the experience had left me shaken.

My concern deepened as I began to suspect that Charlene was making excuses for me not to see my father. His ability to speak for himself and make his own desires known continued to decrease as the weeks went by, and I knew that as his wife and primary caregiver, Charlene had a lot of power over Dad.

When I called the house in the days that followed, I tried to convey a casual cheerfulness as though nothing had happened. During visits, I put on a happy face for Dad and went out of my way to be as helpful to Charlene as I could. But her unexpected lashing out had left me wary of even the simplest gestures. If I saw something I thought Dad might like, a soft lap throw or a cashmere neck pillow, I'd pause, wondering if the gift might offend Charlene in some way. *This is crazy*, I thought. *I should be able to give my dad whatever I want to give him*. But I weighed each decision carefully in an effort to avoid angering my stepmother.

Despite my attempts to make nice, it started to become harder to see Dad. Calls went unanswered; messages inquiring about his health were not returned. If I stopped by the house, Charlene would be visibly annoyed at my presence. Jackie was still friendly to my face, but she never made any extra effort. When I texted her asking about Dad, her typical truncated answer was, "All's well."

I'd been telling Dad about a great Mexican restaurant in Santa Monica called Gilbert's. Dad loved Mexican food, and he had a doctor's appointment the following week close to the restaurant, so I suggested we all go to lunch afterward. My treat.

On the day of Dad's appointment, no one answered my calls. I drove over from my place in Malibu to Santa Monica, figuring I'd catch up with them after they saw the doctor. No one called me back. I went to their house, but no one was there.

Finally, as I was heading back home, Jackie called. After giving me a perfunctory summary of Dad's appointment, she mentioned they had all gone to lunch. At Gilbert's.

I felt angry tears welling in my eyes. It had been days since I'd seen Dad, and being excluded from an outing that had been my idea stung.

"You went to Gilbert's?" I said. "Gosh, Jackie, I just told Charlene that I wanted to take you all there. I thought we were going to have lunch together after his doctor's appointment."

"Oh," Jackie said. "Well, your dad was hungry, and we just kind of decided to go last minute."

"Did you and Charlene not get my calls? I've been driving around Santa Monica for the past couple of hours, waiting to hear back from you."

Jackie didn't answer. I was starting to choke up, so I said good-bye and hung up the phone. There was no way I was going to cry on the phone with Jackie.

As I drove home, all the anger I'd been holding inside came to the surface. For months, I'd felt like anything I did for Dad was not wanted, and that my presence in his life was only grudgingly tolerated. I had no idea about the plans for his medical care, or even the results of his tests. I sensed that I was being edged out of my dad's life at a time when he needed me the most.

There was no way in hell I was going to let that happen.

Chapter 22

"WE'RE SELLING THE HOUSE," CHARLENE ANNOUNCED ONE DAY.

"Are you serious?" I said, looking over at Dad. He gave a sad smile and shrugged.

We were sitting at the bar in the game room. It was decorated with Dad's favorite antique signs and photographs on the walls. All the video games my brothers and I had loved for so many years, and the pool table, were still there.

I wondered if moving Dad out of his familiar space into a new home was wise, considering his increasing confusion and mobility problems. And Dad loved the house. It was his sanctuary, filled with all the things that made him happy. Why make a change now?

"The business manager said it's a good time to sell," Charlene said, as though she were reading my thoughts. "Property values around here are through the roof. Even just the lot is worth a small fortune."

Dad shook his head. "I don't want to sell this house to someone who will tear it down."

Many charming, old houses in the area were being torn down to make way for enormous modern homes that often took up the entire lot. These "McMansions" were destroying the character of the city's older neighborhoods. Dad would be devastated if that happened to the house he'd put so much love into for more than three decades.

When he'd bought the house after my parents divorced, it was in such terrible shape that Dad hadn't wanted any of us kids to see it. But after a few months of work, he had transformed it into a comfortable home decorated with all the things he loved. There was a big backyard with a pool and a workshop where Dad spent hours tinkering on his many projects. But the office was Dad's favorite room. He'd upholstered the walls in green-and-blue-plaid Ralph Lauren fabric, and with the big mahogany desk and leather chair, it had the cozy feel of an English library.

"It's getting to be a lot for us to handle," Charlene added. "I think we would be better off someplace that doesn't need as much upkeep."

Though I could tell Dad was reluctant about parting with his house, Charlene had a point. And there was no hurry to sell, so they could take their time to find the perfect new place.

As it turned out, the house was put on the market quickly and it sold within days. Suddenly, Charlene was scrambling to find them a new home with only a few weeks until the closing. She settled on an apartment on the twelfth floor of a large building on the Wilshire Corridor, between Beverly Hills and Westwood. The apartment was nice, but the transition was a big shock for Dad. He went from a private, comfortable house on a quiet street to an apartment overlooking a busy intersection. The tiny balcony in the apartment only let in the sounds of honking and car exhaust. Cars had to be parked by valet in a cavernous, underground garage, and it often took several calls to the valet stand before someone finally answered. You could smell what the neighbors were cooking in the narrow hallways outside the elevator. Dad hated it.

Charlene was thrilled. "I've always wanted to live in the Wilshire Corridor!" she exclaimed, because it was close to shops and restaurants. Carol Burnett had a sprawling condo in a luxurious building just up the street. It might have been a fun place to live for people who were healthy and active—but not for Dad and Charlene.

I'd begun to notice that Charlene was sleeping a lot during the day. She took pain pills for her back and knee pain, exacerbated by her increasing weight gain. I couldn't help but notice a connection between the many bottles of pain pills on the kitchen counter and Charlene's increased sleeping. There were days I'd come to visit and Dad would be sitting alone while Charlene slept in the bedroom.

Jackie, who'd moved into the apartment with them, was also in the habit of sleeping late. I'd knock on her door to ask a question, and she'd open it to reveal a room filled waist-high with clothes, dirty plates, and other stuff. There was a little path cleared among the junk from the door to her bed. Jackie had never been a neat person, but her lack of any personal organization alarmed me. This was the person who was supposed to be taking care of my dad.

I noticed that Dad was losing weight. He had never been a big eater, and he sometimes would forget to eat when he was preoccupied with other things. Now the doctors told us that it was important that Dad ate regular, healthy meals. In spite of this recommendation, for Dad's breakfast Charlene would hand him a cup of coffee and a single, plastic-wrapped biscotti. It was clear no one was putting much effort into encouraging Dad to eat a healthy diet.

One day when I was visiting, I looked in the refrigerator for something to make him for lunch. "What about some of this eggplant parmesan, Dad?" I held up one of the dishes.

Dad grimaced and shook his head. "No thanks, I'm good." I realized the Italian meals Charlene cooked were too rich for him. But the refrigerator didn't have many other options.

The next day, I stopped at a deli and picked up two turkey sandwiches and a big container of vegetable soup. Charlene was sleeping when I got to the apartment, so Dad and I sat at the table and had lunch together. I was overjoyed when Dad ate every bite of his sandwich.

"This is delicious!" he said. "I didn't realize just how hungry I was."

I started bringing food every time I visited, simple, healthy meals that I knew Dad would want to eat. He especially loved the open-faced turkey sandwiches with stuffing, mashed potatoes, cranberry sauce, and gravy from Gelson's Market. It was fun deciding what meal I would surprise him with. But I always came ready with an excuse in case Charlene happened to be awake. I'd say that I'd picked up lunch for myself, but couldn't eat it all, so I'd given some to Dad. I was always relieved when Charlene was napping in the bedroom because then I didn't have to make up a reason why I'd brought food over.

There was a month when I didn't have a car because I'd sold mine and hadn't yet decided what car I wanted to buy next. Instead of renting one, I decided to embrace the challenge of being car-free in Los Angeles. My Malibu neighborhood had shops within walking distance, and I could take a car service for work. I studied the bus schedules and learned all the routes to get from my place at the beach to Charlene and Dad's apartment in Westwood. This made stopping at the deli for Dad's favorite turkey sandwich a little more complicated, but I was dedicated to making sure he got enough to eat.

One day Dad and I were sitting at the table eating the lunch I'd brought when Charlene emerged from the bedroom. When she saw the turkey sandwiches and soup, her face darkened with rage. She picked up the takeout box Dad was eating from and hurled it into the trash.

"Whoa, whoa, whoa!" Dad cried. "What's going on?"

"You know what, Kelly?" Charlene snapped. "You can stop bringing fucking food into this fucking house." She stalked into the kitchen and started slamming pots on the stove.

Dad and I were stunned.

"I'm sorry, Charlene," I said. "I'm not trying to offend you. Dad likes it when I bring lunch."

"He'll eat what I make," she said, dumping a jar of red sauce into a skillet.

I looked at Dad, but he just shook his head.

"Char," he said with a sigh. "Just relax." He didn't have the strength to rock the boat.

Although I hated not seeing Dad, I kept away for a few days, thinking about how I could approach Charlene to discuss our rapidly deteriorating relationship. It also gave me time to reflect over the past year and piece together a picture of how dramatically things had changed, mostly for the worse. Charlene was increasing her pain pill intake and slept all day. She was lashing out at me. And Jackie, who was supposed to help Dad and Charlene, was becoming more erratic in her behavior, too.

I noticed that Jackie had become distracted and almost hyperactive. She jumped from doing one thing to another, leaving tasks unfinished all over the house. She would go out to run an errand and be gone all day. If we ordered a pizza and Jackie offered to go pick it up, Charlene would roll her eyes and say, "Guess we won't be eating for a few hours." We never figured out where she went.

Once, Jackie was late coming home for a family dinner. When she arrived, she breathlessly described how she had stopped at the grocery store and the power went out, preventing the sliding doors from opening.

Everyone was trapped in the store for hours until the electricity came back on. Suspicious of this story, I later called the store and asked if they had experienced a power outage earlier that day. They had no idea what I was talking about. I couldn't figure out why Jackie would say this.

Jackie was in charge of Dad's doctors' appointments. When I began hearing from the doctors that some appointments were being missed, I asked Jackie about it. She admitted that she'd forgotten to write them on the calendar.

A few days after Charlene had thrown out the lunch, I drove over to the apartment for a visit. Charlene answered the door without a greeting and walked back into the kitchen. Dad was taking a nap, and Jackie was out.

"Can we talk?" I asked Charlene, and she gave a curt nod. We sat across from each other at the kitchen table.

"Charlene," I said after a moment of silence, "is there something you want to talk to me about?"

"No," Charlene said. She picked up her mug of tea and frowned. "I just don't want you sneaking food in here, Kelly."

"I'm trying to help you and Dad, Charlene. I know there are days you can't get out of bed, and I want Dad to have some healthy food."

"But I prepare meals ahead of time. It's not about helping, Kelly, even though that's what you say. You have control issues. You think I don't feed your father."

"Charlene," I said, "that's not true. All I care about is making sure that Dad has enough to eat."

"Didn't you sneak soup in here after I told you not to bring food in?" She was getting angry.

"Yes, "I said. "I brought two quarts of that soup you love from Gelson's. I was going to leave one with you guys and take the other home. I really didn't think that was a problem."

Charlene put down her mug and folded her arms.

"Look," I continued gently. "I just don't understand why you dislike me so much. We've had a great relationship for over thirty years."

"Why I dislike you?" Charlene said. "Because you lie and try to make me feel bad about your dad."

"Tell me how I've lied."

"You lie about bringing food in the house."

"Charlene, you have asked me to bring food over—and even thanked me for it! Even when I was taking the bus and had to get off at multiple stops to get all the things you wanted, I did it. Gladly!"

"I'm not talking about when I *asked* you to bring food. I mean the other times when you snuck it in behind my back."

I sighed. "Look, I bring food over for Dad because he eats it. Isn't that the most important thing? Why does that make you so mad?"

"Because you're just trying to control us."

I threw up my hands. "No, I'm not! I just want to make sure Dad gets something to eat when he's hungry, especially when you're not feeling well and need to sleep."

"That doesn't mean I don't get up to feed him," she snapped. "And even if I don't, Jackie is here."

I laughed bitterly. "Jackie leaves to go get a loaf of bread and is gone for six hours. You know that as well as I do."

Charlene slammed her fist on the table. "He's my husband. I'm the one who will make his meals. You're not his wife."

"But I'm his daughter."

"There's a big difference between a wife and a daughter, Kelly." She smirked at me across the table. "You've been a tremendous pain in my ass ever since I've known you."

"So you're saying you've resented me from the start?"

"Yeah," she said. "Actually, even before I married your father."

I couldn't believe what she was saying. All those decades, I had considered Charlene a close friend. We had traveled together, laughed together, shared a lot of great times. I was always so grateful to her for how happy she'd made my dad. I had loved Charlene and thought she felt the same for me. Her words stung.

"Kelly," Charlene said with a tight smile, "I don't care what you, or anyone else, thinks I'm doing wrong for your father. You're not in charge."

"Charlene, I still need a reason for why you don't like me."

"Because you lie."

I met her gaze. "Tell me one lie I've ever told you."

"Do you want me to make a list from the past thirty years?"

"Tell me one lie."

We both knew there was nothing.

"Well," she muttered. "I didn't write them all down."

"Tell me one, Charlene."

She pushed back from the table.

"I'm done here. You can see yourself out. But let me just say this: I'll never try to keep you from your dad." She started toward the kitchen, then turned back. "Because you'd be the one to take me to court if I did."

Chapter 23

CHARLENE CONTINUED TO VACILLATE BETWEEN THREATS TO LIMIT MY access to Dad and, in the next breath, declaring that she would never try to keep me from him. She gained more control over the situation as Dad's physical health declined and his confusion increased.

Over the decades of their marriage, Dad had always joked that Charlene was the "boss." She was barely five feet tall but strong in personality and attitude. In the past, I'd accepted Charlene's brusque manner as just part of her Jersey-born, rough-and-tumble Italian background. There might have been times when her abruptness hurt my feelings, but I'd never doubted that she loved and cared for me. Neither had I believed she had anything but the best intentions for Dad. But these beliefs were now crumbling before my eyes.

Charlene had made it clear that she would curtail my visits if I continued to bring food to Dad. But, oddly, she didn't seem to mind if I offered to make meals when I was at the apartment as long as it was from items in their pantry. And she still accepted my offers to grocery-shop for them, as long as I stuck to the list that she gave me.

Around this time Dad and Charlene hired caregivers to stay with him in the apartment. Sometimes they would text me, asking if I could bring a sandwich and soup over because, as they'd say, "there's nothing suitable for your dad to eat here." I would wait until I was sure Charlene was asleep and then I'd bring the food over. Then I would take the empty containers away with me so she wouldn't see them in the trash. The caregivers would sometimes quietly pass on information to me about Dad's medical progress. The turnover for caregivers was very high because Charlene would inevitably get angry with them over something and fire them. I'd show up for a visit and someone completely new would be there.

One of the new doctors recommended another surgery to replace Dad's brain shunt. The doctor didn't think the shunt was adequately draining fluid from his brain and could be causing many of his symptoms. I hated the thought that Dad would have to undergo another major surgery, but clung to the hope that his quality of life might improve.

He was admitted to St. John's Hospital in Santa Monica for the procedure. It turned out that the original shunt was not the correct size for an adult man. After the surgery, he stayed in the hospital for a month while the doctors monitored the new shunt.

Santa Monica was close to where I lived, so I visited Dad at St. John's every day while he recovered. He was placed on a private floor in a hospital suite with a kitchenette. Jackie, in her manic style, transformed the space into a kind of dormitory. She cluttered the tables with an electric teakettle, a coffeemaker, magazines, candles, and a humidifier. There were boxes of takeout food and snacks, enough for a party of ten. Plugged into the various outlets around the room were her laptop, iPad, and two phones. Jackie wasn't working at the time, so I could never figure out why she needed so many devices. She crammed the mini-fridge with snacks and drinks, and whatever didn't fit was stored in an insulated cooler bag. The couches were piled with throws and pillows. The television blared all day and night. And there, in the middle of it all, was Dad. He lay on the bed, weak and confused from pain meds, unable to escape the chaos.

I could tell the hospital staff was annoyed by the clutter in Dad's room. There was always something in the way when they tried to roll a cart into the room. Charlene and Jackie treated the nurses like hotel staff, asking for extra blankets, pillows, and once, a fan, because they said the room was too hot. When the nurse replied that they didn't have any fans, Jackie rolled her eyes.

I was always relieved when I stopped in and found Dad alone, with Jackie out on one of her "errands" and Charlene away. Then I could turn off the TV and sit with Dad, holding his hand, talking about things that made him smile. Since Charlene liked the room very dark because she slept most of the time, I would open the blinds to let in some sunlight. I'd tell Dad a funny story about something at work, and it made my heart burst to see him laugh.

I'd noticed that since Dad had fallen ill, both Charlene and Jackie had become obsessed with researching medications and alternative treatments on the internet. Jackie would tell the nurses and doctors that they should adjust some of his drugs based on something she'd read online. Once when I was there, she tipped up Dad's head and fed him a large pill that he could hardly choke down. When I asked what it was, she told me it was vitamin D. She'd heard on a television show that vitamin D could help Dad's symptoms. I couldn't help but think that if the blinds in Dad's room were occasionally opened, he would get some vitamin D the natural way.

By the second week of Dad's hospitalization, it was clear the staff were fed up with Charlene and Jackie's presence. While I didn't want Dad to ever be lonely, I knew that he couldn't get the rest and quiet he needed with the two of them always there. My dad was the kind of person who would never ask anyone to leave the room, no matter how tired he was. When he and Charlene were entertaining, Dad would always be an attentive, gracious host even when a guest had long overstayed their welcome.

I was familiar with St. John's Hospital because I'd had two surgeries there in the past few years. A couple of the doctors and some of the staff remembered me and would come by to say hello when I was visiting Dad. I'd also become friendly with the hospital's resident Catholic priest during my stays. I ran into him one day in the hospital lobby and asked him to come with me to meet Dad. I knew my father would like this friendly, red-haired man who told great stories in a lilting Irish accent.

When we got to Dad's room, Charlene turned and gave the priest a withering glare.

"What's this—a priest? For fuck's sake, Tim doesn't need his last rites read."

I was mortified by her rudeness, but the priest gave a gracious laugh.

Dad grinned from his bed. "Really?" he quipped. "Am I dead yet?"

The priest sat and visited with Dad for a few minutes, and the two men soon had each other cracking up. Meanwhile, Charlene glowered from her recliner. I couldn't understand why she wasn't happy that Dad appeared to be enjoying himself.

Charlene's grasp on Dad's routine tightened in the coming days. I still visited almost every day, but I could tell she loathed my presence.

Jackie always acted friendly, but I knew it wasn't sincere. One day I overheard Charlene and Jackie talking about me when they didn't realize I was standing outside the door. They were annoyed that I was coming in so much and half-joked that maybe Dad's next surgery should be done out of state so I couldn't be there.

One day, when I had a rare moment alone with Dad, a nurse slipped into the room to check his IV line. I was sitting quietly in a chair next to the bed while Dad slept. The nurse looked down and smiled. "You know," she said, "I can tell how much your father loves you."

"Aw," I whispered back. "Thank you. I love him so much, too."

"All the nurses say it. When you come in, he just lights up. And then when you leave, he says to everyone, 'That was my daughter, Kelly.' He's a proud papa." She lingered by the bed, tucking Dad's blanket around his shoulders. "But these other two . . ." she shook her head, gesturing around the room at the piles of blankets, magazines, and takeout boxes.

As with the caregivers, Dad's doctors seemed to change frequently. I heard from the staff that Charlene and Jackie often argued with them over Dad's medications, and when the nurses didn't give in to their demands, they'd be replaced.

After his month in St. John's Hospital, Dad was moved to a rehabilitation center in Century City. Four weeks in the hospital had already taken a toll on his mental and emotional health, and the rehab was even drearier. Dad became more confused, forgetting where he was. A doctor told me about "sundowner syndrome," when older people can't sleep at night and become disoriented. They can start to hallucinate and even wander outside and become lost. I looked around Dad's dark, cluttered room at the rehab center and thought about how being confined to such a space could make any person delusional.

I'd been working long hours on a commercial shoot but still called in to check on Dad a few times a day. One day, after being unable to reach Charlene or Jackie, I called the rehab facility and talked to one of the nurses. She said Dad had been agitated and confused. He had crying spells and would repeatedly ask for Magi and Papa.

By the time I hung up the phone, I was sobbing. I sent Jackie a desperate text, saying I'd heard Dad wasn't doing well and begging her to call me back. An entire day went by before she returned my call. Dad had gone through a "rough patch," Jackie said, but was doing better. No more details were offered.

As soon as I could get away from work, I drove to the rehab center. Charlene and Jackie weren't in the room, and Dad was sleeping.

I spent the next few hours sitting by his bed, holding his hand and talking to him softly whenever he opened his eyes. "I'm right here, Dad," I whispered. "You're not alone."

One morning about a week later, I woke up to a phone message from Dad's rehab center. A nurse had called my phone in the middle of the night, saying they were having a problem with Charlene. When I called the facility back, the nurse told me what had happened.

Around two a.m., a staffer had found Charlene sitting on the floor in the hallway outside Dad's door. She was saying the same phrase over and over again: "I want a biscuit. I want a biscuit. Where's the biscuit?" After taking her vitals to make sure she wasn't having a medical emergency, such as a stroke or diabetic shock, the staff tried to get Charlene off the floor and back into Dad's room. They asked her if she knew where she was.

"I want a biscuit," she said.

They asked her if she knew her name.

"My name is Poo-poo," she replied.

They suspected that Charlene was, as the nurse on the phone put it, "high as a kite."

During the incident, the staff had tried to call Jackie, who was listed first on the emergency contact list, but she didn't answer. Second on the list was Karen Beatty, Charlene's former stepdaughter, but she didn't pick up either. The third name was me, and I'd slept through the call, too.

Unable to reach anyone and not wanting to call the authorities, the staff decided to let Charlene fall asleep on the recliner in Dad's room.

"Charlene," I said when I saw her the next day. "What happened last night?"

"Oh, I was sleepwalking," she said with a dismissive wave. "It was nothing."

"Mom's always been a sleepwalker," Jackie added.

In the thirty years I'd known Charlene, I never once recalled that she had ever been a sleepwalker.

After two weeks in the rehab center, the doctors said it was okay for Dad to go home.

Shortly before he was discharged, I ran into one of his doctors out in the hall.

"Hi!" I said. "How's my dad doing?"

"Actually," the doctor said, "your dad's doing great." Then he jabbed his thumb over his shoulder toward Dad's room, where we could hear Charlene and Jackie talking loudly over the TV. "It's everything else in there we're having a problem with."

Even then, I had no idea just how much worse that problem would get.

Chapter 24

AFTER THE SECOND SURGERY TO REPLACE THE SHUNT IN HIS BRAIN AND the weeks of hospitalization that followed, Dad's symptoms didn't improve. Back home at the apartment, every day seemed to drain a tiny bit more of his strength, mental clarity, and coordination. Though he still liked to tell jokes, his speech was slow and labored as he tried to voice his thoughts. He could walk from the sofa to the kitchen, but every step was fraught with imbalance. Dad didn't like to use his walker, and each time I watched him make his way across the room unaided, I was ready to spring up to catch him if he fell. The doctors had warned that a fall could be a serious setback, and I was worried that one stumble could cost him the last bit of physical freedom he had left.

It was strongly recommended that Dad continue physical therapy after he went home from the rehab center, but Charlene didn't like having people come into the apartment, so physical therapy fell by the wayside. When I visited, I would encourage Dad to do some simple exercises to increase his strength and flexibility, such as sitting and standing in a chair a few times, or lifting a few light weights. Sometimes I would walk with him up and down the hall outside of the apartment. After all of my ski accidents, I was no stranger to the benefit of physical therapy. I knew it was vital to maintaining Dad's muscle strength and balance, both of which he was rapidly losing.

Charlene tolerated my presence, and some days she even acted friendly. When she was in a good mood, I would hope that maybe there was a chance to repair our fractured relationship. I missed the closeness we'd had for all those years, and I wanted the Charlene of those times back.

But just when I thought that things might get better, Charlene's attitude would suddenly change. And even Dad wasn't spared when she was in a foul mood.

Once when I was visiting, Dad opened the blinds to let in some sunlight into the dark living room.

"Tim," Charlene snapped. "Keep those drapes closed!"

"Whoa," Dad said. "Sorry, I just thought we might want to see the sun for once." He closed the blinds.

My brother Tim lived in Los Angeles, so he and his wife, Jennifer, and their daughter Sophia often visited Dad on weekends. We would watch a football game or a movie, and for a few hours, the apartment would have a lighthearted, fun vibe as everyone laughed and ate snacks. Tim also took Dad out to the racetrack. Like Dad, Tim loved horse racing, and a day at the track had long been a favorite outing for the two of them. There was nothing Dad enjoyed more than a day watching the horses tear past, with hot dogs for lunch and a stack of tickets in his hand. Tim and Dad made visits to the track until Dad became too incapacitated to leave the apartment. To this day, I am so happy that he had these great times with my brother while he still could.

Our other brothers lived farther away, so I kept them updated on Dad's progress. Patrick, who'd become more eccentric as he got older, lived out in the Mojave Desert and surfaced only occasionally. Seann was still living in Steamboat Springs, Corey was in Arizona, and Jamie lived in San Diego.

At a certain point, I began to notice a marked increase in Charlene's hostility toward me. I sensed that her anger was about something specific, but I couldn't figure out what.

One day when Dad was taking a nap, I confronted her in the kitchen.

"Charlene," I said. "Did something happen?"

She slammed down a pan that she'd been wiping. "Yeah, something did happen. Did you call and have someone do a welfare check on us?"

"What?" I was stunned. "I have no idea what you're talking about."

"Someone reported us. And they sent out a social worker to make a surprise check on your dad. I know it was you."

I shook my head. "Charlene, I swear I didn't call anyone. It wasn't me."

"I know how much you want to take him away from me."

"No!" I protested. "I don't want that! Dad loves you, and you love him."

"You know, Kelly," she continued, "they could have decided to just take him away from here. Just like that."

"Char, I didn't do it."

"Of course you're not going to admit it," Charlene said. "But Jackie and I both know you did it."

"All I care about," I said, fighting back angry tears, "is that Dad has the happiest and most comfortable life he can have. That's it. I *don't* want to take him from you, Charlene. I know that would break his heart."

"Whatever, Kelly," she said, turning away. "You just better be glad nothing came out of it. They didn't find one thing wrong."

Charlene and Jackie never stopped believing that I had called in the welfare check. It was another severe blow to our already-shattered relationship, but nothing I said would convince them otherwise. Although I never discovered who had made the call, I couldn't help but feel a kind of validation that my concerns about Dad were genuine. Someone else had been worried, too, so much so that they had made that phone call. I wasn't overdramatic or controlling. Other people saw the problems, too.

The welfare check may not have uncovered anything severe enough to remove Dad from his home, but his quality of life was rapidly deteriorating. Charlene was still sleeping most of the day, and Jackie would confine herself to her room when she was home. That left my dad, helpless to do much of anything for himself, being left to sit in a dark, cheerless apartment.

While I was regularly in touch with my brothers throughout Dad's illness, I think in many families it is the daughters who are most closely involved with the daily care of parents. As the eldest child and only girl in our family, it felt natural for me to assume this role. Even so, I found that I desperately needed someone to talk to, and the person who immediately came to mind was Karen, Charlene's former stepdaughter and Jackie's half-sister.

Karen and I had been friends since we were little. Her father, Roger, had been a writer and associate producer on *The Carol Burnett Show*, and Karen was one of the kids I'd run around with on the CBS lot when our parents were working. She and her sister, Colleen, were regular guests at the Conway home for birthdays and swimming parties. Even after

Charlene divorced Roger and later married Dad, she remained close friends with both Roger and Karen. Karen had maintained a good relationship with Charlene over the years, and spent a lot of time with our family. She and my dad adored one another.

Karen had become an ER nurse for Ventura County Emergency Medical Services. As Dad's illness progressed, she used her extensive medical knowledge to help out in any way she could. Although she knew that my relationship with Charlene was strained, Karen always kept me in the loop regarding anything she knew about Dad's care. Rational, intelligent, with a strong sense of right and wrong, Karen would have walked to the ends of the earth to help my dad, and I knew that I could confide in her.

Karen admitted that while she'd also been concerned about Charlene and Jackie's erratic behavior, she hadn't realized just how bad the situation had become. Although she was still close to Charlene and Jackie, she was worried about their ability to properly care for Dad.

"Document everything you see," she said. "This could get legal. You need to have all your ducks in a row."

I soon had another incident to add to my growing list when one of the doctors came by the apartment to check up on Dad. As the doctor was preparing to leave, Charlene asked him to write her a prescription. When he refused, she reached over and grabbed his leather doctor's bag and, while we all watched in amazement, began digging through it.

"Oh, come on," she said. "I know you have your prescription pad in here. Just write me the script."

The doctor swiftly took the bag from Charlene. "Excuse me," he said. "That is mine." Clearly rattled, he left quickly.

A few weeks later, I got a call from a nurse from the same doctor's office. She informed me that a family member had told them I had stolen some of her pills and was demanding a refill to make up the loss. I was so shocked that I nearly dropped the phone. Except for a few short periods when I'd been recovering from surgery, I had never taken pain pills. That this "family member" would flat-out lie to a doctor and accuse me of such a thing made me realize just how desperate she'd become.

The nurse went on to tell me that they had found the story suspicious and had refused to fill the prescription.

"We didn't think for one minute that you stole the pills," the nurse said. "But that's a serious allegation, and you need to know what's being said behind your back."

I was furious. I grabbed my car keys and got ready to drive over and confront the likely culprit. But just as I was about to get in my car, I stopped.

Charlene had already been making it hard for me to see Dad, and I didn't want to make things even worse. If I were to confront Jackie, Charlene might lock me out for good. There was no way I could let that happen. For now, my anger would have to wait.

Throughout all of this, Karen became my lifeline, confidante, and advisor. We met for lunch or coffee every week to share notes on what each of us had observed.

Jackie was still obsessed with researching medical treatments for Dad, and Karen tried to reason with her about what would help and what wouldn't. Karen told me that Charlene and Jackie believed that Dad needed a third surgery to replace his brain shunt, even though all of the specialists they had consulted advised against it. Karen explained what I already knew—that in Dad's condition, another major brain surgery could be devastating.

In the meantime, Charlene decided to move them all out of the Wilshire Corridor apartment. A fire had broken out in the middle of the night and forced all the residents to evacuate. In all the panic and confusion, Charlene could barely get Dad down the many flights of stairs to safety. Although the fire was extinguished quickly, it was a terrifying experience. Charlene had already soured on the inconveniences of apartment living, and the fire scare was the final straw.

To my delight, Charlene rented a condominium back in Encino, only three blocks from our old family home on Magnolia. Perched on a hill in a beautifully landscaped, gated community, their three-bedroom condo was spacious, with sliding doors that opened onto a large, sunny balcony that afforded sweeping views of the Valley.

Encino had always been home to Dad, and the moment they moved in, I could see a positive change in him. He would sit for hours on the balcony looking over the Valley, basking in its relaxed, warm familiarity.

When I visited, I would help him walk down the sidewalk under an arch-way of mature trees. We would sit by the community pool and enjoy some quiet time together.

Even Charlene seemed happier in the new condo. I resumed making healthy meals that I knew Dad would like, using only the things found in their kitchen. Charlene didn't seem to mind. Jackie, ever the double agent, was playing both sides. To my face, she was gregarious and chatty, but I hadn't forgotten her lies about the pills. I knew I could never trust her.

For a while, things looked brighter. I clung to the hope that the peace would continue so Dad could have the happy home and care that he deserved, surrounded by the family he loved.

I should have known better.

Chapter 25

AFTER MOVING TO THE NEW CONDO IN ENCINO, DAD WAS HAPPIER than I'd seen him in months. There was space for the familiar things he loved, such as his antique signs and framed photos of his favorite race-horses. His Emmys sat on a shelf next to mementos and awards from his long career. There was the *SpongeBob SquarePants* statue he'd been given in recognition for his voice work as the show's character, Barnacle Boy, sitting next to a framed Bob Mackie sketch of his Mr. Tudball costume. A candid photograph of Dad and Harvey laughing together from their days on *The Carol Burnett Show* had pride of place over his desk.

Though his weakening health made talking difficult, Dad was determined to engage in conversation. He was a man who loved to communicate, whether it was discussing a current event in the news or simply cracking jokes. Even if his body was slowing down, his mind remained mostly intact, full of memories and opinions he needed to share. It might have taken him a few beats to recall the name of an old colleague, but the man famous for his perfectly timed sense of comedy was still totally present. As long as I could see that familiar twinkle in his eye, I knew that Dad was okay.

But without continuing physical therapy, Dad's health continued to get worse. I asked Charlene about bringing a physical therapist into the home a few days a week, but again, Charlene didn't think it was necessary. Karen had told me that Charlene and Jackie had found a new doctor who recommended that Dad spend a few weeks at a rehabilitation center in Thousand Oaks. "It will help him get stronger," Charlene had told Karen. "The doctor says it's one of the best centers in the state." A few days later, Dad left the condo for a two-week stay in the center, to get physical therapy.

The moment I stepped through the rehab center door, I knew they had made a terrible mistake. The smell of urine was like a smack in the face. People sat hunched over in their wheelchairs along the narrow hallway, and many were crying or moaning. Some would try to grab your arm as you walked by. This was the place that was supposed to help my dad get stronger?

I was already in tears by the time I reached Dad's room. The small, dreary space was littered with Charlene and Jackie's familiar junk: a tea-kettle, a reading lamp, mounds of cartoon-colored pillows, and cheap polyester throws. I noticed that they opted to go home to sleep instead of staying overnight, as they had done in other places Dad had been. I couldn't help but speculate that the drab, stinky environment had some-thing to do with that; this place was a far cry from the VIP suite at Cedars-Sinai Medical Center.

I sat next to Dad's bed and took his hand.

He opened his eyes and smiled. "Hi, Pal."

"Hi, Daddy," I said, bringing his hand to my face and kissing it. "How are you?"

I forced myself to be cheerful and bustled around the room, tidying up and opening the dusty blinds to let in some light. But inside, I raged. *Why are you here?* I thought. *There's no reason for you to be in this horrible place!*

Later, it was time for Dad's physical therapy session. As we walked down the hall, a woman who was visiting with another patient looked up.

"Tim Conway?" she said.

Dad was sitting in his wheelchair, and she bent over to examine his face. "You're Tim Conway, right?"

Dad nodded.

Another woman approached. "Oh, wow, I'm a huge fan! Mind if we take a selfie?" Both women were already taking out their phones.

I wanted to say something, but Dad smiled and agreed to the picture. It wasn't uncommon for Dad to be recognized by fans. Sometimes he would be stopped in a store or on the street, and other times people would interrupt when they shouldn't, like during a restaurant meal. This intru-sion of privacy makes some celebrities nuts, and they will often curtly refuse to talk or sign an autograph.

Now that everyone has a cell phone, many fans will demand a selfie no matter what the place or situation. My dad was always gracious to fans. It was part of who he was—a genuinely nice human being who recognized that much of his success was due to his fans' devotion. Still, it burned me to watch these two ladies hold out their phones and snap pictures with Dad when he was obviously in a compromised position. Another facility would have immediately stopped this intrusion of a patient's privacy, but the staff here didn't blink an eye.

The facility's physical therapy room was a windowless basement with worn-out equipment and torn furniture. I cheerfully coached Dad along with the therapist, but I couldn't see anything special about the routine. It was difficult to believe that this place was one of the "best" in the state for physical therapy, as Charlene and Jackie had claimed. Dad should be getting physical therapy at home, in the privacy of his comfortable condo. Not in a dreary rehab facility with neglected patients practically falling out of their wheelchairs.

I forced myself to keep smiling as Dad wearily finished the session, and we walked him back to his room.

"Charlene," I said when she arrived later, "this place is awful. It's filthy, and people were taking selfies with Dad in the hall. Please"—now I was begging—"can't we just take him home and let him have the physical therapy there?"

She fixed me with a steely gaze. "Jackie researched this facility," she said. "It's one of the best in the Valley. That's why he's here. Now butt out."

One day I walked into Dad's room and found two strangers there. One was leaning over Dad's bed so that the other could take a picture with him.

"Excuse me," I said. "This is not appropriate. You need to leave now."

They scurried out of the room and I slammed the door after them.

Sinking into the chair next to Dad's bed, I held his hand and tried to hold back the tears that I could feel welling in my eyes. I glanced at the table where I'd set a vase of fresh flowers the day before. They were gone. The caregiver said that Charlene had thrown them out, muttering something about his allergies. Dad had never been allergic to flowers. More likely, she just didn't want any reminders of me in the room.

As I drove home, I thought back to all the world-class medical centers Dad had gone through. The Cleveland Clinic. UCLA Medical Center. Cedars-Sinai. Institutions where the best specialists in the world had examined him. All those doctors, removed from Dad's case, one after the other, for reasons I could never understand. And even though I was his daughter, the doctors and nurses told me that they were instructed not to share any details of Dad's health care.

One day I was sitting with Dad at the rehab center when a nurse walked in.

"Hi," I said. "I'm Kelly, Tim's daughter."

The nurse gave me a tight smile and turned back to her tray of medicines. A few awkward minutes went by, and she didn't say anything.

"So," I ventured, "how do you think my dad's doing today?"

Wordlessly, the nurse picked up her tray and left the room.

I was still processing this baffling silent treatment when a doctor walked into the room.

"Oh, hi," he said. "You must be Tim's daughter?"

"Yes, I am."

We shook hands.

"Look," he said, glancing at his chart. "I've discussed this again with my team, and we are still advising against another surgery for your dad. As far as we can see, replacing the brain shunt wouldn't alleviate his symptoms. And quite frankly, the risks far outweigh any possible benefits."

I nodded, amazed at what I was hearing. After so many opinions from one specialist after another saying that another operation would be dangerous, Charlene and Jackie were still fighting for it.

"I completely agree with you, Doctor," I said. "I don't think my dad should have another operation."

The doctor looked at me with surprise. "You don't? Oh, that's great. From what I understood, you and your mother—"

Suddenly the nurse appeared. "Stop!" she said. "We've been given strict orders by the patient's wife not to talk to this woman."

The doctor was confused. "But this is his daughter, right?"

"It's the *wrong* daughter," the nurse said. "This one has been causing a lot of problems."

"Doctor," I said, "I appreciate your advice. And I couldn't agree with you more. But unfortunately, my stepmother feels otherwise." I looked at the nurse. "And just for the record, Jackie is my father's stepdaughter. *I* am his daughter."

The doctor gathered up his chart and fled the room.

——◦——

I had hoped that the many doctors who opposed another surgery for my dad had finally convinced Charlene and Jackie not to pursue it, but that was not the case. I soon discovered that the doctor who had mistaken me for Jackie was eventually let go, too.

And then Charlene and Jackie found a doctor who agreed with them.

Ever since Dad had first gotten sick, Charlene had proudly referred to Jackie, who had no medical background at all, as "Tim's doctor." Jackie had convinced herself that some miracle cure for my dad existed, and she would be the one to figure it all out. She had barraged Dad's doctors and their staff with the information she'd read on the internet, and when they ignored her "advice," Charlene had replaced them. Charlene and Jackie continued to believe that Dad needed another surgery to replace his brain shunt, even though every doctor they'd consulted thus far had adamantly disagreed.

This new doctor felt differently, however. He also thought that Dad should have the shunt replaced. Charlene and Jackie were elated.

I begged them to reconsider. Karen came over to the condo and attempted to reason with them, explaining that the surgery could seriously jeopardize Dad's condition.

"That's if he even lives through the surgery!" Karen said. "At this point, Tim should be living his life in comfort, surrounded by the family he loves—*not* undergoing another very complicated operation that all the top specialists have advised against."

The only way I knew what was going on was through Karen. Because she was a nurse, Charlene and Jackie allowed her to read all of Dad's charts. Later, Karen would fill me in on what she'd learned. Being careful not to arouse suspicion, Karen and I gave each other code names in our cell phones. That way, if Charlene or Jackie happened to look at our phones, they wouldn't realize how frequently Karen and I were talking.

But no matter how much Karen tried to dissuade them about another surgery, Charlene and Jackie had made up their minds.

"It's going to cure him," Jackie said earnestly. "The doctor says that after the surgery, he'll be able to go on tour again!"

The stay in the rehab center had only served to weaken Dad further, and he was helpless to decide for himself. I knew this was not what my dad wanted, but I had no legal authority in the matter at all. And at this point, Dad didn't have any say, either.

On Easter Sunday, I brought Dad a potted white lily and a card that had a bunny on it with the words, *Have a Happy, Hoppy Easter!* I pinned the card on the corkboard by Dad's bed so he could see it. When I came in for my next visit, the lily and the card were gone.

Charlene had left me a handwritten note: "Nothing—absolutely *nothing* goes up on the walls. Tim gets agitated looking back—consider the condition he's in now. Cards that say 'Happy' anything are insensitive, as he will not have a 'Happy' anything, ever. If you knew him at all you'd realize oldies but goodies bring him pain—not joy."

He will not have a "happy" anything, ever? I was stunned at the message. How could Charlene say or think such a thing about Dad? Yes, his life had changed dramatically due to his illness, but that didn't mean he couldn't still experience happiness and joy. And it was up to us, his family, to do everything in our power to make that happen. Charlene's angry words claiming that Dad was incapable of ever being happy again infuriated me.

Dad's brain shunt operation was scheduled at Los Robles Regional Medical Center in Thousand Oaks. The day before the procedure, I waited with him by his bed until late that night. While I was there, Dad's new doctor swept into the room for a few minutes, chatting with Charlene and Jackie, who were both enamored of him. He patted Dad on the shoulder, like they were about to embark on some great adventure together.

When it was time to leave, I leaned down and hugged Dad for a long time.

"I love you, Daddy," I whispered. "I'll be here all day tomorrow, waiting for you to wake up."

Dad hugged me tightly. "See you tomorrie, Pal," he whispered. It was a phrase we'd used only with each other ever since I was little.

"See you tomorrie," I repeated. And when he finally closed his eyes, I left.

After the operation, my dad never spoke again.

Chapter 26

After the surgery, Dad stayed in the hospital for almost two weeks. Even though it was only about twenty-five minutes from their condo, Charlene and Jackie decided to book a suite at the luxurious Four Seasons Hotel in Westlake Village. This shaved about ten minutes off their drive.

Seann came to visit a few days after the operation, and we stayed late at the hospital with Dad. I was driving Seann to the airport early the next morning, so Charlene grudgingly invited us to stay in Jackie's room at the hotel because it had two beds. Jackie pouted when she realized that she'd have to give up her room to Seann and me while she slept on the sofa. I was too tired to care.

None of us had eaten dinner, and we were hungry when we arrived at the hotel around midnight. After glancing at the prices on the room service menu, I suggested we order a pizza instead. Charlene waved me away and picked up the phone. She ordered almost the entire menu, about three hundred dollars' worth of food. It was far more than the four of us needed, and when we went to bed, most of the food lay untouched and spoiling on the table.

Although no one wanted to admit it, Dad's miraculous recovery didn't happen. It soon became clear that the surgery had done more to worsen his condition than improve it, just as the specialists had warned. Dad still managed to smile, but no matter how hard he tried, he couldn't form words. The doctor who had done the surgery breezed in and out, full of assurances that we would see an improvement in a few weeks. Charlene and Jackie eagerly accepted this, but I was devastated at how much Dad had declined since the operation. Still, I kept up a happy face for Dad and spent every day that I wasn't working at his side.

On the day of Dad's discharge from the hospital, a nurse asked us to sit down to go over his postsurgical care. It was one of the few nurses who hadn't been afraid to stand up to Charlene and Jackie when they had made ridiculous demands and were rude to the staff. Not coincidentally, I had developed a sort of quiet camaraderie with the nurse. We often exchanged knowing glances, and I could tell she understood what I was going through.

As the nurse opened her laptop, I sat with my pad and pen, ready to take notes. She looked up and smiled. "No need to take notes," she said. "I'll give you a printout of everything you need. But I love that you're so prepared. Now, who is going to be in charge of changing Dad's bandage?"

Charlene was reading a *People* magazine on the lounge chair.

"Jackie is in charge of Tim's care," she said without once looking up. "But show Kelly, too, in case Jackie is out or something."

Jackie was sitting on the other side of the room, looking at her phone.

"Jackie," the nurse said. "Can you come over here so I can show you how to change the bandage?"

Jackie got up and stood behind me.

"This bandage must be changed every day. There's a very high risk of infection in this area, so it has to be kept very clean." I saw her glance at Jackie. I looked up and saw that Jackie was busy scrolling through her phone.

"Hey, Jackie?" I said. "Can you please pay attention? This is really important." I wanted to grab her phone and throw it out the window.

Jackie shoved her phone in her pocket and watched as the nurse demonstrated the steps for changing Dad's bandage. There was special tape used to adhere it and antiseptic wipes to clean the wound. The entire time, Charlene never looked up from her magazine.

The nurse held out a plastic bag full of the bandages, and Jackie took them. "Remember," she said, "it absolutely must be changed every single day."

Dad had two exceptional caregivers at home, Anna and Jason, watching over him day and night. They were both from the Philippines and possessed a gentle, kind, and knowledgeable bedside manner. Jason had been with my dad before his operation, and the two had become very close. Anna and Jason both called him "Papa."

Charlene's treatment of Anna and Jason was horrendous. Once when I was visiting, Anna walked out of the front bathroom. Charlene was waiting for her.

"That bathroom is not for the help," she snapped. "You can use the one in the back."

I knew that Dad never would have tolerated anyone in his family treating people so terribly, and I later apologized profusely to them.

When Anna and Jason quietly asked if they could have my cell-phone number, I gladly gave it to them. I told them to call me anytime, day or night. With two competent caregivers on hand, Charlene could sleep the day away and Jackie could disappear for hours and I'd still be comfortable, knowing Dad was in good hands.

A few days later, I was in South Los Angeles, working on a shoot for a major client. I'd taken a lot of time off work to spend time with Dad, so I was grateful for the job.

I was steaming some pieces of the wardrobe when my phone rang. It was Jason, and he was frantic.

"Kelly, your dad isn't doing good. He has a fever."

"Do Charlene and Jackie know?" I asked.

"Charlene is asleep," Jason said. "Jackie has been gone all day. I think his surgical wound is infected."

"Has Jackie been changing the bandage every day?"

"No, I don't think it's been changed in a few days."

I felt a tightening in my throat. Neither Jason nor Anna could change Dad's bandage because they hadn't received the detailed instructions from the nurse. That was Jackie's responsibility.

"Do you see the clean bandages?" I asked. "Jackie has a bag full of them."

I waited a few minutes while Jason looked.

"I can't find them," he said when he got back on the phone.

I thought of the bag the nurse had handed to Jackie, most likely lost somewhere under the heaps of junk in her room.

"Jason," I said, "I'm leaving work now, and I'll be there as soon as I can."

As I hung up, the producer, who is also named Kelli, walked over. Kelli and I had worked together on so many jobs that we'd become great friends. She could tell immediately that something was wrong.

"Hey, what's going on?" she asked.

I blinked tears away, trying to get my thoughts in order.

"My dad is really sick, and I need to go to him." We were right in the middle of the shoot, and it was a day when I didn't have an assistant working with me.

"Go," Kelli said. "You already have everything picked out for the rest of the shoot, so we can take it from here. Don't worry about anything except being with your dad."

I hugged Kelli and raced to my car. Leaving a job in the middle of a shoot was unheard of, but this was an emergency.

Before I drove off, I sent a quick text to Charlene. She would be mad if I showed up without telling her first.

"Hi!" I texted. "I got off work early, so I thought I'd stop by and see Dad for a bit."

A few minutes later, I received her curt reply: "Fine."

Jason called again when I was on the way to Encino.

"Kelly," he said, "Jackie's home now, but she can't find the bandages."

"She can't find them?" I repeated. "I saw her take the bag from the nurse. She *has* to have them."

"I'm fucking looking for them!" Jackie screeched in the background.

"Jason, I'll stop and get some more bandages. I'm still in south LA, but I'll get there as fast as I can."

It took almost two hours to drive up to Encino with a stop at a medical supply store to buy more bandages and tape.

When I arrived at the condo, Charlene's bedroom door was still closed, and Jackie, Jason, and Anna were in the living room with Dad. Two workmen were hanging new wallpaper in the powder room.

"Oh my God," I breathed, gently pulling up one side of the bandage. It had been on so long that it had stuck to the incision. Jason and Anna both said it was the same bandage the nurse had put on at the hospital three days before.

"Okay," I said to Jason and Anna. "Let's get this taken care of."

Gently, I peeled away the bandage. Jason held a length of tape for Anna to cut as I cleaned the wound and centered the new dressing over it.

Just then, the master bedroom door opened.

"What the fuck are you doing?" Charlene said.

We all looked up. I was holding the bandage to Dad's head and Jason was handing me a piece of tape.

"We're changing Dad's bandage," I said, trying not to sound as angry as I felt. "It hasn't been changed in a few days."

"Get your hands off my husband," Charlene growled. "And get the *fuck* out of my house."

"Charlene," I said. "Dad's bandage has to be changed. Now."

Charlene suddenly descended upon me, clawing at my face and arms. Anna screamed as Jason rushed to pull Charlene off.

"Get the fuck out of my house!" Charlene screamed. "Get the fuck out! Jackie, call the police!"

Dad was facing away from the room and couldn't see what was happening, but he heard it.

"My God, Charlene," I said, backing away. "This is not normal. This is not normal!"

Charlene jerked her arm from Jason's hands.

"If I had a baseball bat," she said, between gasps for breath, "I would beat you right now and watch you bleed to death on the floor. Nothing would make me happier."

"I'm calling the police," said Anna.

The two men hanging wallpaper had come out and were staring back and forth between Charlene and me as paste dripped from their hands.

"I'm leaving. Jason, please be sure the bandage is taped on Dad's head like I showed you."

As I passed Jackie's bedroom, I could see her gathering bottles of pills and stuffing them into a bag, which she then shoved under her bed. She had heard Anna say she was calling the police.

Outside in my car, I flipped down the visor mirror. There were four rows of bright red marks swelling up on my right cheek, where Charlene had scratched me. There were also bloody marks on my arms where her sharp nails had dug into the skin. I stared at my face, still not believing the stepmother I'd once loved so much had done this. It was a clear and sunny day, but the world looked blurry. I was in shock.

Somehow, I got the car started and drove a few blocks to the Encino Fire Department. I needed to tell someone what had happened, and even more important, I had to make sure Dad was going to be taken care of. Sitting in my car in front of the firehouse, I broke down into heaving sobs.

A couple of the firemen came over to the car. I was shaking so hard that I could hardly get the story out.

"I don't care about me," I said. "I'm just so worried about my dad. He's not being taken care of."

"We can call the police," one of the firemen said, "and have them go over there. But you have to understand that once you go that route, there's no going back. I doubt they would arrest your stepmother, and because of her age, they'll probably take her word over yours."

I took a few deep breaths, pressing the antibacterial cloth they had given me against my cheek.

"Let me think about it. Thank you, guys, so much. I'm just going to go home."

I was just about to head back home when I turned off the freeway and into the West Valley police precinct parking lot. Inside, I calmly filed a report of physical assault against my stepmother. I told them I didn't want Charlene to be arrested, but I needed the incident to be on file. Sitting under the glaring fluorescent lights while a policeman took photos of my face and arms, I realized just how helpless I was to protect my father.

When I left the precinct, the sun was dipping low over the hills. Instead of heading home, I drove around and looked at all the places so familiar to me from my childhood. The hardware store where I'd tag along with Dad on Saturday mornings, and the Baskin-Robbins where he would take my brothers and me for ice cream when we had pushed Mom to the brink and she needed a little time by herself. The school where Dad had found me in the playground that first day of class, crying and forgotten.

I remembered something that Charlene had said a few years back. I'd brought my boyfriend at the time to dinner over at Dad and Charlene's house. Dad and I were joking with each other, and my boyfriend had commented on how close our relationship was.

"Oh, you have no idea," Charlene said. "She idolizes him, and he idolizes her. I've never seen anything like it in my life."

Then I thought of the two wallpaper hangers back at the condo. Knowing that the wallpaper had been changed, but not Dad's bandage, filled me with unbearable sadness.

I drove down Ventura Boulevard to our old house on Magnolia. The owners had painted it a different color, but the trees, the iron balcony, and the shrub-lined driveway beyond the gate were all the same. The past year of hurt, anger, and frustration had left me in a fog of uncertainty, but sitting there on Magnolia outside my childhood home, all the confusion melted away, and the realization of what I had to do became clear. As I watched, a single light switched on inside the house and brought me out of my daydreaming.

I put the car in gear and headed home.

Chapter 27

FATHER'S DAY 2017 ARRIVED A WEEK AFTER CHARLENE ATTACKED ME. While I recovered from the shock and figured out my next steps, I stayed away from the condo.

During that time, Charlene sent me a text: "I will not keep you from your dad on Father's Day," it read. "But I won't be here when you visit."

Dad and I had always agreed that our celebrating Father's Day wasn't a big deal since we talked or saw each other almost every day. I still needed some time to process what had happened, so I didn't go on this particular day.

On the Sunday of Father's Day, I got a call from Jason.

"Kelly," he whispered into the phone. "Papa's not doing good. He hasn't been eating, and I think he's dehydrated. I said something to Charlene, but she told me not to worry about it."

As soon as I hung up with Jason, I called the police on the nonemergency line. I told the dispatcher that I was seriously worried about my dad's well-being and asked if they could conduct a welfare check, adding that he might also need an ambulance.

An hour later, my brother Tim called. He was furious. He'd been visiting Dad at the condo when the paramedics, accompanied by a pair of police officers, had knocked on the door. Tim had allowed the paramedics to check Dad while assuring the police that everything was fine. The EMTs didn't think Dad needed to go to the hospital, but they agreed that he was dehydrated. They made Charlene promise that she would get him to a doctor the next day.

"Kelly, what's going on?" Tim demanded. "Why are the police over here?"

"Tim, Dad is not being taken care of," I said. "You don't realize just how bad things have gotten." My relationship with Tim had become tense over the past year. He often thought that I was overreacting and "crying wolf" about Dad's health.

"Dad's fine, Kell. Jen and Sophia are here, and we're all watching the game. I'm about to order a couple of pizzas. Why don't you just come over?"

"There's no way I can be around Charlene right now. As long as you think Dad's okay, I'm good."

About a month later, Charlene moved Dad to Topanga Terrace, a care facility in the Valley. To my relief, it was a lovely place. The lobby was like a luxury hotel with big arrangements of fresh flowers and polished marble floors. Visitors had to check in with the staff at the desk before entering, to ensure the patient's privacy. Dad's room had its own small corridor so that no one walking by in the hall could see in when the door was open. And the room itself was immaculately clean and decorated like an elegant home, not a hospital, with large windows and plenty of comfortable seating.

Jason was there as Dad's round-the-clock caregiver, sleeping on the recliner chair. Dad had always been fastidious about being well-groomed and neatly dressed, and Jason made sure to give him regular shaves, always keeping him dressed in clean, pressed shirts. He was instrumental in helping Dad to retain his dignity.

It had been almost two weeks since I'd seen Dad, and I covered his face and head with kisses.

"Look at that!" Jason said. "I haven't seen Papa smile so big in ages!"

Since Dad's last brain surgery he still hadn't regained his ability to speak, so we spent the day watching our favorite television shows, like Jerry Seinfeld's *Comedians in Cars Getting Coffee*. Dad loved this show, and when one of the comedians said something funny, he'd smile and turn his head to look at me. I'd also brought copies of *McHale's Navy* episodes and old movies that I knew he liked.

When I noticed Dad was drifting off to sleep, I'd mute the television and read while he napped, or I'd go out and chat with the staff, who were all wonderful.

Jason told me that Charlene had seen one of the stand-up comedy DVDs I'd brought in to watch with Dad. She had become angry, insisting that Dad's watching other comedians "fucked with his head." Jason tried to reassure her that my dad loved watching the shows, but Charlene grumbled and said she would put a stop to it. Despite her threat, she never said anything to me about the DVDs, and even if she had, I still would have watched them with Dad. The few pleasures he had left in his life were becoming more and more precious.

Dad was receiving speech therapy each day to help him recover his voice. He also got physical therapy in Topanga Terrace's clean, sunny, and well-equipped gym. We hoped the physical therapy would keep his body flexible enough to do certain things for himself. I knew Dad was declining, and no miracle would be coming along to transform him back into his former physical self. I just wanted him to have the best life he could have.

One day I arrived for my scheduled visit and was surprised to see that Dad was wearing a stained T-shirt. When I looked in his closet to find a clean one, there was only a hamper overflowing with dirty clothes. Jason explained that Charlene had refused to allow Dad's clothes to be washed by the facility's laundry services, saying that she and Jackie would take them home to launder there. But since they hadn't visited Dad in nearly ten days, Jason said, he'd run out of clean clothes.

I took the hamper to a local laundromat that day, where I washed, dried, and folded the clothes, returning them to Dad's room.

At this point, Charlene was not texting me directly. Instead, she would text Jason and have him relay her messages.

A couple days after I'd done the laundry, Jason showed me a text Charlene had sent him, for me: "Don't take your dad's laundry again. That's our job."

I started to text back that she and Jackie had left Dad without clean clothes for days, and that the two of them were woefully inadequate when it came to doing their "job," but I stopped. I worried that any recourse was futile and might only make things worse.

To give Dad some things to look at in his room, I brought in a few framed photographs of him with my brothers and me. One was a large photo of just me and Dad from a few years earlier. In it, we are both looking at each other and laughing. After asking the administrator if it was okay, I hung them on a side wall by Dad's bed so that he could turn his head and see them. Jason told me that Dad would stare at the photographs for hours. And sometimes, Jason said, he would cry.

"Do you think I should take them down?" I asked. I didn't want to make Dad upset.

"No," Jason said firmly. "Keep them up. He loves looking at them. I think it would kill him if you took them down."

I wondered if Charlene would take the pictures down, but for some reason, she never did.

Although Dad was in a top-tier facility and receiving excellent care, I knew that things could change at any moment. Through Karen, Jason, and certain staff members, I heard that Charlene's behavior was still erratic.

For a while, Charlene and Jackie had employed a doctor who they called Dr. Z. The doctor readily prescribed them any pills they wanted. But now, Jason told me, they were also getting this doctor to prescribe medicine for Dad, even though Dad wasn't Dr. Z's patient. This was against Topanga Terrace's rules, which required any medical care for its patients to go through their primary physicians. Later, we found out that Dr. Z had had his license revoked for prescribing narcotics without sufficient documentation.

Dad was on a variety of medications, and mixing them with other pills could be very harmful.

Karen was floored when I told her.

"We have to do something, Kelly," she said. "This can't go on."

I started to think about Casey Kasem and his daughter Kerri's fight over his medical care conservatorship. Casey had physically and mentally deteriorated after being diagnosed with Lewy body dementia, a Parkinson's-like disease. In 2014, the children from Casey's first marriage attempted to get custody of their ailing father from their stepmother, Jean. It became a vicious battle in the courts and a feeding frenzy for the tabloids when Jean took a seriously ill Casey from a medical facility against doctor's orders and hid him at a friend's house over a thousand miles away. Reading through the case's details, I couldn't help but see many similarities to what was happening with Dad.

Casey died in 2014, but the family continued fighting a wrongful death suit against Jean until it was settled in 2019. I had never met Kerri, but I reached out to her through Instagram and explained the situation with my dad, saying that I'd be grateful if she could provide any advice. She messaged back right away, and we began to text and talk on the phone. Kerri told me to document everything—take notes, save texts and e-mails, talk to medical staff, and take pictures.

Around this time, I learned that Charlene was planning to move Dad from Topanga Terrace to another facility in Ventura County. I couldn't understand why she wanted to take Dad from where he was so comfortable, and where he was afforded much-needed privacy.

Karen lived in Ventura County, so she offered to go check out the facility Charlene was considering. When Karen called back, the news wasn't good.

"It's just a house," Karen said. "And the patients are in the bedrooms. This place is not a skilled facility equipped for someone as compromised as your dad. And there isn't any real nursing staff, either. It's just a few health aides taking care of the patients."

Karen said the house was in an area that had been ravaged by wildfires a few months earlier, and most of the homes and buildings around it were gone. There were no trees, and the air still swirled with ash when the wind blew.

"Jackie told me that the owner is the sister of someone your dad and Charlene knew from the racetrack," Karen said, adding, "Kelly, this is absolutely the *worst* place for your dad."

For over a year, I had been contemplating hiring a lawyer to help me fight for a say in my dad's care. I'd kept putting it off in hopes that things would get better. But when I learned that Charlene planned to move Dad from Topanga Terrace, I pulled the trigger. Filing a suit would cost a lot of money, and the lawyer was honest with me when he said it would be a long shot. I didn't hesitate. If there was any chance I could legally help my dad, I was going to do it.

I spent an entire day in the lawyer's office preparing a suit to ask the court for two things: first, to prevent Charlene from moving Dad from Topanga Terrace; and second, to change the conservatorship of Dad from

Charlene to me, based on the belief that Charlene was not mentally stable enough to make decisions for his care. I'd spent hours documenting all of the evidence that Karen and I had collected, including Charlene and Jackie's unauthorized medicating of Dad, the worsening neglect, and the nonstop firing of his doctors. Also included was the police report from when Charlene had attacked me, and witness declarations from Karen and Jason, Dad's caregiver.

More than anything, I wanted to keep the case out of the press. I knew about the people who made a career searching through public court records for information they could sell to the media. These people sat hunched over portable desks they set up under a big tree in the square outside the LA courthouse, poring over the newly filed court documents for a celebrity name they could sell to a tabloid.

To protect his privacy, we decided to use my dad's actual first name, Thomas, instead of Tim, in the suit. Dad had started going by "Tim" professionally shortly after moving to California when he realized that another actor named Tom Conway was already registered in the Screen Actors Guild. I hoped that the name Thomas Conway would not pique the interest of the courthouse tabloid suppliers.

The lawyer told me it would take a week for the suit to go through the court system, and before anything would happen.

I asked him if I should cancel a long-planned ski trip to South America.

"Go on your trip," the lawyer said. "You'll drive yourself crazy sitting around thinking about this all week. I don't need you in court, and it's actually better if you're not present."

I left for Chile and spent a week skiing in Portillo with my friends. Then my friend Yvonne and I headed to Argentina, where we planned to ski a few extra days in the Andes.

After dinner the first night there, my cell phone rang. It was my brother Tim.

"Are you kidding me?" he yelled when I picked up. "The lawsuit you filed is all over the goddamn papers and the internet. And then you leave the country while the shit hits the fan?"

"What?" I was floored. "The lawyer told me to go. This was all planned. We filed the suit under Dad's real name. He said nothing would happen."

"Well, it did. And it's happening. You need to come home. Now."

I caught the next flight out to Los Angeles.

Tim wasn't kidding. The news was everywhere—online, in the newspapers, and in all the trade publications. People I hadn't talked to in years were trying to call me. Reporters filled my voicemail with requests for interviews.

As soon as I got home, I called Tim.

"Look," I said before he could start yelling. "I know you're pissed. But please, talk to Karen about what's been going on with Dad. I promise that you'll understand why I had to do this."

Since Father's Day, when I'd called in the welfare check on Dad, Tim and I hadn't spoken. He was still livid, but he agreed to talk to Karen. He loved and respected Karen and would listen to her.

After talking with Karen, Tim called me back. "Jesus. This is absolutely nuts. I had no idea how bad things had gotten." He sighed. "Okay, I get it now. I'm in."

I was so relieved that Karen had been able to convince Tim when I hadn't. After being alone in this long fight with none of my family except Karen behind me, it meant everything that Tim was also lending his support to protect our dad.

"I just hope you're ready," Tim said, "because you know Charlene. This is going to be one hell of a fight."

Chapter 28

THE HEARING TOOK PLACE A FEW DAYS LATER ON A SWELTERING AFTER-noon in late August. Tim, Karen, and I sat on one side of the room with my lawyers. On the other side was Charlene and Jackie, surrounded by about fifteen friends, many of whom I'd known since childhood. They threw us nasty glances and whispered among themselves until the judge called the room to order.

My attorneys had submitted witness declarations from Karen, Jason, Katie, the speech therapist, and a former caregiver named Diana as evidence. The statements detailed the poor decision-making and neglect of Dad's medical care that each person had witnessed. When Charlene found out that Jason had submitted a declaration, she was livid. Jason was in the process of becoming a US citizen, and Charlene had threatened to report him to immigration if he cooperated with me. Although he was terrified that this could compromise his citizenship, Jason did it anyway. Knowing she was under scrutiny, Charlene didn't fire Jason immediately, but we all knew it was only a matter of time.

Karen's willingness to make a witness declaration destroyed her relationship with Charlene. She had been eight years old when Charlene became her stepmother. Karen, who spent time in both her parents' homes, came to know and love Charlene, and even when Charlene had divorced her father, Roger (also Jackie's father), they remained very close. Just like me, Karen mourned the Charlene she had loved for so many years. But my dad had been like a second father to her, and she never wavered in her support.

The hearing was over in fifteen minutes. The judge acknowledged that Dad had been bounced from one facility to the next without good reason. He approved our request for a temporary restraining order to keep him in Topanga Terrace while the court decided about his conservatorship. When questioned, Charlene denied that she had been planning on moving Dad to another facility in Ventura County. Then her attorney stood up and asked if there were any exceptions for removing Dad in the case of an emergency. The judge confirmed that he could be taken to a hospital in case of a medical emergency. It wasn't until later that I realized how significant that question was.

I still had my weekly visit with Dad. It was hard to know if he fully understood what was going on. His face always lit up when I walked into the room, and he smiled at funny things we watched on television. But his communication was limited to gentle hand squeezes or a raise of the eyebrows. I chose not to talk to him about my fight with Jackie and Charlene because it only would have made him feel even more helpless and sad.

The following Monday, Labor Day, I was at a friend's house when I got a text from Jason. "They're moving Papa!" It read. "Charlene made up an emergency, so they are moving him."

When I reached Jason on the phone, he told me that Charlene had claimed Dad was choking and demanded he be taken to the hospital. The nurses had examined him and didn't find anything that they felt mandated an emergency. Jason said that Charlene ignored them and made arrangements to have Dad taken to Cedars-Sinai Medical Center. He also mentioned that she was going to meet a woman named Georgina there.

As I drove to the hospital, Jason kept me posted on what was happening. Two men in an unmarked white passenger van had arrived at Topanga Terrace, rolled Dad out on a gurney, and drove off with him. Charlene and Jackie had followed. Jason sent me a picture of the van so I'd be able to identify it.

When I reached the hospital, I parked near the emergency entrance and put on a hooded sweatshirt and a pair of dark sunglasses. I found the white van parked outside, but no one was in it. Inside the lobby, I looked around to see if Charlene or Jackie were there, but didn't see them.

I noticed a woman who looked familiar standing by the information desk. She was with another woman, and they were talking to the receptionist. As I looked closer, I realized it was Tia, a friend of Charlene and

Dad's from the racetrack. The woman with her was her sister, Georgina, who owned the nursing home in Ventura County where Charlene wanted to move Dad. It was the place that Karen had checked out and found to be dismal and remote, lacking the resources necessary to care for a patient in my dad's condition.

It had been years since I'd seen Tia, and with my sunglasses and hoodie on, I was confident she wouldn't recognize me. I lingered by the desk as they got Dad's room number. Then I followed them to the elevator and when the doors opened, I stepped in after them. They were talking about my dad, so I turned on my phone recorder. It seemed like a plan was in place to get Dad moved from the hospital into Georgina's facility.

"Let's just stop in the room and say hi to Charlene," Tia said. "We probably shouldn't hang around."

When we reached Dad's floor and got off, I turned and walked in the opposite direction. Then, concerned that Charlene might see me, I returned to the elevator and went back down.

I was shaking as I sat in my car and listened to my recording of the women's conversation. If there truly had been an emergency, Dad would still be down in the emergency room, getting immediate care. Instead, he'd been taken straight to a hospital room once the van had arrived. I knew this only happened when preparations had been made with the hospital in advance. It was proof that Charlene had falsified an emergency to get Dad out of Topanga Terrace and into the hospital. From there, she planned to have him moved to Georgina's nursing facility in Ventura.

Later, I learned that Charlene had fired Jason before they'd left Topanga Terrace. He never saw my dad again. Jason had been more to my father than merely a hired caregiver. He'd been his friend and companion, making sure Dad was always neatly groomed and dressed. Jason had slept by Dad's bed every night, and when he did take a rare day off, he would call the substitute caregiver for updates. His presence had been one of the reliable comforts Dad had in his life, and now he was gone. Jason would later get a tattoo of Dad's autograph on his arm to honor their time together. I'll always be grateful to him for giving "Papa" so much love and dignity, when he needed it the most.

I immediately called my lawyer to tell them about Dad's removal to the hospital and the conversation I'd recorded in the elevator, which confirmed that Charlene still intended to move him to Ventura County, despite what she'd told the judge. When my lawyer inquired about my visitation days for the hospital, he was told by Charlene's lawyer that she wasn't allowing any visitors. But after some pressure, she relented and said I could see him once a week.

I went to see Dad at the hospital on the first scheduled visit. He was very weak and thin, but he smiled and held out his hands when he saw me. I assured him that we would get him back to his cheerful room at Topanga Terrace once the doctors had given the okay, and he smiled.

When I visited the following week, a strange man was sitting in Dad's room. When I introduced myself, the man said his name was John.

"Are you Dad's new caregiver?" I asked.

"No."

"Then why are you here?"

"I'm a friend of Charlene's," John said.

"Okay. How do you know Charlene?"

"I met her in a bar on Ventura Boulevard. I'm a musician."

Charlene, who slept most of the day, was going to bars? Exactly who was this man?

"Okay." I could feel anger rising, but I forced myself to stay calm. "Well, John, would you mind stepping out for a while so that I can visit with my dad?"

"I can't. I promised Charlene that I wouldn't leave the room." He seemed genuinely sorry.

A little while later, John had put his headphones on and seemed to be dozing off. Sitting by the bed, I took Dad's hands in mine and rested my head on his arm.

"Dad," I said, "I don't know why you're here. I don't know why things have become so terrible. Just know that I love you so much, and all I want is for you to be happy and comfortable." When I looked up, tears were streaming down his face. I took a tissue and gently wiped his face, and mine, too, since I was now crying. "I promise I'm doing everything I can to help you, Dad."

Later I got a call from my lawyer.

"I just heard from Charlene's attorney," he said. "She's trying to stop your visits because she says you upset your father."

"Upset him?" I said. "Yes, my dad cries, yes. But it's because Charlene's terrible decisions are making his life miserable."

"Well, this is no reason to deny your visits. They're just grasping at straws. But I wanted you to know."

One day when I was visiting, a new doctor came into the room. John was sitting in his usual chair, reading a magazine. I said hello to the doctor, waiting for him to ignore me. But instead, he held out his hand.

"I'm Dr. Gonzales," he said. "You must be Kelly."

"May I ask you a few questions about my dad?" I said, after our introductions.

Dr. Gonzales nodded.

"Okay. First, why is Dad here in the hospital?"

"Because he's having more tests done."

"And after the tests are done, can he go back to Topanga Terrace? He was really happy there, and I think that's where he should be. They're even holding his room for him."

"Which facility he goes to is not my decision to make. But in his current condition, it needs to be a skilled facility, not an assisted living home."

"You do know that my stepmother wants to move him to a place in Ventura County, right? We have looked into it, and we don't think it is suitable."

"That facility is not the level your father needs," Dr. Gonzales said. "I would not authorize him to go there."

I sighed in relief. "Thank you, Doctor."

Before he walked out of the room, he turned to me.

"Look, I know what's going on with you and your stepmother," he said. "And I want you to know that I'm not here to be anyone's friend or take sides. I'm here to give your dad the best care I can, and that's all I care about."

"I'm so relieved to hear that," I said. "That's all I want for my dad."

"I can see right through your stepmother and your stepsister," he continued. "They certainly have their opinions about what should be done, but I will do what I can to protect your father." His words filled me with hope. Finally, a doctor who wasn't going to be bullied by Charlene and Jackie.

Dad stayed in the hospital while the judge decided the case. My lawyer said that getting legal conservatorship from Charlene would be difficult, but he thought we had a chance. I also stated that my intentions for getting guardianship of Dad had nothing to do with financial gain. Money is often at the center of high-profile legal battles, and I wanted to make it clear to the court that it never once played a role in my actions to protect my dad. As far as I was concerned, Dad's bills and expenses could be handled by a third party. But as our battle became public, Charlene would go on to spread lies that I was only after Dad's money.

After Dad had been in Cedars-Sinai for about a month, I got word that he had been discharged and moved to another nursing facility on the edge of Van Nuys. After another round of lawyer calls back and forth to find out the address and arrange new visitation days, I drove over to see him.

Before I even got out of my car, I was devastated. The facility was in a part of town with graffiti-covered abandoned buildings and trash-strewn vacant lots. Inside, the smell of urine and unwashed bodies filled the stifling air.

I found Dad's room with the door wide open to all of the chaos and noise in the hall. He was asleep, so I tiptoed around the room and took photos. Mildewed broken tiles in the bathroom. Dirty linen piled up in the corner. A tray of old food with a fly buzzing around it. Outside the grimy window, cars on busy Sepulveda Boulevard honked and roared by all day and night. All I could think about was the bright, clean room back at Topanga Terrace that was still available for Dad.

A place like Topanga Terrace was costly, but money wasn't the issue for my dad. I knew the reasons why Charlene would never send him back there. She and Jackie had quarreled with the primary doctor and staff at Topanga Terrace when they'd been prevented from having their way. Topanga Terrace was a place where Dad could have lived out his life in comfort and privacy, but it wasn't going to let Jackie play doctor. And for Charlene and Jackie, having that control was far more important. Even if Dad had to pay the price.

Chapter 29

Dad's new caregiver matched the grim surroundings of the Van Nuys nursing home. She spent most of her time with her eyes glued to her phone except when she lifted them to shoot me a scornful glare. She didn't speak, not even to answer my greeting when I walked in the door. The shadow that her sullen presence cast against the loss of bright, dependable Jason was a terrible blow for Dad. Someone—Jackie, I guessed—had dragged an air mattress into the room and wedged it in the small space by Dad's bed. The caregiver would lie on it with her phone, never moving an inch when I stepped around her to sit by Dad. It took everything in my power not to give her a hard kick.

A few days later, I arrived for my visit and found Dad's bed empty. My heart pounded in panic as I searched the halls for someone who could tell me where he was. One of the nurses said that Dad had gone to the emergency room, but she didn't have any further information. Tears dripped onto my phone as I called my lawyer, who then put a call into Charlene's lawyer to find out what had happened. Three hours later, my lawyer called back. He'd learned that Dad had been taken to a local hospital after the nursing home had given the wrong dose of medication.

Dad was sent to the emergency room four times during his stay at the Van Nuys facility. Each visit was determined to be caused by the mismanagement of his medication by the staff. Through my lawyer, I pressured Charlene to find a more-suitable place for Dad. "They're going to kill him at that place," I told Karen. "It's only a matter of time." Meanwhile, I was visiting Dad every day that I was allowed. When a nurse walked in to give him medication, I stood over her shoulder to watch.

One day I walked in and found Dad's room empty once again. The air mattress was gone, and the bed was stripped of its sheets. The staff said

Dad had been sent to the ER, again, and added that he wasn't coming back this time.

Tim called Charlene to try to find out what had happened to Dad, but she never picked up or called back. My lawyer couldn't get an answer. Karen hit the phones and called all of the hospitals in Los Angeles but couldn't find a trace of Dad. Two agonizing days went by when we had no idea if Dad was dead or alive. I couldn't eat or sleep, wondering if I would ever see him again.

On the second day, I broke down and went to the police station to file a missing person's report. After listening to my story, the police officer told me that Dad wasn't technically a missing person.

"He may be missing to you," he said. "But he has a wife who you admit is his legal guardian, and she would have to be the one to file a report. If he's missing to *her*, that is."

"But I'm his daughter!" I said. "And I'm extremely concerned about his well-being."

The officer gave me a sad smile. "I realize that. But under the law, he's not considered a missing person. I'm sorry."

Again, my hands were tied. Charlene could whisk Dad anywhere she wanted and not tell me a thing. As his daughter, but not his guardian, I had no rights whatsoever.

At the end of day two, an e-mail from the lawyers arrived in my in-box. It said that Dad was in a new facility in another part of the Valley called Lake Balboa Care Center, and that I could visit him the next day between eleven a.m. and two p.m. There was no other information. I was furious that the message had been sent by e-mail instead of a phone call when we were all so desperate for news, but was nonetheless flooded with relief, knowing that Dad was still alive.

The Lake Balboa facility was across the street from my old high school. It was not nearly as nice as Topanga Terrace, but it was somewhat of an improvement over the last place. A cheerful young woman greeted me at the front desk. When I told her who I was there to see, she scanned her computer to find Dad's room number.

I was nervous walking into his room, not knowing what condition I'd find him in. A new caregiver was sitting next to the bed where Dad lay sleeping. She looked up and gave a welcoming smile.

Just then, Dad opened his eyes and turned his head. When he saw me, he beamed in recognition, and I rushed over and hugged him as tight as I could.

Dad was weaker than I'd ever seen him, but his eyes sparkled, and he squeezed my hand as I talked to him. The newest caregiver, Mena, brought a chair for me to sit next to the bed.

"Mr. Tim is so happy to see you," Mena exclaimed. "I think he has been waiting all this time just for you!"

I could tell Mena was a gentle and attentive person and that she was taking good care of Dad. I was so grateful for her kindness to him, and to me, that I nearly cried. The air mattress was there on the floor, but this room was a little bigger so it wasn't in the way. Mena had made the mattress up neatly, where the other caregiver had just piled it with wrinkled blankets and pillows.

A few minutes later, a woman stepped into the room.

"Mena," she said, pointedly not looking at me. "Is everything okay in here?"

"Yes," Mena said. "Everything is fine. Tim's daughter is here visiting."

"Would you mind stepping out for a moment? I want to show you, umm, where we're keeping the graham crackers now."

Mena and I glanced at each other as she walked out into the hall.

As soon as the door closed, I jumped up and pressed my ear against the crack to listen.

"We are not supposed to let her in here!" the woman said.

"Why not?" Mena asked.

"Because she's crazy!"

I opened the door and smiled innocently. "Is everything okay?"

"You're not on the visitation list," the woman said. "You should not have been let in. I'm going to get my supervisor."

"Yes, go get your supervisor."

As I watched, she marched down the hall into the lobby, where I could see her gesticulating angrily at the friendly receptionist who had given me Dad's room number.

I went back in to sit with Dad, and a few minutes later, a man walked in. He introduced himself as the facility's administrator and asked me to come to his office.

"What did you say your name is?" he asked once we were seated.

"I'm Kelly Conway. Tim Conway's daughter. And I have the legal authority to visit him."

"Well, we were given strict orders by Mrs. Conway not to let anyone in to see Mr. Conway whose name is not on this list." He handed the sheet over to me. "Do you see your name here?"

I was trembling in anger. I didn't need to see this list to know my name wasn't on it.

"I don't care," I said, handing the list back. "The court said I could see my dad. And I'm going to see him."

The administrator sighed.

"Look, if you're allowed to see your dad, I will not keep you from it. But can you give me a few hours to make some calls and get this straightened out? I'm just trying to do my job. Give me your number, and I'll call you once I get everything cleared."

"Okay, I'll go out for a little while. But if I don't hear from you in two hours, I'm coming back to see my dad."

On the way out, I caught the glance of the friendly receptionist.

"I'm so sorry," I mouthed, and she smiled. I felt terrible that she had been yelled at because of me.

I spent the next hour sitting in the empty football stadium of my old high school across the street. I thought back to my high school graduation, and how angry I had been at both of my parents for not sitting together. And then my relief when Dad later married Charlene, giving me a stepmother I knew and loved.

Now, so many years later, here we were, a family torn to shreds. And Dad was helpless to do anything about it.

My phone rang. It was the administrator telling me I could return to Lake Balboa to see Dad. After a back-and-forth with the lawyers, my name was added to the visitation list.

I went to see Dad every day that I didn't have to work. By now, Mena and I had become friends, and I would bring her a coffee and pastry when I came.

Mena was from Belize, and she and her husband were raising a teenage daughter. Mena doted on Dad, and I could tell he liked her, too. I gave Mena some DVDs of Dad's shows, and she told me that her daughter sat and watched them for hours. "Mr. Tim has a new fan!" she said happily.

Dad was fading. He was getting thinner and slept a lot. I brought movies I knew he liked, such as *Field of Dreams*, *Big*, and *Breakfast at Tiffany's*. Mena told me Charlene didn't want me to watch them with Dad, but I continued because I knew he enjoyed them.

When my visiting time was over and I said good-bye, Dad would start crying. Sometimes I would be so upset that I'd have to sit in my car in the parking lot until I'd calmed down enough to drive home. Even though I was getting no new information from the doctors about Dad's status, I could tell he was slowly slipping away. It fired my determination to make what life he had left as comfortable and happy as possible.

Dad's room at Lake Balboa had no decorations, pictures, or color. I decided to put my talent and skills as a stylist to work and make over Dad's room in the same style as his old home office. I bought a roll of green plaid fabric and sewed a pair of curtains, which I hung on a brass rod. Then I spread two plaid patchwork quilts and matching throw pillows over Dad's bed and the air mattress. There was a small corkboard against one wall that Dad could see if he turned his head, so I put up some photos of Dad with my brothers and me, a picture of him with Harvey.

I'd found a shelf that looked like a smaller version of the beautiful oak bookshelf Dad had had in his old home office. It was just big enough to hold the DVD player, one of his vintage toy trucks, and some framed photos of Dad with friends and family. I also left a couple of empty frames with a sticky note for Charlene and Jackie to put in their photos if they wanted.

Finally, I splurged on a thick cable-knit cashmere throw for Dad, similar to one he'd had at home. I worked quietly and quickly so as not to disturb anyone while Dad watched from the bed, smiling when I looked over at him.

"Amazing!" Mena exclaimed when she saw the room. "See, Mr. Tim, now you have photos of your beautiful family to look at. Kelly, I think your father is very happy."

I couldn't visit Dad the next day because I had to work, but I went the following morning.

When I walked into Dad's room, I froze mid-step. All the decor I had so lovingly added was gone. The plaid curtains and throw pillows I'd sewn, the pretty bookshelf with the vintage toy truck, and all of the framed photos. Even Dad's cashmere throw was missing.

Mena looked at me sadly from where she sat next to Dad, who was sleeping.

"She take it all down," she said. "Miss Charlene says it makes your dad very sad to see all of these things."

Mena stood and opened a closet. Inside, all of the items were balled up and stuffed into the small space. I blinked back tears, picking up the soft cashmere throw heaped on the closet floor.

"Even this?" I said softly. "He can't even have his throw?"

"She says he has allergies to it," Mena said, shaking her head. We both knew that was bullshit.

Later as I was driving home, my lawyer called.

"What's this about curtains and pillows in your dad's room?" he asked, sounding irritated.

"I just wanted his room to look nice," I shot back. "What's wrong with that?"

"Well, it was pretty bold of you."

"Bold?" I repeated. "Because I wanted to make my dad more comfortable?"

"Kelly, you had to know this would piss off your stepmother. You're not helping your case if you keep pushing her like this."

"This is ridiculous," I said. "It has absolutely nothing to do with me trying to piss off Charlene. I'm just trying to make Dad more comfortable. That room is like a prison cell. He lies in that bed every day and stares at a blank wall. What is the harm of having things around that he recognizes and loves?"

After we hung up, I was furious at my lawyer's contempt. Wasn't he supposed to be on my side? I wondered how much money that one phone call would cost me. I'd used up a lot of my savings to hire the lawyer, and every time he called me, or called Charlene's lawyer, or sent an e-mail, hundreds—even thousands—of dollars were added to the bill. Wanting to spend as much time with Dad as I could, I had turned down jobs that were out of town or required too many days away. Tim had offered to help, but he was supporting a family, and I said I would cover the legal fees on my own. But I wasn't sure how much longer I could continue.

"I talked with Charlene's attorney," the lawyer told me a few days later. "He says she's agreed to try mediation to see if we can work some things out."

"Mediation?" I said. "Fine. I'm willing to try anything. I just hope we can work something out soon, because honestly, I don't think my dad has much time left."

Chapter 30

Mediation is when two parties voluntarily negotiate terms through a trained go-between, an impartial third party. An entire mediation industry has been built around people's inability to speak face-to-face without coming to verbal or physical altercations. The idea is to get each side in the same building—but not the same room—where the mediator can go back and forth between the two parties during the negotiations. It is often a last attempt to get each party to agree before resorting to a long and expensive court battle.

The night before the mediation appointment, my lawyer phoned and said Charlene had canceled due to illness. We set another date for a week later, but she canceled that one, too. I was livid because, in both cases, I had turned down a job in order to attend the mediation.

Eventually we scheduled a third appointment, and this time, Charlene and Jackie showed up..

The mediation office was located in a high-rise in downtown Los Angeles. Karen was along to lend support, but my heart was pounding as we stepped off the elevator, anxious about coming face-to-face with Charlene and Jackie. A receptionist immediately whisked us into a conference room where my attorney was waiting. He explained that all of the meeting rooms were spaced on opposite ends of the office to keep the mediating parties from ever seeing each other. The room was very comfortable, with leather chairs, a mini-fridge filled with drinks, and glass walls offering stunning views across the city to the hills beyond.

The mediator came in and introduced himself as Judge Powell. He was a silver-haired retired LA judge, friendly and talkative. We went over my requests which he would present to Charlene. I'd put in everything that I wanted, from the number of visitation days with Dad to access to his medical records. I knew that Charlene would probably not agree to everything I had asked for, but I was confident that Judge Powell could get us somewhere in the middle.

When he left to talk to Charlene about the first term, visitation, Karen and I glanced at each other and smiled nervously.

Judge Powell returned about an hour later.

"Mrs. Conway won't negotiate on visitation," he said.

"What do you mean?" I asked.

"She doesn't want you to have any visits with your dad."

"That's not happening. She has to give me some visitation."

"Look, try not to get upset," the judge said. "Sometimes it takes a while for people to ease up. Why don't we go on to the next item, and we'll come back to visitation later?"

I looked at my lawyer, and he nodded.

Judge Powell left to go speak with Charlene again, and while we waited for him lunch arrived on a rolling cart. The plates held a selection of gourmet meals—seared scallops, ravioli with shaved truffles, dandelion and apricot salads, and other delicacies you'd expect to find at a high-end restaurant. When Karen joked that everything looked good and she couldn't choose, the attendant told us to take as many plates as we wanted.

So far, I was feeling optimistic about the mediation experience. Maybe Judge Powell was right, and Charlene just needed a little more time to soften up before she started to play ball.

Judge Powell returned, and I thought he looked a little more deflated than before.

"Well," he said, "she won't budge on allowing you access to the medical records."

"She won't budge?" I repeated.

"No, she doesn't want you to see any of them."

"If she had a good reason to keep me from seeing his records, I would agree with it. But she doesn't."

"Well, she has power of attorney, so it is her right." The judge sighed. "Let's move on to item three, your immediate notification of any serious change in your dad's health status."

By the time the coffee and dessert tray rolled around, I started to think the entire mediation process was just a huge waste of time. Still, my attorney urged me to stay optimistic.

"It's just a quarter past one," he said. "Sometimes things come together at the last minute. Charlene's just trying to intimidate you."

Hours later, after Judge Powell had come and gone countless times, we had accomplished nothing. Charlene wouldn't even counter my requests. She simply refused to give me anything.

I had arrived that morning feeling confident that this would be the day I'd finally achieve something in my fight for access to and better care for my dad. But now, we had wasted an entire day for nothing. We should have been with Dad, but instead we were all cloistered in this office sipping cappuccinos as our lawyers racked up their bills.

"Fuck this," I said to my lawyer. "I want to go to trial."

As I began shoving my folders into my bag, I could feel the ghost of my mother, defiant and impenetrable, filling me with blind courage. Dad used to joke that I became "Mary Anne 2.0" whenever I got really angry.

"Kelly," the attorney said, "if you go to trial, it will cost you a fortune. And you'll probably lose anyway."

"I don't care. I'll live in a box under that highway if I have to." I pointed out the window to the 110 freeway, choked with rush-hour traffic. "If she won't even give me one day with my dad, I want to go to court."

"Let's try this one more time," the lawyer begged. "I know Charlene's attorney is pissed that she won't cooperate, and I'm sure he'll try to talk some sense into her. Come on, one more time."

I agreed to one more mediation a week later.

The back-and-forth had been exhausting and only added to my frustration, not to mention my attorney's fees. But if anything, I was becoming stronger. There was no limit to the lengths I would go to protect my dad.

Before the next mediation, I spent a few days making a visual storyboard around each of my requests. I'd printed out all of my notes and neatly pasted them onto foam-board panels, along with photos documenting the squalid places Charlene had placed Dad. There was a list of every doctor who'd been replaced, charts showing the timeline of Dad's move from one facility to another, and statements from witnesses. If Judge Powell was going to fight for me, he needed to see the whole story.

On the morning of the next appointment, I arrived almost an hour early. Karen wasn't with me this time, but the nervousness I'd had at the first session was gone. At the first mediation, I'd hoped that I wouldn't run into Charlene because it would have been awkward. Now, I almost wished she'd walk in so that I could look her in the eye.

In the meeting room, I set up my displays along the length of the window ledge. When Judge Powell came in, he looked each one over carefully.

"You've certainly done your homework," he said.

"Yes, I have. And here's what I want." I pulled out a freshly typed list of my requests and pushed it across the table:

- Visiting hours every day, from 9:00 a.m. to 3:00 p.m.
- Full access to health providers and records on Dad's health care.
- In case of severe decline in condition, access to see Dad any time of day.
- Immediate notification if Dad is moved to a hospital or another facility.

Judge Powell took the list and left the room. A little while later, he came back.

"Okay. She will give you four visitation days a week."

"I want five," I said.

He left and came back.

"She agreed to three-hour visits five days a week. But no weekends."

"I have to have a weekend day. For football. My dad and I have always watched football together."

The judge shot me a look of irritation. "Are you kidding me? I just got you five visitation days, and you're worried about football? Why don't you just record the game and then take it to watch with him later. He'll never know."

"I can't believe you just said that. That is an awful thing to say about my dad."

The judge flushed to the roots of his gray hair.

"I apologize. Let me see what I can do."

Again, he left the room.

"Okay," he said when he came back, slapping the paper on the table. "I got you Monday-night football. Instead of seeing him Monday morning, you can visit him that evening."

I thought for a minute. "As long as Charlene is gone by five so I can be there for the pregame shows, I'll accept that."

"Well, I'll be," Judge Powell said. "We finally agreed to something."

For the rest of the day, we negotiated back and forth down the list. When the lunch cart came around, I shook my head. I didn't want their gourmet food, and was disgusted that so much money, and two full days, had been wasted on something Charlene and I should have been able to do ourselves. All I wanted from this place now was to get my requests approved and documented and get back to spending time with my dad.

By the end of the day, we had a list of agreed-upon terms that both Charlene and I had signed off on. I could see Dad five days a week for three hours each visit. I'd be notified immediately if Dad's health took a turn for the worse. A new doctor would be hired to replace Dr. Z, who I suspected was giving Charlene and Jackie pain pills. The agreement also stipulated that Dad would only receive medications prescribed to him by his acting physicians, effectively barring Charlene and Jackie from giving him any drugs on their own. I would have access to his medication list. We also agreed that an independent care manager, called an ICM, would be assigned as a go-between for Charlene and me. The ICM would manage our visitation schedules and pass on information to me about Dad's care from his doctors. In return, I agreed to stop the lawsuit against Charlene seeking Dad's conservatorship.

I left feeling exhausted but relieved. With signed legal documents in place binding Charlene to the terms, I could concentrate on just being with Dad.

The very next morning, Charlene broke one of our agreements.

As soon as I arrived at Lake Balboa, I asked to see Dad's medication list. I wanted to copy it to go over it later with Karen. The nurse hesitated and left the room, returning with the administrator in tow. Before he said anything, I pulled a copy of the signed agreement from my bag and handed it to him.

"I have the legal authority to see my dad's medical records." I handed him the document. "This is a signed and legal copy of the agreement from our mediation."

"I understand," he said. "But we still cannot give medical records to anyone unless Mrs. Conway signs off on them. And she hasn't done that yet."

"Okay, can you please try calling her?" Even though it was eleven a.m., I doubted Charlene or Jackie would be up yet.

A few minutes later, the administrator returned.

"No one answered. I'm sorry, but that is our rule. I cannot give you the records until she signs off."

"Please keep trying to call her. She has to pick up eventually. I'll be with my dad in his room."

Although I was angry about being denied the records, I was happy to see Dad five days a week. When he was awake, I would tell him about things that were going on at work or what my brothers were doing. We watched movies and TV shows, even though Charlene had texted Mena to tell me that I couldn't watch them with Dad. She had thrown away the movies that I had brought.

From her phone Mena read a message from Charlene: "Kelly should do things with Tim that she's good at, like watercolors or something." I was astounded at Charlene's warped sense of what would bring my dad enjoyment. I knew he liked watching the old shows and movies, and we continued to do so.

Each day I visited, Dad was weaker. I desperately wanted to see his medical records to share with Karen, who would be able to explain them to me, but Charlene still hadn't given her permission. I was also anxious for the independent care manager to come on board.

At the end of the week, I e-mailed my lawyer.

"It's been over a week since we signed the agreement," I fumed. "And Charlene has already broken one of the terms. Also, where is the ICM? I could really use their help. My dad is getting worse."

He wrote back: "I know what the agreement says; I wrote it. These things take time. Try to be patient. The judge was hoping that you and Charlene would work together until the ICM is on board."

Now I was mad.

"The judge was *hoping?* I had no idea that our justice system was based on hope. I am following all the rules, as was agreed. I wasn't allowed to visit my dad this past weekend, and his caregiver told me that no one else visited him either. So he was there alone for two days. If I had gone to visit on the weekend, Charlene would have a restraining order placed on me. And you want *me* to be patient?"

The lawyer promised to look into it. Two weeks later, after the lawyers went back and forth, I was able to see Dad's medical records. But a month went by before I got a call from the ICM, a woman named Annette. We made plans to meet at Dad's facility.

Annette came across as friendly and professional. She explained that Dad's new doctor, Dr. Meyers, would be taking over his care. Annette was also responsible for managing visits to Dad, and I would inform her when I had to miss one of my scheduled visits due to work conflicts.

When I asked if we could go over the agreement list signed by Charlene and me, I was surprised that she didn't have a copy. I had started keeping extra copies in my car, just in case, so I ran out and got one.

Over the next week, Dad was heavily sedated and slept most of the time I was with him. I needed to speak with Dr. Meyers, but I could only reach him through Annette. She informed me that some of the new drugs Dad was taking were causing his extreme drowsiness, and that she, too, was concerned.

"I'll talk to Dr. Meyers and get back to you," she texted. But days went by without an answer.

I received a job offer from a longtime client to shoot in San Diego for a few days. I hated to miss even one visit with Dad, but I needed the money.

Before accepting the job, I tried to get ahold of Annette to be sure there was no reason I shouldn't leave town. I couldn't reach her by phone for more than a week, and her voicemail was full. I sent numerous texts and e-mails. Finally, I sent her an e-mail that I was going out of town for a few days for work but would be accessible by phone any time, day or night.

Before I left for San Diego, I visited Dad and sat with him while he slept. Mena was there too, and she promised to take good care of him while I was gone.

"I know you will, Mena. You're incredible to my dad."

I looked down at his sleeping face. "Do you think he knows I'm here, even though he's so sedated?"

"Oh, yes," Mena said. "He always knows when you are here, Kelly. I am with him so much of the time, and I can tell by his face when he is happy or sad. And when you are here, he is very, very happy."

Chapter 31

I was up early in my hotel room in San Diego, preparing for the day's shoot, when Annette texted me.

"I hate to tell you this over text," the message read, "but your father is not doing well. I found out that he's been put on hospice."

I called her back immediately.

"What exactly does this mean?" I cried when she picked up. "Does he have hours left? Days? Are you telling me that he's dying right this minute?"

"I'm not completely sure," she said. "But you might want to come and see him today."

"I'm in San Diego, but I'll leave now and can be there by eleven." I was already pulling on sweatpants and throwing things into bags with my one free hand.

"You're in San Diego?" Annette asked.

"Annette, I told you that I was taking a job out of town. I called, I texted, I e-mailed, and I never heard back from you. If I'd known Dad was getting worse, I never would have left. You haven't answered my messages in over a week!"

"I just found out about it myself," she said defensively. "Charlene refuses to talk to me, so I have to get information from her lawyer."

"Well, I'm entitled to that information, so please try to find out more. I'll call you later."

After cramming my belongings into my suitcase, I dragged a luggage cart loaded with boxes of supplies and a rolling rack of costumes down to the lobby. I called my friend Mark, who was also booked on the job, and told him that I had an emergency and would leave everything for the shoot at the front desk.

The lobby was crowded, with people sitting around drinking coffee and others waiting to check in. My tear-stained face and haggard, half-dressed appearance drew curious looks.

The drive back to Los Angeles was the worst two and a half hours of my life. I wasn't sure if my dad would still be alive when I got there, and I cried nearly the entire way, pausing only to call Karen, Tim, and some of my other brothers. I also tried reaching Annette to see if she knew anything more, but she didn't answer her phone.

At eleven a.m. I pulled into the Lake Balboa facility and rushed inside.

Dad was sleeping, but his eyes flickered when I held his hand.

"Hi, Daddy. You would not have liked how fast I drove to get here from San Diego."

A new caregiver was sitting in the room. I could tell immediately by her demeanor that she would not talk to me, so I just ignored her.

While Dad slept, I looked over the medication list and noticed many new drugs on it, including morphine and Ativan. I took some notes so I could consult later on with Karen and, hopefully, the hospice nurse. Then I opened the closet and looked through Dad's shirts and sweaters. I took out a dark green polo shirt, a color that brought out the green in his eyes. Tears welled in my eyes, and I folded the shirt up and slipped it into my bag. I had no idea if this would be the last time I'd ever see my dad, and I desperately needed a piece of him to take with me.

I sat down next to his bed. His face looked drawn and tired, even when asleep.

"Daddy," I whispered. "If you need to go now, it's okay. I'm fine. I have Tim close by, and so many wonderful friends, and they will all take good care of me. I love you so much. And we'll see each other again." I leaned down and rested my head against his shoulder. "And by the way, I'm stealing your green polo shirt."

I stayed with Dad until the very last second of my visitation time.

In the parking lot, I sat in my car and sobbed for a few minutes. Then I called my lawyer.

"What do you mean, no one told you that your dad is on hospice care?" he said. "This is absurd. I'm calling Charlene's lawyer right now."

As soon as I hung up, a text from Annette flashed on my phone.

"What's this about you taking clothes from your dad's closet? Why would you do that? This does not help your situation. As of today, your visiting rights have ended."

I was shocked. It had only been twenty minutes since I'd left Dad's room. I realized that the new caregiver must have called Charlene and told her I'd taken Dad's shirt.

My whole body was numb as I redialed my lawyer.

"They can't do this," the lawyer said. "Keep visiting your dad during your regular visiting hours. I have a call in to Charlene's attorney to get this straightened out."

When I got home, I called Dr. Meyers. He told me that Dad had been placed on hospice care eight days before.

"Why did no one tell me this?" I said. "Or tell one of my brothers? This is our father!"

"You must have known this was coming, Kelly," Dr. Meyers said. "Your dad is suffering from a terminal disease, and this is how these things progress."

"I realize that. But no one will tell me anything about what's going on. I have no idea if he's expected to live another day or another month. Why can't anyone just talk to me?"

Dr. Meyers sighed. "I think you and your stepmother should just work this out between the two of you."

I gave a bitter laugh. "Doctor, with all due respect, nothing's going to get worked out. Do you have any idea what's been happening?"

"Well, this is the end of your dad's life. Maybe if you two could just sit down—"

"Can you please tell me which hospice is taking care of my dad?" I interrupted. "I have some questions for them."

He hesitated. "I can't give you that information."

"Have you even been to see my dad lately?"

"Well, not in a few weeks, but—"

"Never mind."

I hung up the phone.

On the way home, I stopped at a bookstore and bought a couple of books about hospice. I was reading one of them when Annette called a few hours later.

"I'm still going to see my dad," I told her. "No one is stopping me from that. But I want to talk to the hospice nurse who is taking care of him, because I have some questions."

"Per Charlene's lawyers, I cannot give you that information," she said.

"Yes, you can, Annette." I was trying hard not to explode. "If you refer to the agreement list that we both signed—I gave you a copy, remember?—it says I am to have access to his health-care records. It also states that I'm to be notified immediately should my dad be placed on end-of-life care, but that rule was broken over a week ago."

"I can only tell you certain things, Kelly," she said. "And Charlene won't talk to me herself. I go through her lawyer."

"Regardless, you're supposed to be working for *both* of us. And I don't think you are being completely honest with me."

"Charlene is paying me," Annette said abruptly. "And those are my orders."

"It doesn't matter who is paying you. And besides, it is my dad's estate who is paying you, not Charlene."

"It is what it is. I can't tell you anything else."

"So, when does the independent part of your job kick in? Aren't you supposed to be neutral in all of this? You may be a care manager, but you're definitely not independent. In fact, it all sounds pretty unethical to me."

"I'm about to meet with another client," Annette said. "We can talk about this later."

The next morning when I arrived for my visit, I was half expecting the staff to try to bar me from Dad's room or run to call the administrator. But no one said anything.

I was relieved to find Mena was the caregiver on duty, and we talked quietly while Dad slept.

"I just don't understand what's going on," I confided to Mena. "I understand why my dad has been put on hospice, but no one will talk to me. Isn't hospice also supposed to be a support for the patient's family?"

I'd spent the night reading my book about hospice care, trying to learn more.

"Yes," Mena said. "They are. But Charlene, she makes it so hard for you. I don't know why."

"They won't even tell me the name of his hospice! I spent the entire morning calling all the hospices in the LA area, but none of them has Dad as a patient. And there are so many—I don't think I could call every single one."

"They may not tell you anyway, Kelly. You know, with the privacy laws. If I knew, I would tell you. And I wouldn't care if Charlene got mad." She reached over and squeezed my hand.

Throughout the week, my brothers came to see our dad. Although none of us mentioned it, they understood that they were probably saying good-bye.

I kept calling Annette to ask questions, and she continued to be evasive. From my books, I learned that many hospice patients are allowed to die in the comfort of their own homes, surrounded by familiar things and people. I hated the thought of Dad spending his last days in the nursing home, with its dark rooms and institutional smells. I remembered how much Dad had loved looking out the big window at their condo, quietly taking in the view of trees, distant hills, and blue sky. Hospice would provide in-home medical care, and the caregivers could do everything else. Why couldn't Dad go home?

I asked Annette if she thought there was a chance that Dad might go home on hospice care, and she replied that she didn't think so. She did agree with me that he should be moved someplace better than Lake Balboa. "I'm talking to Charlene's lawyer about this now," she texted.

My hopes were dashed when Annette messaged me a few days later. "Charlene doesn't want to move your dad. And I agree with her."

When I wrote back asking why they had come to this decision, her reply was abrupt.

"We just don't want to move him. There's no negotiating this."

I realized that Dad would never get out of Lake Balboa.

A few days later, Annette e-mailed me. She said that Charlene wanted to be with Dad every day and would even sleep in his room, so now my visiting hours were cut from three hours each day to just one. Our mediation agreement had stipulated that when Dad was in the end-of-life stage, I would get more time with him, not less.

But I was tired of fighting. Now all I wanted was the chance to be with Dad peacefully, without the stress of battling Charlene.

One day I walked into Dad's room for my one-hour visit and was startled to find Charlene there. I hadn't seen her since the day we were in court, nearly two months before. For a moment, we just looked at each other as I stood frozen in the doorway. Then she put her book down and stood up.

"Hello, Kelly. I'm going to leave now so that you can visit with your father." And she walked past me out of the room.

Mena told me that Charlene had been staying with Dad all day and spent the nights sleeping on the recliner next to his bed.

At one point, I left Dad's room to find some clean washcloths and saw Charlene sitting in the lobby. She looked tired and sad. For a moment, I had an impulse to go over, kneel next to her, and hug her. If only one gesture could erase all of the anger and ugliness that had come between us, and we could be the close friends that we had once been. We were the two women that Dad loved more than anything, and he needed both of us. Working together, we could have made this time so much brighter for him. And we could have supported each other, too.

Oh, Daddy, I thought as I turned away. *How very, very different things could have been.*

Chapter 32

My dad left this world on the morning of May 14, 2019.

A few hours later, the media began to pick up on the news and my friend Jill, three hours ahead in New York, saw it and immediately texted me. When she realized that I hadn't heard yet, Jill felt terrible. But I was glad that I had learned it from a dear friend before I'd turned on the television or looked through the news on my phone.

Charlene hadn't bothered to call, or even text, me or any of my brothers when Dad passed away. It was the last punch to the gut in a long and painful battle.

As they learned about Dad's passing, friends and family reached out, wanting to know when the memorial would be so that they could make plans to fly into town. My lawyer contacted Charlene's lawyer to get the information, but there was no reply. In the meantime, Roger Neal, who had been Dad's publicist, helped me send out a release acknowledging Dad's passing on behalf of my brothers and me. I spent a lot of time calling friends and relatives while we anxiously waited for news. We still had no idea if Charlene planned to have Dad cremated or buried, when there would be a funeral, and if we would even be invited.

Finally, nearly five days later, my brothers and I received a group text from Charlene: "Your father's funeral will be May 23 at the Good Shepherd Church in Beverly Hills. Visitation for me and my family is the day prior, but none of you are invited to it." She went on to say that we could visit Dad the following day for one hour before the funeral Mass, in the chapel at Pierce Brothers Memorial Park in Westwood.

Charlene added that a wake was planned after the funeral at the Four Seasons Hotel in Beverly Hills, down the street from the church. She said that my brothers and I would be allowed one guest each for the wake.

We realized that the people flying in for the funeral, and others who had known and loved our dad, wouldn't be able to attend. Tim and I decided that we'd plan our own wake for Dad so that everyone could come. We chose Barone's Italian restaurant in the Valley, which had been one of Dad's favorite places for decades. My brothers and I had memories of eating there from when we were little, and the cozy, unpretentious atmosphere seemed like the perfect setting to celebrate Dad's life.

My friend Beth immediately said that she would take over planning the wake. Beth has been my friend since we were thirteen, and she had gone above and beyond to be there for me during the past year. "You have your hands full," Beth said. "Let me take care of this." And my friend Natalie flew in from her home in Virginia to be with me. Natalie had supported me during the difficult past year, and her comforting presence during this time was a godsend.

On the morning of the funeral, I drove alone to Pierce Brothers for my visitation with Dad. The cemetery is world-famous for the people who lie at rest there. Marilyn Monroe, Ray Bradbury, and Truman Capote are there, and Dad would be in the company of some of his old friends, like Dean Martin, Merv Griffin, and Don Knotts. The grounds are like a secret garden surrounded by the towering high-rises and condominiums of Westwood. There are fountains, ponds, and flowering shrubs offering a peaceful oasis amid a bustling city. It is a popular place for tourists, with its many famous inhabitants, and as I walked toward the small, A-frame chapel flanked by palm trees, people were wandering through the grave markers and posing for pictures.

A chapel attendant was standing by the front door. When I told him my name he opened it and let me into a small foyer.

"Your father is at the altar," he said, gesturing toward the aisle. "Please take all the time you need."

The pure white interior of the chapel seemed to glow with an ethereal light. Dad's casket sat in front of the altar illuminated by a beam of sunlight that poured in through the tall windows. The upper half of the casket was open, and I knelt next to it on a small kneeler. Dad had on the black tuxedo that he'd worn during his live shows, and his face showed a restful expression, as though he was in the depths of sleep.

I put my hands over his and cried softly for a few minutes.

"God, I'm a mess, Dad," I said softly. I laughed, wiping my nose on the back of my sleeve. "What am I going to do without you? You're the only one who always knew where I was and what I was doing. But I'm going to be fine. Really. And I'll see you in Heaven someday."

Then I pulled two small framed photos of Dad and me from my bag: one, when I was little, and another, more recent.

"Here, Dad," I said as I tucked them down the sides of the casket. "Now, I'll always be with you." Finally, I took six shiny dimes from my pocket that I had taken from my dime jar at home.

Ever since Dad was little, my grandfather, Papa, had advised him to keep a dime in his wallet to make a phone call in case he was ever stranded. Later, dimes became a kind of inside joke with Dad and me because we always found them in random places. Dad would say, "Hey, Kell, I was meeting with the trainer at the stables today, and I looked down and saw this dime lying in the hay. I'll hang onto it for you to add to your collection."

I gently tucked the six dimes into the pocket of Dad's tuxedo jacket. "Here's six dimes for you. One for each kid." I leaned over and kissed his head before turning and walking back up the aisle.

At the door of the chapel, I hesitated. I worried that Charlene and Jackie would find the two framed pictures in the casket and was certain they would have them removed if they knew they were there. I asked the attendant when they would be closing Dad's casket. "Visitation for your father ends in five minutes," he said, glancing at his watch. "So, they will close the casket as soon as you leave."

"Yeah, I think my brothers are too upset to see him. So I'm the last one. Do you think," I asked tentatively, "that you could close the casket while I'm here?"

"Of course," he said kindly. "Let's go do it now."

I stood by watching while the attendant gently closed the lid of Dad's casket. Although it may have seemed morbid to some people, being the last person to see Dad laid to rest was a finality that I hadn't realized I needed. I'd always promised him that I'd be there until the end, and I was.

There were still a couple of hours until the funeral Mass, so I went to Natalie's hotel to change clothes and grab a quick lunch. As we drove to the church, I fiddled with the radio to find the country station I liked. Suddenly Willie Nelson's voice filled the car, and I gasped. It was the song, "Angel Flying Too Close to the Ground," that Dad had said he wanted to be played at his funeral.

"Natalie, this is the song I was telling you about!"

We looked at each other in amazement. The song was at least three decades old and wasn't played very much on the radio anymore. I couldn't help but feel a thrill that some divine intervention had just taken place. Even though Dad's song would not be played at his funeral, the station's DJ had selected it out of thousands of songs to play, at this exact moment. I turned up the volume and sang every word.

The Church of the Good Shepherd is classic Mission Revival Style, white stucco with twin bell towers topped with golden domes. It was beautiful against the clear blue sky, with palm trees on each side.

Karen met us in the church's parking lot, and we walked together toward the main entrance facing Santa Monica Boulevard. But when I saw the crowds of people filing up the stairs, I stopped.

"I don't want to go in the front with all of those people there," I said. "I've been to this church a few times, and I think this side door will take us right in to the altar."

An usher was posted by the door with a guest list. Over her shoulder, I could see Charlene and Jackie standing at the front of the church by the altar. I gave the usher my name and she said, "Oh, Conway! You and your guests are on the right side."

"There's sides?" Natalie muttered. "I thought that was only at weddings."

"Is that stage right?" I asked.

The usher looked confused.

"I mean, are we on the right side facing the priest, or on the priest's right side?"

"Umm, I think you're on the priest's right side if he's looking out at the people," she said.

"I'll catch up with you later," Karen whispered. "I see someone I want to say hello to."

Natalie and I headed down the aisle to find a seat. The church was packed, and people were sitting in the pews and standing in the aisles. I looked for my brothers but couldn't find them in the crowd. The first five rows of pews, which were reserved for family and cordoned off with velvet rope, were all full.

"Shouldn't you be sitting in one of the front pews?" Natalie whispered. "I mean, you are his daughter."

"I'm lucky I'm allowed to be here at all," I whispered back.

Natalie and I found a place in a pew about ten rows back and sat down.

The front of the church was filled with flower displays, dominated by the towering, five-foot-wide mass of white roses that Carol Burnett had sent.

Charlene and Jackie stood at the altar, greeting a line of mourners. I saw so many people from *The Carol Burnett Show*. There were writers, producers, and other people who had worked with Dad over the years. Carol was sitting near Vicki Lawrence. George Schlatter, the well-known producer of *Laugh-In* and countless other hit television shows, and a dear friend of Dad's, was sitting in a pew close to the front. I'd thought that I would have been closer to the front of the church, too, but somehow felt serene where I was.

Suddenly, someone was shouting, startling me out of my meditative peace.

"Don't start this shit with me today!"

I looked up to see that it was Charlene, still standing at the altar. She was pointing in our direction. The people in front of us turned around, so Natalie and I looked over our shoulders, too.

"Yes, Kelly!" Charlene shrieked. "I'm talking to you! Get on *your* side of the church. Don't fuck with me today. Not today!"

I stared back in stunned silence as every person in the church stopped what they were doing and looked at us.

"Come on, Kelly," Natalie said, taking my arm and pulling me out of the pew. "Jeez," she whispered. "I knew you and Charlene didn't get along, but to curse like that in a church, at her husband's funeral? Who does that?"

We found the same usher standing by the door.

"I think you put us on the wrong 'right' side," Natalie said sarcastically. "Think you can find us a seat on the *right* right side this time, please?"

Shaken, we slid into a pew in the first row on the other side of the church, next my brothers. I saw that our friends and extended family were all sitting on this side of the aisle, as well. My cousins Danny and Casey smiled sympathetically at me when I glanced back.

"I bet Charlene thought you sat on that side on purpose," Tim said.

"Really?" I said. "I would never have done that on purpose. Especially today."

Just then Tim's wife, Jennifer, walked up. She was sobbing.

"Jenn!" I cried. "My God, are you okay?"

"No, I'm not okay! I'm leaving!"

"What happened?" I pulled her down next to me and we gathered around to listen.

My sweet sister-in-law, who had never had any quarrel with Charlene, had gone over to offer her condolences.

"Get away from me," Charlene had said. "You drank Kelly's Kool-Aid. Just get the fuck out of here."

Although she was extremely upset, Jennifer calmed down and sat back in the pew next to Tim.

A moment later, Karen appeared. She too was in tears.

She had approached Jackie, her half-sister, hoping that, just for a moment, they could put aside their differences. "Just go fuck yourself," Jackie had said before walking away.

"God Almighty," Natalie said, putting her face in her hands. "We're going to have to set up an emergency hotline for Charlene and Jackie victims."

Even for this one day, when everyone had gathered out of love and respect for my dad, neither Charlene nor Jackie could bring themselves to be civil.

I was relieved when the music started and everyone fell silent.

Dad's casket was borne down the aisle, followed by the priest and rows of altar boys swinging their censers.

When the priest had finished saying Mass, a few people got up to eulogize Dad, including Bob Newhart, who had been a dear friend of Dad's for many years, and the world-famous jockey, Chris McCarron. After Charlene's cruel outburst, it was comforting to hear all of these people speak so lovingly about my dad.

When the service was over, people got up and mingled on their way out of the church. I noticed that some of Dad and Charlene's old friends—many of whom I had known since I was little—averted their eyes when they walked by. It hurt, but after Charlene's earlier behavior, I'm sure many were scared to be seen talking to me.

"Let's go outside," I said. "The hearse will be leaving soon."

But when we walked out, we found that Dad's casket had been driven away so quickly that none of my family had a chance to watch it leave. At the front of the church, we handed out flyers that Beth had printed with directions to Dad's wake at Barone's.

I lost count of how many toasts were given to Dad that night at Barone's, but almost everyone present had some memory of him they wanted to share. We had a large banquet room for our guests, with red leather booths lining the walls and crisp white cloths on the tables. Waiters carried out platters of pizza, spaghetti and meatballs, and salads, which were served buffet- and family-style. Drinks were poured from behind the vintage wood and brass bar. More and more people arrived to pay their respects, and after such a hard day, the feelings of love and camaraderie were beautiful.

A group of us were still there telling stories and sipping red wine when the wait staff was closing up for the night. We thanked them for helping to make the event so special.

As we walked out, I spotted a corner banquette on the far side of the dining room, and suddenly I was transported back thirty years to that same table, where all us kids had sat with Dad and Mom, eating pizza and spaghetti. I turned to my brother Seann.

"Remember how we used to make Mom crazy in that booth over there?"

Seann laughed. He and his wife, Tracy, had stopped by the Four Seasons before coming to Barone's, and he remarked on how different the two wakes were—theirs was solemn and formal, ours, rowdy, relaxed, and full of laughter.

We had no doubt which wake Dad would have wanted to attend.

Chapter 33

At its core, I think love is help. Everybody is having a hard time, so love is really devotion to their struggle. It's when you're committed to helping somebody with their life. Helping them to suffer less . . . helping them to manage their mind and their emotions. When you love someone, you want them to feel good. You want them to be happy. I think love is giving and sharing our gifts for the purpose of nurturing them.

—WILL SMITH

Helping them to suffer less. This line from actor Will Smith, where he defines what he believes love to be, was an epiphany for me. This is the kind of love that is rarely acknowledged. It's easy to love when life is good. The purest form of love comes when we have to fight for the people we love, facing whatever demons arise and never quitting no matter how long or hard the battle gets.

I knew my dad was going to suffer as his disease progressed. I just wanted to do whatever I could to help him suffer less.

During the fight for my dad, there was a point when I wondered if my efforts had been in vain. Most of my money had been spent on lawyers. I'd become estranged from part of my family. But worst of all, I was still unable to help Dad live a happier and more comfortable life. It was an exceptionally low moment during a time of very few highs, and I didn't know if I could gather the strength to continue. Will Smith's words brought clarity to all the pain, frustration, and heartache that I had experienced over the past few years. It was the lift I so desperately needed in order to carry on.

In the end, you could say that I didn't win the battle for my dad. I lost the court case that would have granted me the right to have some say in his end-of-life care. I could not get him back home, where he could have lived out the last of his days in peace and privacy, surrounded by familiar things he loved. And I'd been unable to stop the multiple invasive surgeries that likely contributed to his rapid decline.

But if you ask me if I regret any of it, the answer is no. Fighting for my dad is something I'll be proud of for the rest of my life.

The joyous spirit of Tim Conway lives on through his work, and a whole new generation of comedy enthusiasts is discovering him. He also lives on through the memories of his fans. When someone shares a memory of Dad with me, it's like they're giving me a gift. I could fill another book with all of the stories that Dad's fans have told me over the years. I have come to realize that Dad didn't just belong to me, even though, as his only daughter, I often felt that he did. Dad's love, humor, and kindness reached people whose only access to him was through his shows. He transcended the two-dimensional world of a television screen and truly touched the people who watched him. My dad was as present in their lives as he was in mine.

Some stories were poignant. A very famous actress once took me aside to share a story about my how my dad's comedy had affected her family when she was young. She had grown up in a house with angry, alcoholic parents who fought constantly—except on Saturday nights from ten to eleven p.m. During that hour, her mother and father sat together on the sofa, completely absorbed in *The Carol Burnett Show*. "It was the only peaceful moment in our house," she said, "and I'll always be thankful for that."

I love to think about the joy he brought to people through his comedy, but what makes me really proud is how Dad lived his life. Never once have I heard that he was unkind to anyone, either in his professional or personal life. Dad was generous, loyal, and always aware of other people's feelings. It didn't matter if you were a powerful studio executive or the man who cleaned up the set after everyone had left. Dad liked and respected people for who they were.

Dad rests in a peaceful alcove on the far end of Pierce Brothers Memorial Park. I could find the space blindfolded, but anyone else searching for Dad's grave wouldn't have been able to locate it, because, for nearly two years, it lay behind a blank slab of marble without any nameplate identifying the man within.

After the funeral, I figured it would take some time for the nameplate to be ordered, made, and mounted. But months went by, and the plot remained unmarked. I always brought fresh flowers to fill the small brass vase attached to the slab, but it bothered me that Dad's resting place didn't have his name on it. When a year had passed and there was still no nameplate, I e-mailed Charlene's lawyer, asking if there were plans for one. I never received a reply.

I decided to take matters into my own hands and order the nameplate myself. Again, I wrote to Charlene's lawyer that I was putting in an order and asked if there was anything in particular that Charlene wanted on it. This time, the reply was quick and to the point: "This e-mail is a cease-and-desist notice regarding the grave marker for your father. You have no right to interfere with anything having to do with the marking of his burial place."

Just as I was finishing this book, I visited my dad's grave and saw that a nameplate had been installed. After almost two years of anonymity, it's comforting to know that Dad's resting place now bears his name.

The vase for Dad's flowers is too high for me to reach, so I use a special hook the cemetery provides to take it down, remove the old flowers, and put in the fresh ones. I talk to my dad about what's going on in my life. I'll describe a funny thing that happened on a recent job, or tell him how his granddaughter, Sophia, and all my brothers are doing. And sometimes I'll just quietly sit on the ground, looking up at his name, lost in memories.

My brothers have scattered over the Western part of the country and have their own lives and families. The oldest of the five, Tim, lives in Los Angeles and hosts a popular radio show, *The Tim Conway Jr. Show*, on KFI. Tim, his wife, Jennifer, and my beautiful niece Sophia are a regular part of my life. Patrick, Jamie, and Corey are all living in Arizona. Seann still lives in Steamboat Springs, where he moved with our mom years ago, and co-owns three restaurants there.

In telling my story, I hope to accomplish two goals. One is to share the private side of the man who dedicated so much of his life to his family while also bringing happiness to millions of fans. The other is to help people who may find themselves in the same situation I was in. People trying to help an elderly parent or grandparent from being neglected or abused by the people who should be caring for them. Before my dad got sick, I never dreamed that I would become embroiled in such a ruthless fight with people in my family who I'd once loved and trusted. But it happened to me. It could happen to anyone.

My wounds have begun to heal. I have a wonderful life, filled with family and friends. Just as I assured Dad shortly before he passed away, they all take good care of me.

In many ways, my brother Tim has stepped into my life to take over where Dad left off. He's always there with his toolbox to help me fix something when I need it, and when I make a long drive to visit friends or ski, it's Tim who calls to make sure I arrived safe and sound. Knowing that he's close by is a great comfort.

I work hard in a career that is challenging and rewarding. And if there's snow on Mammoth Mountain, which is just a few hours' drive from my home in Malibu, then that's where you will find me.

Spending a day on that mountain has done more for my emotional well-being than any psychologist ever could. On the chairlift ride up, I smile to myself, knowing that I'll soon be 11,053 feet closer to my dad. At the top, before I push off, I speak to him, and I know that he can hear me.

My life is now peaceful and filled with happiness. I walk the beach, hang out with my niece Sophia, and spend time with my friends. I take flowers to Dad and, standing up on my toes, wipe the dust from the marble surface of his grave. Not an hour of the day goes by that I'm not thinking of him.

What a lucky, lucky girl I have been.

THE END